to Evan

A Regulator's Sign-off: Changing the Taps in Britain

The Monetisation[1] and Privatisation of the Water and Wastewater Industry

by

Ian Byatt

Director General of Water Services from Privatisation in 1989 to 2000

and

Chairman of the Water Industry Commission for Scotland 2005 to 2011

[1]Water Services became commercial businesses in England and Wales in 1974, and in 1996 in Scotland, when they were removed from local authority management, becoming Nationalised Industries. The English and Welsh Water Authorities were privatised in 1989 and became subject to external regulation, by a newly-created Office of Water Services (Ofwat), of their prices and the quality of their drinking water and wastewater services in conjunction with a newly created national Rivers Authority and an up-graded Drinking Water inspectorate. In Scotland, water services remained publicly owned but as in England and Wales were externally regulated, first by a Water Commissioner for Scotland (Alan Sutherland) and from 2006 by an independent Water Industry Commission for Scotland (WICS). The three Scottish Water Authorities were subsequently amalgamated into Scottish Water and in 2006 divided into wholesale and retail businesses. In Northern Ireland Water Services were separated from Local Authorities, but little else changed.

Published by Sir Ian Byatt 2019

© Sir Ian Byatt 2019

ISBN 978-1-5272-4233-3

Printed in Great Britain by Short Run Press Ltd, Exeter

To Antonia and Deirdre

Acknowledgements and thanks

I am grateful to David Hume for pointing out, 250 years ago that "a man cannot write about himself without vanity": to my daughter Antonia, who told me that I was never going to finish the draft I had started on leaving Ofwat: to my wife, Deirdre Kelly, who pointed out this alternative and who, despite her busy life, both encouraged me to put this book together and was very helpful in drafting the Prologue: to Nicky Mehta for finding the publishers and working with them, to Paul Luffman at Short Run Press for typesetting and to the initial publishers for permission to republish on a scholarly, not-for-charge, basis.

Prologue

The Content and the Context

These essays are republished versions of lectures given and papers written during and following my terms of office as Director General of Water Services (Ofwat) and Chairman of the Water Industry Commission for Scotland (WICS) and subsequently. They show the development of the strategies of Ofwat and WICS for regulating the privatised Water Companies in England and Wales, and the publicly owned water company in Scotland. They do not cover the situation in Northern Ireland.

They are:

Chapter 1
Pre-privatisation perspective from the Treasury

1   1.1   The Framework of Government Control. In: *Strategic Planning in Nationalised Industries,* Ed. John Grieve Smith, Macmillan, London 1984, pp 67-87   *Page 1*

My view on Nationalised Industries, written, before privatisation became government policy, from my perspective as a Treasury official, part of a team trying to make financial sense of the inefficient, covertly political remains of the post-war nationalisations of the "commanding heights of the economy"

Chapter 2
The Ofwat papers[2]

2   **2.1   Extracts from my statement as Director General of Water Services, issued on appointment on 8th August 1989; in** H_2O; *The Water Share Offers by Schroders on behalf of the Secretary of State for the Environment and the Secretary of State for Wales; Prospectus,* **1989, pp 42-45**   *Page 29*

I wrote this, as newly appointed regulator, for inclusion in the sale Prospectus, setting out my strategy for the regulation that would accompany privatisation. It was designed to pin down the regulatory risks associated with the world's first full privatisation of water services, both the supply of water and the collection and disposal of waste water

2.2   The Regulation of the Water Industry; the Office of Water Services: Structure and Policy. *David Hume Institute, Edinburgh.* **Hume Paper No.16, May 1990**   *Page 37*

A lecture to the David Hume Institute in Edinburgh, setting out:
• the complex structure of regulation: the links between price control and customer service:
• between the monitoring of the quality of drinking water by the Drinking Water Inspector:
• the importance of environmental objectives: both those underlying the regulation of waste water disposal in rivers and coastal waters by the National Rivers Authority, subsequently the Environment Agency: and the implementation of European Community (EC), subsequently the European Union (EU), Directives

2.3   Economic Regulation in a Political Climate: the case of the Water Industry. *Manchester Statistical Society, 7 November* **1992**   *Page 57*

In a lecture in Manchester, I set out the importance of the political, rather than the administrative and economic, aspects of privatisation and the political interface between the Regulator and Ministers

[2]These papers were all discussed with colleagues in the Office and benefited from their comments and suggestions.

2.4 The impact of EC Directives on water customers in England and Wales. *Journal of European Public policy, 3: 4 December* 1996   *Page 79*

This paper deals with the impact of EC, subsequently EU, Directives on standards of drinking water and wastewater, and the implications of these standards, typically adopted without regard for costs, for prices to customers

2.5 Taking a view on Price review. A Perspective on Economic regulation in the Water Industry. *National Institute Economic Review*, Number 159: Jan 1997, pp 77-81   *Page 93*

Against the background of the price limits set by Ofwat in the 1994 Periodic Price Review, in a National Institute seminar, I looked ahead to the second Periodic Price Review which would set much tighter price limits from the year 2000

Chapter 3
Recollections and appraisal

3   **3.1 The water regulation regime in England and Wales. In:** *Regulation of Network Utilities: the European Experience; Ed: Claude Henry, Michel Matheu and Alain Jeunemaitre, Oxford University Press,* 2001   *Page 109*

Written for a wider audience and published in a collection of work on the new approach to the regulation of water utilities in several countries

3.2 Water Regulation: *Centre for the Study of Regulated Industries (CRI), University of Bath, Regulatory Review 2000/2001, Millennium edition,* 2001   *Page 131*

Written after I had left Ofwat, setting out my views on the position of the industry after the 12% cut in prices achieved in the 1999 Price Review

Chapter 4
The Scottish Papers[3]

---

[3]These lectures focussed on the regulation of the public water services in Scotland, when I was chairing the WICS. They were both given in Edinburgh and had benefitted from comments by my fellow Commissioners and by the staff of the Office.

Chapter 5
Regulation of publicly owned utilities

Chapter 6
The lost decade; unfocussed regulation, 2000–2012

Chapter 7
The story and the lessons

Chapter 8
The story and the lessons

Epilogue

Foreword

These papers, written after more than a decade after I left Ofwat, set out my account of the regulation of the water industry, and its successes and shortcomings, in changing circumstances. I look forwards as well as backwards as the privatised companies, especially Thames Water, deservedly become increasingly unpopular.

Nationalisation is now back on the political agenda, but, despite the putative attractions of the political perspective, history shows that a reversion to nationalisation is neither necessary, nor in the interest of customers. I have every expectation that the current Ofwat team, Chairman Jonson Cox and Chief Executive Rachel Fletcher can put things back on the right course at the 2019 Price Review, so that customers come first and water companies are seen as their servants.

CHAPTER 1

Pre-privatisation perspective from the Treasury

1.1 The Framework of Government Control

in *Strategic Planning in Nationalised Industries*
ed. John Grieve Smith, Macmillan, London 1984

> The efficient allocation of resources . . . subject to social and
> sectoral considerations. (Cmnd 7131)

As the nationalised industries are very diverse and have a wide
range of social obligations, any framework of control has
inevitably to be either very general so as to be applicable to all
the industries, or differentiated between industries and tailored to
the particular circumstances of each. In practice the framework
adopted has been of the former kind. It has, by and large, been a
financial framework, but one that has evolved over the years, from
an obligation to break even 'taking one year with another' to a
complex mechanism involving short-term external financing limits
(EFLs), mediumterm financial targets and performance aims. It is
likely to develop further in the coming years.

Successive governments – or perhaps one should say successive
Treasuries – have seen the overall control of nationalised industries
as being concerned with three main objectives:

(1) ensuring that nationalised industries conform to macro-
economic policy objectives, in particular that they do not pre-
empt too much of the nation's savings and investment;

The views expressed are not necessarily those of the Treasury. But I am grateful
to Treasury colleagues for valuable suggestions for improving my text.

(2) ensuring that nationalised industries contribute to the efficient allocation of resources, in particular that their pricing polices are properly related to their costs and they earn an adequate return on investment;

(3) ensuring that nationalised industries are internally efficient and provide adequate services while keeping their costs low.

These objectives are obviously linked. What constitutes the 'correct' allocation of investment resources to nationalised industries depends on the return achieved, which in turn depends on prices and costs. In principle, it is possible to have a set of instruments which can be used to pursue these objectives in a coherent and consistent way. But, in practice, differing emphasis has been placed on the macro-economic, resource allocation and internal efficiency objectives at different periods of time. Hence the differing emphasis given to different instruments.

THE EVOLVING SYSTEM

This section sets out, in broad terms, how the system of government control has developed, under the three objectives. The strengths and weaknesses of the system and pointers to further developments are discussed in the next section.

(i) Macro-economic Issues

Much of the writing on nationalised industries adopts a micro-economic approach. But the control framework cannot be understood unless it is related to macro-economic issues. In part this results from the dominance of macro-economic policy in the post-war period. Also the importance of the nationalised industries in the national economy makes it impractical to imagine that they will not play a rather different role in macro-economic policy than do large corporations in the private sector.

The focus of interest has changed over the years, with changes in the focus of policy. In the 1950s the main concern was with the nationalised industries' call on investment resources, especially for electricity. This was associated with relatively low prices and hence reliance on borrowing, initially directly from the capital market and, after 1956, from the government. It is against this background that the first of the three nationalised industry White Papers, that of 1961, is to be understood.[1]

In the 1960s the emphasis shifted as macro-economic policy switched towards the direct encouragement of economic growth. Nationalised industry investment totals were planned within total public expenditure, but regarded, alongside private investment and net exports, as a prior claim on the growth of national income before considering the split between public and private consumption. In the period of the National Plan,[2] the investment policies of the nationalised industries were explicitly linked with the growth target for the economy. Despite the tone of the 1967 White Paper,[3] that relationship was a macro-economic one, depending more on an overall statistical relationship between investment and output (the incremental capital:output ratio) than on the appraisal of individual investment projects.

As rapid inflation developed in the early 1970s, it was not surprising to find the nationalised industries asked to make their contribution to counter-inflation policy. Nationalised industry prices could no more fail to respond to the CBI 5 per cent limit on price increases than could their investment programmes fail to respond to the growth targets of the national Plan. In both cases, they found themselves on their own, leading to results which were as bad *ex post* as the cynics had predicted *ex ante*.

As the deficits mounted, and investment, encouraged by low prices, surged ahead, macro-economic alarm bells began to ring. In 1975–6, when the Public Sector Borrowing Requirement (PSBR) rose to an unsustainable level, about one-third of it was accounted for by the public corporations. 'Self-financing' once more became fashionable; hence the efforts to raise nationalised industry prices in the years 1976–8. Counter-inflation policy remained an objective, but was thought to be more appropriately pursued by limiting deficits than by limiting prices.

The period from 1972 to 1976 also saw an increase in government intervention in the economy in an attempt to combat rising unemployment and flagging growth. As part of this policy, shipbuilding and aerospace were nationalised, and Rolls-Royce and British Leyland became dependent on the government for their survival. The National Enterprise Board (NEB) was established with a remit to develop mixed ownership by state participation in private companies. But Rolls-Royce and Leyland absorbed most of the NEB's financial and management resources.

During the second half of the 1970s, macro-economic policy switched away from direct concern with output and employment towards the establishment of intermediate targets such as the money supply, expressed in nominal rather than real terms. Consistent with this, the treatment of nationalised industries in the Public Expenditure Survey (PES) was changed, shifting away from investment towards the external financing of such investment. Just as public expenditure programmes were expected to keep within their cash limits, nationalised industries were expected to live within external financing limits (EFLs). As these EFLs were part of the PSBR they had to conform to macro-economic policy.

The establishment of EFL's soon led to the argument that nationalised industries should be 'taken out of the PSBR'. Many of the industries felt that there was a danger that investment would be reduced below the amounts justified on micro-economic criteria. Problems of statistical definition apart, the arguments amounted to a plea for (some) nationalised industries to be allowed direct access to the capital market. For macro-economic reasons, the government rejected arguments for direct borrowing from the market, arguing that such borrowing would increase either interest rates or prices and so 'crowd out' some private expenditure – although not necessarily by an equivalent amount. The issue was examined by the Parliamentary Committee on the Treasury and Civil Service Department,[4] who came down against direct market borrowing by the industry. However, the possibility of direct borrowing was left open if it could be shown that this would be likely to improve micro-economic efficiency. This last question was investigated by the government, The National Economic Development Council, and the City, but practical progress has proved elusive. The British Telecom bond was one idea of this kind. But 'Buzby bonds' were soon overtaken by a decision to privatise BT.

(ii) Resource Allocation

For those industries with some power over their prices there are two, inevitably overlapping, key issues. First, how should nationalised industry prices be set if costs, including the opportunity cost of capital, are to be met? Second, how should the structure of prices be related to the structure of costs, i.e. how much cross-subsidisation should there be? For the industries operating in competitive markets, the 'price takers', resource allocation issues are focused on the level of output, and so on the scale of existing operations and on the volume of investment.

In considering these matters, resource allocation economics should not be divorced from accounting considerations. But the relationships between accounting and economic considerations are both confused and confusing.

Most nationalised industries began life with an obligation to break even. Subsequent experience has revealed the inadequacy of this obligation. The most obvious problems have arisen in relation to borrowing and investment. The interest on government or government-guaranteed loans has only a limited relationship to any calculation of the 'opportunity cost' of capital – that is, what the resources would have earned in other uses. In most circumstances, debt interest is likely to be significantly below the opportunity cost of capital; over most of the post-war period, although not at the moment, real interest rates have been low by historical standards.

The government's response was to devise an 'appropriate' rate of return on investment. The 1961 White Paper raised the issue of comparable returns in private and public industry, concentrating on the point that nationalised industries should cover supplementary depreciation, provide for replacement of assets, and should achieve a degree of self-financing. The 1967 White Paper argued that nationalised industries should make a return on capital broadly comparable to that sought in the private sector, and a test discount rate (TDR) for the appraisal of investment projects was established. This was set initially at 8 per cent in real terms, and subsequently raised to 10 per cent. The 1978 White Paper[5] reaffirmed the need to earn the opportunity cost of capital and introduced a required rate of return (RRR) of 5 per cent in real terms on an industry's investment programme as a whole.

These approaches implied a financial target which would take precedence over the break-even requirement. But because such targets usually do not have a statutory basis, they are agreed with an industry and not imposed on it. They have usually been set as a required return on assets as a whole. Some translation from a return on investment to a return on capital employed has therefore been required. This has not been easy to determine in practice.

Financial targets have also been used to accommodate situations where a nationalised industry is in a position to earn economic rent, or has loss-making social obligations. The 1978 White Paper argued that targets should be related to a whole set of objectives, but in practice this has not been done in any detail.

The 1967 White Paper was noteworthy in advocating marginal cost pricing. It carefully pointed out that the 'relevant' marginal cost would vary with circumstances, and left the development of operational rules to the industries aided by the National Board for Prices and Incomes (NBPI), which was given a new remit to conduct efficiency studies in the nationalised industries. Initially things seemed to be going well. But the abolition of the NBPI and the policy of price restraint set the clock back.

Progress has varied between the industries. In the case of electricity, where considerations of marginal cost go back to the Hopkinson tariff of 1892, much high-quality work has been carried out using systems models. But even so, broad-brush approximations have been used to estimate the capital element in the bulk supply tariff. In the other industries much less analytical work has been done although there has been some progress with systems modelling.

The 1976 report by the National Economic Development Office (NEDO)[6] pointed out the difficulties in calculating marginal cost, casting a good deal of doubt on it as an operational concept. The 1978 White Paper sought to reinstate it by developing the RRR as a broad-brush measure of (long-run) marginal cost, which could be calculated from information derived in the course of corporate planning. But progress in developing the RRR as a determinant of the financial target has been hesitant.

Traditionally, cross-subsidisation has been an important element in the operation of public utilities. The White Papers of 1967 and 1978 spoke out against the practice. But little seems to have changed. It is difficult for those outside the industries to know the extent of cross-subsidisation, partly because of conceptual difficulties, partly because little information is available on the (marginal) costs of individual activities. But casual observation suggests that there is quite a lot.

(iii) Internal Efficiency

Over the last two decades, concern with the level of nationalised industry costs for a given level of service output seems to have grown. The 1961 White Paper contented itself with pointing out that costs would be affected by the extent of commercially unprofitable activities. The 1967 White Paper had a whole section on costs, drawing attention to the need to look for cost savings, especially labour savings, and to increase efficiency. It referred to the strengthening of the NBPI to enable it to make inquiries into the efficiency of industries whose proposals for price increases were referred to it. It stressed the need to develop performance indicators, which would be used in the course of the annual Investment Review discussions with the industries.

But little happened. The NBPI was abolished. A system of

performance indicators was not forthcoming. In its 1976 report, NEDO reiterated the arguments for performance targets as well as financial targets for the nationalised industries. The 1978 White Paper took up the challenge and asked the industries to include suitable cost and service aims in their reports and accounts. This time there has been some progress. Performance targets have been agreed with some industries and results monitored.

By 1980, the Price Commission has been given powers to investigate nationalised industry efficiency. Since then it in turn has been abolished, and powers to investigate nationalised industry efficiency vested in the Monopolies and Mergers Commission (MMC). Nationalised industries are also encouraged to initiate their own efficiency audits.

The privatisation programme, in so far as it opens up the industries to greater competition, can add a major new dimension to the search for ways to increase the pressure to reduce costs and improve services. But in areas where there is a natural monopoly, privatisation will not automatically lead to cost reduction.

Decision-Taking; the IFR and Corporate Planning

The focus of the present control system is the annual Investment and Financing Review (IFR). The industries submit their investment plans with their proposals for financing them. These are discussed with the sponsor Departments and the Treasury and then brought together in the IFR. The IFR, which is as much concerned with the total call by nationalised industries for external finance as with the claims of an individual industry, is an element in the Public Expenditure Survey (PES) where the case for external finance for the nationalised industries can be set against the claims of the other public sector programmes. The IFR, which covers the three years of the PES, is done in cash terms – in line with the emphasis on mominal magnitudes in macro-economic policy. Before the mid-1970s, the process was concerned with nationalised industries investment, not external finance, and was done in real terms to fit in with the real resource planning of the PES and the economy.

Underlying the IFR, recent years have seen increasing emphasis on corporate planning as a process for improving resource allocation and raising the efficiency of nationalised industry operations. The 1976 NEDO report argued the need for the government and the industries to agree on a business strategy, and recommended the establishment of 'Policy Councils' to carry this out. The 1978 White Paper preferred to increase the importance given to discussions between the government and the industry of each industry's corporate plan within existing institutional arrangements. The 1979 Conservative government took this process further. It began a process of agreeing objectives with the industries, and instituted collective Ministerial consideration both of forward-looking Corporate Plans and of backward-looking Performance Reviews.

Progress will not, however, be easy. The objectives of the nationalised industries are not identical with those of the government. This is not only because business objectives and political objectives differ and because of the different timescales that are involved. The nationalised industries often behave as though they had their own social objectives. This is reflected in cross-subsidisation and arguments about 'national needs'. The government for its part has not simply set social objectives; it has involved itself in issues such as the investment appraisal and the operating efficiency of the industries, which many would argue are matters of business not politics.

Financial Performance

Table 3.1 indicates the macro-economic position of the public corporations over the post-war period. It shows their relative capital intensity. It also shows a sector of the economy which drew relatively heavily on external resources during the second half of the 1950s, but whose call has since declined. But this was more because investment fell then because profits rose. The public corporations return on capital has, however, deteriorated since the 1960s, and it is fairly clear that the public corporations are not

Table 3.1. Macro-economic indicators of UK public corporations

	Percentage share in output[1]	Percentage share in investment[2]	Overall surplus/ deficit (–) as a percentage of GDP[3]	Budgetary burden as a percentage of GDP[4]
1946–49		11.0	-0.7 (-0.8)	0.5
1950–53		21.5	-1.7 (-1.7)	0.3
1954–57		22.4	-2.2 (-2.2)	1.4
1958–61		21.3	-2.2 (-2.5)	2.0
1962–65	10.3	19.8	-1.7 (-2.2)	1.3
1966–69	10.4	20.1	-1.9 (-2.3)	1.7
1970–73	10.0	16.3	-1.7 (-2.1)	0.8
1974–77	11.3	18.7	-1.9 (-3.0)	1.3
1978–81	10.9	17.0	-1.0 (-1.8)	1.2

[1] Share of public corporations' GDP in total GDP at factor cost.

[2] Share of public corporations' Gross Fixed Capital Formation in total Gross Fixed Capital Formation.

[3] Overall surplus/deficit is defined as the difference between (i) revenue plus receipts of current transfers and non-government capital transfers; and (ii) current plus capital expenditure. Figures in brackets exclude receipts of government current transfers.

[4] Budgetary burden defined as government subsidies, transfers, and net lending to public corporations less dividends and interest payments to government.

SOURCE Short, 'The Role of Public Enterprises: An International Statistical Comparison', IMF Working Paper DM/83/34. (Figures taken from NI Blue Book.)

achieving a rate of return commensurate with the opportunity cost of their capital.

CONTROL INSTRUMENTS: THE ANALYTIC ISSUES

This section surveys the analytic issues and discusses the main control techniques used by successive governments. Four main areas of concern stand out – pricing, investment, financial performance, and cost reduction. They are looked at in turn. But they cannot be isolated from the wider context, whose salient features are:

(1) Most nationalised industries inevitably have some political status. They supply basic goods directly to a large number of customers. They are major employers of a declining labour force. Some of them have natural monopoly power. Most are seen by the public to have social obligations which private sector firms do not.

(2) There are severe limits on how far it is possible to go in systematising the relationship between the industries and the government. The 'arm's length' relationship is a pipe-dream. The 'holding company' analogy provides some insights, but has limitations. The 'banker/client' model is again only part of the story. In principle it is possible to have sufficient clarity about objectives to work out a full and systematic relationship, but the different philosophies, styles and timescales of the political and business worlds would make this extremely difficult to achieve in practice.

(3) Information is scarce and the environment uncertain, both at the macro-economic and the industry level. Doubtless the situation could be improved, but this would still leave a very large number of decisions to be based on informed judgements – with a high probability that those judgements can only be generally right and, more often than not, will be precisely wrong.

Pricing in Public Utilities

The message of successive White Papers has been that prices must be reasonably related to marginal cost and that accounting costs must be covered. The potential conflicts have long been recognised and the two-part tariff offered as a form of squaring the circle. But while White Papers have stressed economic pricing, in practice concepts of accounting cost have, I judge, played a larger role – although without assuring prices that always covered costs.

Those who, like me, have been brought up on marginal cost doctrines, are naturally disappointed to see them so little used. But in their present form they are deficient as operational guides. First, it is not possible to calculate a unique number, or set of numbers, for marginal cost. Second, because all marginal cost calculations contain a subjective element, agreement about marginal cost involves compromise. Third, a soundly based compromise requires that all parties have adequate information. If they do not, the results can be biased. Fourth, even if they do, compromise is difficult when the parties have different objectives.

The first point is the key one, because it underlies all the others. What increase in output are we talking about? To estimate long-run marginal cost (LRMC) involves long-term forecasting of a large number of both economic and technological variables and judging a hypothetical situation compared with what would otherwise have happened. The best anyone could hope for is to estimate LRMC as a range. With present information it is often more accurate to describe LRMC estimates as points on a wide spectrum.

In any case it is not always right to base all prices on LRMC. In a world of shocks, mistakes, myopia and fluctuations in output, it often makes sense to optimise over a shorter timescale. How short depends on a whole variety of factors which it is not possible fully to settle *ab initio*. Very often it only proves possible to settle the 'right' time scale in the course of the analysis of a particular problem.

A further difficulty, which perhaps deserves more analytical attention, is the issue of consumer expectations in responding to pricing signals. If, for example, marginal cost is changing through time, resource allocation theory requires consumers, especially when investment decisions are involved, to take account of future prices, i.e. of future marginal costs as well as current ones. But how can pricing signals be used to help consumers form the right expectations? Should changes in marginal cost be anticipated in prices? If so, how far ahead?

Practical men may be able to make sensible decisions about these matters in particular situations, when they can take account of wider considerations. But there are no set rules. It is not, as Arthur Young said of the work of the States-General in 1789, 'as though a constitution were a pudding to be made out of a recipe'.

With the exception of electricity, the nationalised industries themselves have not set much store by marginal cost concepts. They doubtless have their reasons. But if the industries do not calculate marginal cost, what can those concerned with resource allocation, either in the government or outside it, do? Are they to offend canons of good management by second-guessing? Or are they to accept whatever they are told?

It would be wrong to conclude from these arguments that marginal cost concepts should not be used in considering the allocation of national resources in this area. Decisions about the future must be related to estimates concerning the future. But those arguing for marginal cost pricing should beware of putting too much weight on it. Estimates must be broad-brush, both because of the limitations of our knowledge of the future and because of the political context. If they are to carry conviction, forward estimates must be more than pure forecasts of the future.

One of the objectives lying behind the introduction of the RRR was to provide a broad-brush estimate of LRMC using corporate planning data. Corporate plans which showed estimates of output growth and of the investment needed to achieve it could be used to calculate the incremental costs of that extra output. The estimates of the future would be related to the past through the process of constructing a corporate plan which would take the organisation from its historical position into the future. As corporate planning developed, and was complemented by a review process, the data would get progressively better; 'hockey-stick' planning, where the unfavourable trends of the past are miraculously linked to a golden future, would be controlled if not completely eliminated. Corporate planning information would, of course, be common to the government and the industry.

But in practice things have not worked out as envisaged in Cmnd 7131. Increments of output have not been costed in corporate plans. Only where such increments have been large in relation to existing supply, and have therefore required considerable investment, has it proved possible to calculate incremental costs from information set out in the corporate plan. Nationalised industries sometimes provide other estimates of marginal cost, but the basis of these calculations has not always been clear.

Five years on, it may be worth considering a more explicit accounting approach. In a steady-state situation, in the absence of shocks and mistakes, LRMC would be reasonably well proxied by a projection of running costs plus the mark-up required to cover economic depreciation and the RRR on existing assets when adjusted for inflation. But the steady state is an abstraction. Depreciation as calculated in the accounts, even when done on a Current Cost Accounting (CCA) basis, is often an imperfect approximation to economic depreciation. CCA asset values often fail to allow explicitly for the shocks, mistakes, etc. which people the real world.

Despite this, accounting costs (in contrast to planning estimates of marginal cost) have the merit that they are grounded on costs actually incurred. The more the industries' accountants are able to make explicit adjustments to allow for changed circumstances, the more accounting costs and forward-looking marginal cost estimates will be brought closer together. The key requirement is to ensure that, where assets need to be replaced if the business is to continue to operate in the longer term, they are entered in the balance sheet at their current replacement cost.

Carsberg and Lumby[7] have shown how an accounting approach can be used to meet the objectives of Cmnd 7131. But, in practice, accounting and planning approaches to marginal cost will not necessarily produce the same number, so compromise would still be necessary when setting prices. But such a process would involve useful iteration between the two sets of estimates, one based on planning models looking to the future, and one based in accounting costs, grounded in the past, to the benefit of both. Adjusting the accounts to allow for shocks, mistakes, etc. would concentrate the mind of management, and where appropriate that of the government, on what had gone wrong compared with past expectations. Ensuring that forward-looking estimates were explicitly linked to accounting performance would improve the process of monitoring of performance against expectations.

It is often necessary to go below the level of the whole industry. Better resource allocation also depends on how far it proves possible to relate the structure or prices to the structure of costs. The presence of massive cross-subsidisation within an industry can be fatal to any attempt to improve resource allocation.

But there is no generally agreed definition of what constitutes undesirable cross-subsidisation. Even cross-subsidisation itself is difficult to define. Should prices be related to average costs? Or should cross-subsidisation refer to divergence between the structure of prices and the structure of LRMC? Or are short-run marginal costs also relevant? These distinctions are important ones and there are no universal answers. Professions vary in their approaches. Accountants traditionally tend to have an average-cost philosophy; economists dislike attempts to allocate 'overheads'. Again the need is to bring them closer together. It is also necessary to recognise the rather different objectives of the government and the nationalised industries. The government is mainly concerned to avoid medium- to long-term (i.e. LRMC) cross-subsidisation. Yet industries with significant joint costs, facing different demand elasticities, may be more interested in relating the structure of their prices to relative SRMC than to relative LRMC.

If the aim is to reduce divergences between LRMC and price for different elements of a nationalised industry's business, several approaches are possible. Where different operations or activities are involved, separate profit centres (or separate businesses) with separate accounting systems can be developed. But it is not always possible to take this very far. Completely separable activities are rare among nationalised industries, and where they exist privatisation is already well advanced. In an integrated systems industry, cost allocation poses problems, but difficulties with common costs can too often deter the assembly of costing information that could help with decisions. Different industries have given different degrees of priority to cost disaggregation; progress by British Rail shows, however, that useful improvements can be made.[8] Generally speaking, there is a strong case for more and better disaggregated costing information, partly from public policy reasons (the need to avoid 'discrimination') and partly for business purposes. Again Carsberg and Lumby are helpful.[7]

Where operations or activities are integrated, such as the production of peak and off-peak electricity, separate profit centres cannot be established and costs cannot be disaggregated. In these cases, the best structure of prices will be that which is consistent with multi-period output and investment optimisation.

Investment

The 1967 White Paper set the tone for investment appraisal, not only in nationalised industries, but across the whole public sector. But its application was inadequate on three counts. First, not all elements in an investment programme were seen as requiring appraisal by those concerned with the determination of the whole programme: some schemes were said to be for essential replacement, some needed for safety, some to meet statutory requirements to supply. Second, and the two points merge, the TDR did not affect prices; it was more concerned with the composition of investment and the choice of techniques than with the size of the programme. Third, the TDR test was very strict by comparison with the revenue required to cover interest on any associated borrowing from the National Loans Fund (NLF). Projects not yielding the TDR could still pay off in financial terms; those that met the TDR yielded large cash surpluses.

The 1978 White Paper attempted to deal with the first two points by developing the RRR, which was designed to apply to the whole investment programme and to be one of the elements determining the financial target. But it was recognised that there were difficulties in doing the latter. An investment programme yields returns over the long term; it is not easy to identify the return during the period of a medium-term financial target sufficiently clearly for tight monitoring to be possible.

But the switch to a 5 per cent RRR did little, if anything, to deal with the third problem. Because the RRR at 5 per cent in real terms exceeds the real rate of interest on NLF loans, and because inflation during the 1970s greatly reduced the real value of nationalised industry debt, a nationalised industry which earned its RRR on the assets would make a large post-interest surplus. Such surpluses would naturally be used to pay off its debt or be retained as capital for new investment on which it would not have to pay interest. As nationalised industries become progressively less dependent on external borrowing this is likely further to reduce the incentives they have to earn the 'opportunity cost of capital'.

The problem, to which the Public Accounts Committee has drawn attention,[9] could be dealt with within the existing framework if the nationalised industries were to make payments to the government which were related to the return on their investment rather than to the interest on their outstanding debt. There are several ways that this could be done. They would all involve a hard look at the liabilities side of the balance sheet and the role of interest payments. Carsberg and Lumby have shown the relationship between cost estimates, including the cost of capital, financial targets and 'dividend' payments, and have set out proposals which would bring together accounting and economic principles and so achieve a closer relationship between an industries return on capital and its financial target on the one hand, and between its payments to its owner, the government and its cost of capital on the other.

It has sometimes been argued that rather than give nationalised industries access to the NLF, they should be allowed, or forced, to borrow directly from the market. But as any nationalised industry borrowing is virtually guaranteed by the government, implicitly if not explicitly, the interest rate paid would remain advantageous compared with the cost of capital to the private sector.

Financial Targets

All three of the post-war White Papers recognised the need for financial objectives – although only in the case of the water authorities is there statutory provision for one. But practice has been less satisfactory. Many years have gone by when no targets have been in operation. While it is right in principle to stress medium-term (3-5 year) targets, this does reduce the pressure to make some return on capital, even in bad years. Although there are good arguments for basing the financial target on a 'wide range of factors', it makes monitoring difficult.

The 1978 White Paper preserved the formal position by saying that when announcing a target, the government would 'indicate the main assumptions on which it was based', so that 'Parliament and the public' could 'subsequently judge the industry's performance against the target'. But for a number of reasons it seems unreasonable to expect any very precise relationship between the target and the various factors lying behind it, and susbequent history tends to bear this out.

Where an industry is judged to have extensive social obligations or to be a beneficiary of substantial economic rent, it is often better to take explicit account of this, as in the case of Public Service Obligation for the railways, or the Gas Levy. There is a case for extending the concept of explicit subsidies or levies more widely, and in some cases such a move could naturally accompany the reduction of cross-subsidisation. But some 'looseness' in the target, especially in relation to 'social and sectoral considerations', is inevitable.

The arguments for more emphasis on annual EFLs do not, therefore, derive solely from considerations of macro-economic policy. Provided they are consistent with the medium-term target, they also have a valuable resource allocation role. Also financial control is a necessary element in achieving internal efficiency. If macro-economic objectives were to play an *additional* role, the policies underlying EFLs could have taxation as well as resource allocation implications. But the financial performance of the nationalised industry sector as a whole – which is what is relevant for the macro-economic aspects of EFLs – does not suggest that taxation elements have been of quantitative significance. On the contrary: in addition to explicit subsidies there have been implicit subsidies resulting from failure to achieve a return on capital comparable to the private sector.

Cost Reduction

The need to maintain pressures on nationalised industry costs is well recognised. But tools for the job are not easy to find. EFLs have undoubtably had some effect, but they cannot be a precision instrument. Advocates of cost and service measures and targets make a powerful case for them. But should they be aggregative measures, such as labour costs per unit of output for the industry as a whole, or should they be concerned with the detailed operations of a part of the business? Perhaps the government should concentrate on asking the industries to agree and to monitor general performance indicators, leaving them to decide how best to translate general indicators into specific indicators for elements of their businesses.

But regular performance measures need to be backed up by periodic examinations of efficiency by a body such as the MMC. How frequent such investigations should be must, however, depend as much on specific as on general considerations.

A completely new element has now been introduced by the

privatisation programme. Initially the emphasis was on opening up the industries to the disciplines of the capital market. Some of the issues involved have already been touched on in this chapter. But in making proposals for direct borrowing, advocates also argued that micro-economic benefits could be achieved if direct lending were linked to a specific project, so that the return to the lender would depend on the success of the project, and thus that lenders would be concerned with its design and investment appraisal, and possibly with its subsequent management. But so far it has proved impossible to find separable projects where lenders were prepared to be involved on terms that would involve them in significant risk.

But the debate is now shifting towards the role which competition could play in product markets through privatisation. Privatisation can meet a number of objectives, of which increased competition is only one. Beesley and Littlechild[10] have recently stressed this dimension, which is clearly a very important one. As they point out, the introduction of greater competition would involve disentangling the natural monopoly elements of nationalised industries from elements that could operate in competitive markets. This would imply an analysis of what structural changes might be desirable in order to maximise the exposure to competition. It would also imply consideration of the best way to treat the residual natural monopoly elements. If so, it would be for consideration whether the framework of control developed to date for the nationalised industries would apply to those natural monopoly elements or whether new approaches were desirable. Moving in such a direction thus opens up a large new policy – and research – agenda.

SUMMARY AND CONCLUSIONS

The basic framework of government control of nationalised industries is a financial one. The industries have statutory obligations to break even. From time to time statutory or non-statutory mediumterm financial targets have been set, or agreed.

22

Since the mid-1950s nationalised industries have been unable to borrow medium or long term direct from the domestic capital market. Since the mid-1970s annual limits have been set on their use of external finance.

On top of this framework the government has, in the course of the White Papers of 1961, 1967 and 1978, put a layer of non-statutory guidance. This has involved the issues of supplementary depreciation and an adequate contribution to the nation's savings (1961), investment appraisal, marginal cost pricing and financial targets (1967), and corporate planning, the required rate of return on investment and overall profitability (1978).

The government's concern with nationalised industries has covered both macro- and micro-economic issues. The industries have been expected to play a role in macro-economic policy throughout the post-war period. The focus has shifted from control of total investment programmes to control of external borrowing, and from a concern with price restraint to a concern with the PSBR. The focus may shift in the future as macro-economic policy develops. But while the nationalised industry sector is large, this macro-economic concern will persist.

At the micro-economic level the focus has been on pricing and investment. Economic pricing has been defined as marginal cost pricing, subject to the need to cover accounting costs. At the disaggregated level, White Papers have argued that the structure of prices should reflect the structure of (marginal) costs. The direction of government prescription has been against cross-subsidisation and in favour of explicit rather than implicit subsidies. Investment was covered in rather different ways in successive White Papers. The 1961 White Paper concentrated on the effect of prices on the demand for investment and the need for more self-financing. The 1967 White Paper concentrated on project appraisal and the achievement of comparability with the private sector. The 1978 White Paper returned to the influence of the 'opportunity cost of capital' on the determination of total investment and focused on *ex post* achievement rather than *ex ante* appraisal.

It is not easy to characterise the relationship between the government and the nationalised industries. The 'arm's length', the 'holding company' and the 'banker/client' analogies illustrate part of the relationship, although none of them is wholly right. Perhaps the political context of the relationship inevitably involves both fuzziness and conflict. In recent years attempts have been made to improve the relationship in the context of corporate planning. This offers a more flexible model where a common process may be able to accommodate different policies.

A key factor in nationalised industry policy is the need for cost reductions. This is difficult to achieve in industries which either have natural monopoly power or are seen to have non-economic obligations. It is also difficult where cost reductions involve shedding labour and where unions are strong. Financial targets, however necessary, do not guarantee success in this area. The White Papers have therefore advocated performance and service measures. External investigations of nationalised industry efficiency began with references to the NBPI and the Price Commission and are now in the hands of the MMC. In so far as the privatisation programme can be used to increase competition, it will provide a major new tool of cost control.

There is much unfinished business in government: nationalised-industry relations. Much of it is concerned with specific industries and specific policy areas. But at the aggregate level, the following interrelated issues stand out:

(1) What role should the break-even requirement play? How should this be defined in current conditions? How should it relate to medium-term financial targets?
(2) What should be the relationship between forward-looking concepts, such as marginal cost, and an industry's accounting framework?
(3) How can economic pricing be made operationally useful (a) at the level of the whole industry, and (b) in relation to the different products of an industry?

(4) How can cross-subsidisation be made explicit and be controlled? How far should cost allocation go? What are the respective roles of the economist and the accountant?

(5) How can a requirement to earn a rate of return comparable to that in the private sector be made compatible with the nationalised industries' debt structure?

(6) How can the need to earn a satisfactory return on investment be linked to an industry's medium-term financial targets?

(7) How can pressures to reduce costs be best put on industries with natural monopoly power or social obligations? What is the role of performance measures and external and internal efficiency audits?

(8) How can the privatisation programme be best used to increase efficiency and reduce costs? Is it right to think in terms of separating elements which could operate in competitive markets from those with irreducible natural monopoly power? If so, how would those residual elements be best controlled? Is a regulated private monopoly to be preferred to a public monopoly? How can competition be introduced into areas where social obligations loom large? Is franchising[11] a possible answer?

NOTES AND REFERENCES

1. Cmnd 1337, *The Financial and Economic Obligations of the Nationalised Industries* (London: HMSO, 1961).
2. Cmnd 2764, *The National Plan* (London: HMSO, 1965).
3. Cmnd 3437, *Nationalised Industries: a Review of Economic and Financial Objectives* (London: HMSO, 1967).
4. Treasury and Civil Service Committee, *Financing of the Nationalised Industries*, House of Commons (London: HMSO, 1981).
5. Cmnd 7131, *The Nationalised Industries* (London: HMSO, 1978). See also, I. C. R. Byatt *et al.*, 'The Test Discount Rate and the Required Rate of Return on Investment', Government Economic Service Working Paper No. 22 (London, 1979).

6. National Economic Development Office, *A Study of UK Nationalised Industries* (London: HMSO, 1976).

7. Carsberg and Lumby, *The Evaluation of Financial Performance in the Water Industry – The Role of Current Cost Accounting* (London: Chartered Institute of Public Finance and Accountancy, 1983).

8. British Railways Board, *Measuring Cost and Profitability in British Rail* (London: British Railways Board, 1978).

9. House of Commons Session 1980–81, *15th Report from the Committee of Public Accounts* (London: HMSO, 1981).

10. Beesley and Littlechild, 'Privatisation: Principles, Problems and Priorities', *Lloyds Bank Review*, no. 149 (July 1983).

11. Gretton and Harrison (eds), *Franchising in the Public Sector* (London: *Public Money*, 1983).

CHAPTER 2

The OFWAT Papers

These papers were all discussed with colleagues in the Office and benefited from their comments and suggestions.

2.1 Extracts from my statement as Director General of Water Services, issued on appointment on 8th August 1989

in H2O; The Water Share Offers by Schroders on behalf of the Secretary of State for the Environment and the Secretary of Sate for Wales; Prospectus, 1989, pp 42-45

DIRECTOR GENERAL

Other duties and functions

The Director General is required to keep under review and to report annually to the Secretary of State on activities connected with the matters in relation to which undertakers carry out their functions. The Director General also shares with the Director General of Fair Trading certain functions under the Fair Trading Act 1973 and the Competition Act 1980. These functions relate to control of monopoly situations which may exist in relation to commercial situations connected with the provision of water supply or sewerage services and of anti-competitive practices which may arise in connection with the provision of water supply or sewerage services. The Director General of Fair Trading may also require the Director General to exercise certain functions under the Fair Trading Act 1973 for the protection of consumers against courses of conduct detrimental to their interests in relation to the supply of water or the provision of sewerage services by undertakers.

Policy

The following extracts are taken from the statement by the present Director General of Water Services issued on 8th August, 1989, in which he indicated the general principles he would follow in carrying out his duties. References to Appointees or Appointed Companies are to both Water Service Companies and Statutory Water Companies.

General approach

"My primary duty under the Act is to ensure that the functions of water and sewage undertakers are properly carried out and that Appointees can finance them. Subject to that I must protect customers, facilitate competition and promote economy and efficiency. I see these duties as complementary. It would not be in the interest of consumers if Appointees were unable to carry out their functions."

"But, because of the limitations on direct competition, consumers cannot look to market mechanisms to protect them from unnecessarily high charges or a poor service or both. My objective will be to achieve through regulation the same balance as would otherwise be achieved by competitive markets, aided by my ability to compare the performance of 39 separate Appointed companies."

"It is also essential that companies invest wisely to maintain an adequate capital stock to meet the needs of existing and future consumers. Detailed investment decisions are for the companies. But I will ensure that the objectives of investment plans are met, that progress is monitored and, that, when appropriate, plans are brought up to date."

"The Appointed companies must be left with incentives to act efficiently. Subject to meeting the requirements of the regulatory regime, the companies will be free to follow their commercial objectives. They must be able to make management decisions without undue interference, including those concerned with the financing of investment."

"Arms length regulation implies that I must be provided with information which can satisfy me that, in addition to meeting the conditions of their Licence, the Appointed companies are providing an effective and economical service to their customers. This includes information on which I can compare their performance."

Adjustments to charges
Periodic Reviews
"The industry is facing many changes and a new operating regime. At a 5 year review it would be opportune to consider the extent to which the arrangements for implementing the regulatory regime had achieved their objectives and to examine any deficiencies which may have emerged. It would provide an opportunity for reviewing the available evidence on the rate of return which investors and creditors would require, and on the performance (measured against suitable financial ratios) which it would be reasonable to expect from a company, with the same characteristics as an Appointed company, which was well regarded by the City. A review could involve adjustment of K factors for the second quinquennium in the light of events. It would also provide an opportunity for rolling on Ks for a further five years. If Appointed companies did not agree with my proposals the Licence gives them the right of appeal to the Monopolies and Mergers Commission (MMC)."

"Adjustments to K would not be retrospective. If Appointed companies have increased their profit by increasing their efficiency more than was anticipated, they should retain such higher profits. Any such increases in efficiency, across the range of their activities, would be relevant to the judgement I would make concerning the scope for further prospective increases in efficiency by them, and other Appointees, in the future. In reaching this judgement, I will want to undertake my own studies."

Interim determinations
"If substantial expenditure is involved, there will inevitably be a significant element of uncertainty. Subject to that, both Appointees and customers should be as clear as possible about how K will be adjusted between Reviews. Detailed rules are set out in Part IV of Condition B of the Licence. While it may be necessary to exercise

discretion in dealing with unforeseen circumstances in individual cases, it is my intention generally to apply the rules as follows:

(i)   Where there is a relevant item, I am required to judge whether the costs put forward by the Company applying for an adjustment in K are reasonably attributable to the item and whether the amounts and timing of such costs are reasonable. The increase in cost, after allowing for any receipts and savings from other relevant changes, must, in aggregate, then be sufficiently large to make material difference to the financial position of the company. This materiality test is specified in the Licence. Provided that costs are properly attributable, are reasonable and pass the materiality threshold they will be allowed in full, except in the case of land – see (v) below.

(ii) Costs may change, up or down, after K is set for reasons outside an efficient Appointee's control. Where national construction costs change, then this will be reflected through automatic indexation. Additionally, I can adjust K where the cost of meeting a particular obligation or standard has increased substantially. I will have regard to the overall impact which the change makes to the costs of the Appointed Business as a whole. I will also be concerned to ensure that incentives to efficiency are not blunted. I will deal similarly with reductions in cost.

(iii) The Licence allows me to adjust K if the company has failed to take the steps assumed when setting K initially or at periodic reviews. I will pay particular attention to any failure of an Appointed business to achieve the objectives of the capital investment programme underlying its K. Customers have a right to get benefits from the investment which they have financed through their water charges. But if companies achieve their investment programmes at lower costs than assumed in K, they will not be penalised through their own efficiency.

(iv) In deciding what adjustment to K is necessary to finance any increase in costs, I will examine the most up to date evidence which is available on the returns which lenders and shareholders require and on the key financial indicators of financial performance which would be reasonable to expect from a company, with the same characteristics as an Appointed company, which was well regarded by the City. Any adjustment to K will

(a) be based on an assessment of the return required on new investment, and

(b) be profiled (ie adjusted over the years), in so far as is necessary and consistent with all my Section 7 duties, to ensure that key financial indicators, taken as a whole, are kept within acceptable ranges.

In the first 5 years, the Licence requires me to assume that no fresh equity is to be raised to finance additional expenditure. I will therefore examine the evidence which is available on the cost of raising money by other means when, for example, considering the choice of an appropriate discount rate.

(v) In adjusting K for differences between actual proceeds from the disposal of surplus land and those underlying the initial K, I will need to ensure that receipts from land are accounted for separately. I may need to issue guidelines. In operating these arrangements, I will aim to ensure that Appointed companies retain the necessary incentive to make good use of surplus land; if a Company achieves higher net sales receipts from land than assumed when K is first set the Licence allows it to keep half of them.

(vi) The basis on which I make adjustments to K will be clearly set out and the reasons explained."

Unfair discrimination between customers

"I consider that it is an important part of my duties to guard against unfair discrimination. For example, where a company applies to me for K to be adjusted to allow for the costs of metering, I will need to take account of any changes in revenue expected. In doing so, I will check that the tariff does not discriminate unfairly between

33

metered and unmetered customers or between different classes of metered customers."

"In cases where I have reason to suppose that unfair price discrimination is being practised, I will use my powers vigorously."

Standards of service

"Any shortfall in performance against standards will have to be discussed with me. If I am not satisfied that an Appointed business is performing satisfactorily, I will ask the Company to tell me what steps they propose to take to improve the situation. Unless satisfactory action follows, I will ask the Secretary of State to set standards of performance which would then be legally enforceable."

"I recognise that service standards can be too high (because too expensive) or too low, but it is vital that utilities should commit themselves to satisfactory performance and deliver that performance. In my deliberations, I will take account of the views of consumers, in particular those articulated by the Customer Service Committees ("CSCs"), especially if companies propose changes in service standards that involve adjustment to K."

Investment plans

"The formulation of sound plans for the maintenance, and improvement of the long lived assets, especially underground assets, is crucial to the future performance of the industry and hence to the long term needs of customers. The Licence requires the submission of Asset Management Plans in respect of their underground assets. It also requires that they should be kept up to date. I consider that it is also important to develop good quantified forward plans for specialised long lived surface assets."

"The companies are required in their Licence to appoint an Assessor to report on changes to their Asset Management Plans. I will have to approve each Assessor. I will have close contact with these Assessors so that I can be assured that the plans are sufficient to meet statutory requirements. I will also want to be assured that these investment plans are cost-effective without involving myself in matters which are properly the concern of the management of the companies."

"I will require appointed companies to monitor progress in achieving these plans. They should provide evidence not only of expenditure, but of progress in achieving objectives."

Customer Service Committees

"I intend that the CSCs will play a major role in ensuring that the interests of consumers get high priority. They should be effective and streamlined bodies."

"I will meet with all the Chairmen of the CSCs regularly as a group. The CSCs will seek to ensure that the appointed companies deal properly with complaints and queries from customers; they will pursue unresolved complaints which customers take up with them; and they will make representations to the companies on these and other consumer matters. I will also expect them to address more general issues and, from time to time, will ask for their advice. In particular I will want them to review the Codes of Practice which the Companies are required to issue and the Appointee's performance against them."

Comparisons between companies

"Because of the limited scope for direct competition, I will compare the performance of the appointed companies. In particular I will compare their costs, their efficiency and their return on capital."

"Such comparisons can reveal significant differences which can be pointers to ways in which some companies may be performing relatively weakly. Comparisons between Appointed companies can help to promote efficiency and achieve low prices to consumers. In competitive markets, competition brings prices down to those of efficient firms. In the case of water I must set the charges limit to have a similar effect."

Take-over and merger

"I welcome the competitive pressure which can arise because Appointed companies will be subject to take-over by other firms who feel they can make better use of the assets. Mergers between existing Appointed companies may enable economies of scale to be exploited. But mergers will also result in a reduction of the number of comparators. Where a merger is referred to the MMC the Act requires the Commission to be concerned that a merger will not prejudice my ability to make comparisons between companies."

Monitoring

"In exercising my powers to obtain the information I need to carry out my statutory duties, I will seek to ensure that appointed companies provide regular information which is, where possible, comparable across all the companies."

"I will attach particular importance to the provision of current cost accounts as required by the Licence. I intend to use them to compare information both on costs and on financial performance."

"In accordance with the Licence I will issue guidelines for these regulatory accounts."

2.2 The Regulation of the Water Industry; the Office of Water Services Structure and Policy

David Hume Institute, Edinburgh.
Hume Paper No. 16, May 1990

Introduction

The purpose of the Office of Water Services (OFWAT) is to protect the interests of consumers of water and sewerage services. The companies appointed to supply these services are, in many respects, monopolies and there are few 'pure' market pressures on them. Consumers cannot therefore look to market mechanisms to protect them from unnecessarily high charges or a poor service or both. My objective will be to achieve through regulation the same balance as would otherwise be achieved by competitive markets. Where market pressures exist I shall foster them.

I would like to give two examples of how OFWAT proposes to protect customers. One concerns protection against excessive profits. The second concerns protection against ill-considered proposals for capital investment.

I have a duty to ensure that companies can finance their functions. Subject to that, I am to protect customers, promote economy and efficiency and facilitate competition. I see those duties as complementary. Customers benefit if efficient companies remain financially viable.

But the duty placed on me of "securing reasonable returns of [the Companies'] capital", does not mean that I am to guarantee the achievement of a rate of return of any particular size. I consider that it implies that providers of Capital (lenders and shareholders taken together) should be in a position where they can expect to receive a return sufficient, but no more than sufficient, to induce them to make the loans and hold the shares, if the company operates efficiently. This return should be a competitive return in a market situation.

Secondly, customers have a right to know how environmental decisions will affect them. I am concerned to dispel the misconception that environmental improvements are justified irrespective of their cost. Everyone welcomes moves to improve the quality of our drinking water, bathing waters and rivers. However, these improvements require massive capital expenditure programmes. These programmes will be paid for by the customer.

Politicians and environmentalists must be sure that environmental proposals are soundly costed and that the efficiency of different solutions is examined. Costs must be justified. I shall be pressing government to ensure that the consequences for customers' bills are taken into account before major environmental decisions are taken.

OWS: The Main Framework
39 Companies were "appointed" under the Act, on 1 September 1989 to supply the necessary water and sewerage services in England and Wales. The 10 former Water Authorities are now Water and Sewerage Companies WaSCs), whilst the former Statutory Water Companies are now Water only Companies (WoCs). The 10 Water Authorities' previous responsibilities for regulating pollution were transferred to the National Rivers Authority.

The main regulatory instrument is the Water Act of 1989. However the "Appointed Companies" also have to comply with the more detailed requirements set out in the licences which were issued to them on their appointment.

The main control which I can exercise through the Licence is to limit the prices which the companies can charge to their customers. The annual increase is restricted to the Retail Price Index plus an additional factor "K" which has been allocated to the companies on an individual basis for each of the next 10 years to off-set the significant investment programmes which have been necessary to achieve the higher standards which we all seek, but which also include an element for future efficiency savings.

I can also influence the performance of the companies by introducing an element of competition. There are two main examples of this. I can act as a surrogate for the market, comparing the performance of the 39 separate companies and using the example of the best to set a standard for the others.

I can also create partial contestability by making new appointments for greenfield sites within existing allocated areas. These are known as "inset" appointments and can be introduced under Section 12 of the act. However the scope for such appointments may not be large. There is also some scope for large customers to abstract their own water and to treat their own waste. I shall wish to keep these opportunities open.

The Wider Regulatory Regime

The work OWS will be doing to discharge our duty to customers needs to be put in the context of the regulatory regime as a whole. At first sight this is quite complicated, with a number of actors having a role eg Office of Water Services (OWS), National Rivers Authority (NRA), Drinking Water Inspectorate (DWI), Office of Fair Trading (OFT), Monopolies and Mergers Commission (MMC), HM Inspectorate of Pollution (HMIP), Ministry of Agriculture, Fisheries and Food (MAFF), let alone the European Commission. However the actors can be divided into three main groups: the quality regulators, the economic regulators and the supply companies [diagram No 1].

It is then useful to see how the major players, the three "core" regulators, the Secretary of State (drinking water quality), the National Rivers Authority (environmental regulation) and the Office of Water Services (economic regulation) relate to each other and to the other regulators. The arrows in diagram No 2 show the main links and reveal the complexity of the arrangements. They

Structure of the New Regulatory Regime

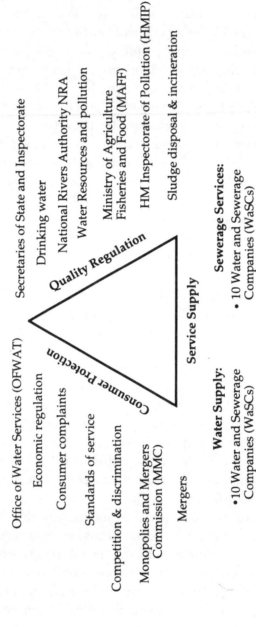

Quality Regulation

Secretaries of State and Inspectorate

Drinking water

National Rivers Authority NRA
Water Resources and pollution

Ministry of Agriculture
Fisheries and Food (MAFF)

HM Inspectorate of Pollution (HMIP)

Sludge disposal & incineration

Consumer Protection

Office of Water Services (OFWAT)

Economic regulation

Consumer complaints

Standards of service

Competition & discrimination

Monopolies and Mergers
Commission (MMC)

Mergers

Service Supply

Sewerage Services:
• 10 Water and Sewerage
  Companies (WaSCs)

Water Supply:
• 10 Water and Sewerage
  Companies (WaSCs)

• 29 Water only Companies
  (WoCs)

Diagram No. 1

40

Structure of the New Regulatory Regime

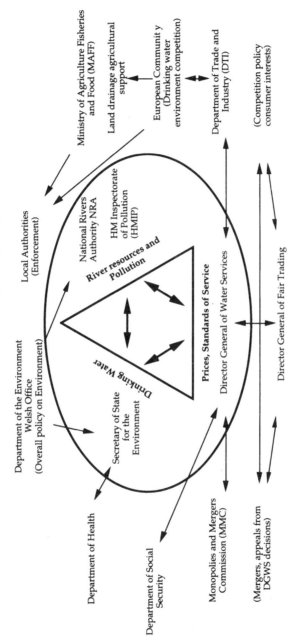

Department of the Environment
Welsh Office
(Overall policy on Environment)

Local Authorities
(Enforcement)

Ministry of Agriculture Fisheries
and Food (MAFF)

Land drainage agricultural
support

European Community
(Drinking water
environment competition)

Department of Trade and
Industry (DTI)

(Competition policy
consumer interests)

National Rivers
Authority NRA

HM Inspectorate
of Pollution
(HMIP)

River resources and
Pollution

Prices, Standards of Service

Drinking Water

Secretary of State
for the
Environment

Department of Health

Department of Social
Security

Monopolies and Mergers
Commission (MMC)

(Mergers, appeals from
DGWS decisions)

Director General of Water Services

Director General of Fair Trading

Diagram No. 2

41

also show how OWS, like the Narrator in 'A la Recherche du Temps Perdu', can tread two different paths to reach the same end point. One route involves environmental and water quality issues; the other competition and industrial issues.

Integration of Economic and Environmental Regulation

Drinking water quality, the life of our rivers and the state of the beaches are major issues of current importance for environmental policy. Although the lead is taken by the Department of the Environment (DOE) and the Welsh Office, I also have an important role to play. My involvement may simply be an exchange of information. But I may also need to take steps to ensure that the interests of water consumers are fully safeguarded – especially when it concerns the size of the bills they pay.

There are important interactions within the core triangle of diagram No 1. If any of the "quality regulators" change either their standards or their systems of measurement this can impose costs on supply companies. Those companies will then apply to OWS for an adjustment to K, as shown by arrows from quality regulators to DGWS. But arrows linking OWS to the quality regulators in the opposite direction are also important. I will impress on the quality regulators the need to ensure that adequate costing is done before higher standards are determined. It would not be in the national interest, if higher standards were imposed without considering the costs as well as the benefits of so doing.

I will also impress on the quality regulators the need to reach efficient solutions, where quality and environmental objective are achieved with the minimum commitment of resources. The test is not just whether solutions achieve their objectives, but whether they do so in a cost effective way.

The water companies have existing 10 year investment programmes which will cost over £25 billion at today's prices – most of which are related to improvements in quality. The government has now announced that it is to phase out the dumping of sewage sludge in the North Sea by 1998. Land based alternatives for disposing of this sludge will have to be found. The costs involved have not yet been fully spelt out nor their implications fully assessed. However there is no doubt that the cost will be considerable, particularly when added to the extra investment which will be needed to meet the proposed new EC Directive on the treatment of sewage discharged to our seas. Those costs will ultimately be borne by the customer.

For avoidance of misunderstanding, I want to stress that my part in the process is to strive to ensure that costings are available and that sufficient solutions have been considered. It is not for me as the economic regulator to decide on environmental policies, but to ensure that decision makers – Minsters and Parliament – have the necessary facts.

As economic regulator, I am also concerned that the companies should be able to plan their investment programmes in a reasonably stable environment. They have a large programme to manage and I am sure that we would all want to avoid a situation where new obligations could crowd out the achievement of the existing priorities.

Economic and environmental regulation of the industry should go hand in hand. There is a belief that the Water Industry can easily take on new requirements because they can apply to me for Interim Adjustments to K. In practice I think that major changes to the demands placed on the Industry should be built into Periodic Reviews not introduced piecemeal through Interim Adjustments. This will avoid excessive bureaucracy and will provide a more stable pricing structure for the customer, as well as a better planning framework for the companies.

Competition and Merger Policy

The links between the director General for Water Services (DGWS), the Director General for Fair Trading (DGFT), the Monopolies and Mergers Commission (MMC) and the Secretary of State for Trade and Industry (and indirectly with the Competition Commissioner in Brussels) are less well known. They operate in three areas:

- Monopoly policy
- Merger policy
- Customer policy.

Monopoly Policy. The DGFT and I have concurrent powers in this area. Section 28(2) of the Water Act gives me power to take action in place of DGFT (with his agreement) where it appears to me that a monopoly situation may exist "in relation to commercial activities connected with the supply of water or provision of sewerage services".

Merger Policy. The Water Act does not inhibit the takeover of an appointed company by another enterprise, unless this involves a merger with another water enterprise operating in England and Wales. The possibility of takeover can put desirable pressure on management to be efficient and make good use of their assets. I welcome the existence of such pressures. In the long run customers can only gain from an efficient industry.

However mergers between existing water enterprises in England and Wales will reduce the number of comparators and may prejudice my ability to make valid comparisons. I therefore welcome the provisions of Section 30 of the Water Act 1989 which introduces a new public criterion, against which the Monopolies and Mergers Commission can judge mergers of water enterprises. If the MMC concludes, on the basis of evidence from me and other interested parties, that a merger prejudices my ability to make comparisons, it is required to consider whether there are public interest benefits which might be expected substantially to outweigh such a detriment. For this to be the case, I believe there need to be benefits accruing to customers, normally in the form of reductions in their bills.

Merger references to the MMC are made by the Secretary of State for Trade and Industry following advice from the DGFT. I have a responsibility to alert the DGFT to developments which may lead to "material influence" or "control". The investigation itself is made by the MMC who will take evidence from interested parties including myself. Enforcement would depend on the decisions of the Secretary of State. But OFWAT would almost certainly be heavily involved. In the case of the Three Valleys merger, for example, the Secretary of State has asked me to see whether satisfactory undertakings can be obtained to offset the detriment to the public interest resulting from the loss of comparators.

MMC is also the body to whom the companies can appeal if they wish to contest my actions relating to:

- determinations on K
- amendments of their Licences
- accounting guidelines.

I also have certain powers to modify the Licences under which the companies operate. I can do this by agreement with the companies. Alternatively I can refer to the MMC any matter relating to the carrying out of functions which operate – or may be expected to operate – against the public interest and which could remedied or prevented by modifications of the Conditions of the Licence.

Customer Policy: Finally I am directly responsible for appointing and overseeing the consumers' champions, the 10 regional Customer Service Committees. I will describe these more fully later on.

OWS: The Levers of Policy

The three main tasks of OWS are to ensure: reasonable prices, satisfactory standards of service and adequate consumer representation. I will take them in turn.

The formula for the limitation of price increases (RPI + K) is becoming familiar – although I think the public has still to appreciate fully the scale of the price increase that will take place year after year. For example in the case of the 10 previous water authorities prices may increase by 5% a year over and above the inflation for the next decade. Some of the early increases for some of the previous statutory water companies are even greater.

The Secretaries of State for DOE and Wales had the responsibility for setting the initial Ks; those for the ten WaSCs in August of 1989 and for the 29 WoCs more recently in 1990. We in OWS inherit those Ks. We will administer them, and, where appropriate adjust them, either at periodic reviews or, if necessary, between those reviews in what will be known as interim adjustments to K.

Periodic Reviews

A periodic review must take place at least every ten years, although the Licence also provides for a periodic review after five years should a company request it or I consider it appropriate. Many people expect there to be a review after five years, but it would be premature to take such a judgement yet. It would, however, be prudent to plan for such an eventuality.

A periodic review provides the opportunity to conduct a 'zero base' assessment both of the situation facing an Appointee and of the Appointee's performance. The review will involve a range of tasks including:

- examining the company's investment programme, in the light of its current obligations and its revised Asset Management Plan
- assessing the appropriate return on this investment (the cost of capital)
- setting efficiency targets in the light of the results of the most recent comparative studies
- reviewing targets for standards of service
- reviewing the extent to which the arrangements for implementing the regulatory regime had achieved their objectives and examining any deficiencies which may have emerged.

I hope that a periodic review can be more streamlined than the lengthy, in-depth exercise involved in setting the initial Ks. But it will, inevitably, represent a considerable exercise.

As I indicated earlier, a periodic review would provide an opportunity to review the implications of policy developments on the part of the quality regulators and to put them into a medium term financial framework for the companies. The scale of new policies concerning quality should influence whether periodic reviews should take place at five year or ten year intervals.

At periodic reviews, price limits (K factors) would be set for the subsequent ten years. If such reviews were to take place at five year intervals, there would always be K factors (albeit subject to adjustment) set for at least five years in the future. This would provide a rolling quinquennial perspective concerning prices and levels of investment.

Interim Adjustments

By contrast, interim adjustments to K will be much more restricted. They will only involve the "relevant items" specified in the Licences, plus items "notified" by the Secretary of State. It would not be appropriate to undertake an examination of the efficiency of the company on such occasions – although its performance in meeting its objectives, for example those of its capital expenditure programmes, would be relevant. The Licence specifies a materiality threshold before interim adjustments to K can be made and trivial items are excluded.

It is entirely right for there to be provision for adjustments to K when the obligations imposed on companies are changed. Companies have no choice in the matter of externally imposed obligations as these are clearly outside the control of prudent management. But there would be risks for the regulatory regime if the provisions of the Licence for interim adjustments to K were to generate a large number of items for consideration each year. This would run counter to the objectives of the new regime, which is to focus on establishing a medium term framework within which companies can carry out their strategies, without being subject to detailed control in the short term.

Charging structures and charging systems

The formula, RPI + K, relates to the average of the charges which a company can make. It is also important to assess the structure of those charges and to relate individual charges to the actual costs of providing specific services. Price discrimination can be an abuse of monopoly power if tariffs are not available to all customers who are in the same, or a reasonably similar situation, and if those tariffs are not reasonably related to costs. The Act and the Licence require the companies to avoid undue discrimination and undue preference. OWS will examine pricing structures and develop general criteria to help identify "undue" discrimination. But the companies will also need to consider the structures of their tariffs as part of their response to the management of the rising costs of water resources and water treatment.

The method of charging for domestic consumers must change as rateable values will not be available in future for new properties, and cannot, under the Water Act, be used as the basis of charge for existing properties beyond the year 2000 for any properties. A number of options have been canvassed – metering, a flat rate charge and banded charges based on various characteristics of the property.

OWS will encourage a public debate on alternative charging systems and tariff structures. The CSCs will play a major part in this work. We propose to publish a Consultative Document on these issues during the autumn. Various issues also need to be debated in addition to the question of future charging systems, such as the charges for installing meters and the options for tariff structures, that is the relationship between standing charges and volumetric charges.

An operational problem that has already arisen in this area concerns the levying of infrastructure charges for domestic consumers. Unique to the water industry, the Government's intention was to see that, "through the [infrastructure] charge, newly connected customers for domestic water supplies or domestic sewage supplies as a group, meet the investment costs of the undertakers in providing additional capacity at treatment works, in reservoirs and trunk mains, and so on, incurred because of the additional demand from those new customers ..." (Earl of Caithness, Hansard Vol 508, Col 56, 22 May 1989).

What, however, in the 1989 Water Act, constitutes a "connection" to a water supply/public sewer of "premises" is not crystal clear, and I have had to raise with the Companies the question of amendments to Licences. I may also, perhaps over a longer time scale, have to consider whether the concept of infrastructure charges is equitable as between new and existing customers.

Service Standards

Companies are required to set targets for three standards: namely water pressure, interruptions to supply and flooding from sewers. These have been set out as:

- properties experiencing pressures of less than 10 metres head;
- properties experiencing interruptions lasting more than 12 hours;
- the number of properties where flooding from sewers occurs more than twice every 10 years.

These targets were taken into account in the initial figures for K and are set out in Levels of Service letters, which are available to the public in the OWS Library.

These are minimum standards. The aim is to reduce the number of properties where the relatively low standards are not met. OWS will also have some concern with standards more generally. For example, we have discussed pressure more generally with the manufacturers of unvented heating systems. We have asked water companies to be forthcoming about the pressures they are maintaining in different parts of their supply areas.

Companies are also required to specify and monitor their performance on other measures of service – eg response to complaints and enquiries. Companies have to notify the Director each year of their intentions during the charging year and to send him an annual Service Target report on their achievements relative to their intentions. Ministers decided to reinforce this regime of Levels of Service with guaranteed standards. This was implemented through The Water And Sewerage Services (Customer Service Standards) Regulations 1989 (S.I No 1159). These entitle customers to a £5 refund if certain standards are not met eg keeping appointments, responding to complaints and giving notice of interruptions in supply (and keeping to it). This was the first statutory scheme for privatised public utilities. If disputes arise, they can be referred by either party to the Director. We are now receiving such references.

Where performance against expectations is unsatisfactory, OWS will discuss those matters with the companies. If it remains unsatisfactory, OWS may ask the Secretary of State to make regulations under the Water Act to lay down standards of performance which will then be enforceable in the Courts.

Service standards can be too high, because they are too expensive, as well as too low. This, and the whole question of assessing the costs as well as the benefits of quality improvements, is one of the issues where I expect Customer Service Committees to contribute to the debate.

Customer Service Committees
Ten Committees have been established in areas matching the areas of the former Water Authorities. Each company (WaSCs and WoCs) has been allocated to one of these Committees. I have now appointed the Chairmen for those committees.

The Committees are an important part of the regulatory regime. Their job is to champion the interests of the consumer. They will have three tasks:

- identifying the main concerns of water consumers in their area
- ensuring that customer complaints are properly dealt with
- advising me on particular issues, such as systems of charging for water.

I will meet regularly with the Chairmen as a group. This will constitute a national Consumer Committee.

It is important that the public know who to turn to when they have problems concerning water and sewerage. All issues, whether concerning customer service or water quality might be referred to the CSCs – we will not turn them away. But we cannot invade other regulators' areas. Matters concerning the rivers are the responsibility of the NRA, who have established their own Advisory Committees; and if the matter concerns water quality it is for the Secretary of State. In such cases we will ensure that the proper body is involved.

Comparative Competition

Unlike other privatised and regulated industries in the UK, the water industry consists of a relatively large number of firms. There are 10 WaSCs and 20 WoCs. This gives scope for comparative competition. Comparative competition can never be as effective as competition in free markets, but it can be a valuable tool to stimulate efficiency and to help the regulator in setting the prices, etc, which might be expected to rule in competitive conditions.

Comparative competition should cover a number of issues. It should cover comparisons of costs – both operating costs and capital costs. It should cover levels of service. It should also consider the whole area of "customer care" – how well, for example, companies explain their services, deal with complaints and develop new ways of meeting customers' wants.

In making those comparisons, it will be necessary to take account of the differing conditions facing companies, which are outside the control of their managements, such as geological and geographical conditions. In making these comparisons it is important to recognise that there may be some factors, such as the inherited pattern of capital equipment, which are outside the scope of management in the shorter term but not in the longer term.

When making comparisons we will also have to take account of the independence of each company's management. Where an appointed business is completely independent, in terms of ownership and management, its managers can be held fully accountable. But where an appointed business is owned by a larger group, with significant activities of its own, the situation is more complex. The scope for comparison will depend on the nature and degree of devolution of management in the wider unit. The more that responsibility is devolved and the more scope there is for independent action on the part of the managers, the more helpful comparisons between companies should prove to be.

In view of the ownership structure of the industry, where four holding companies control fifteen of the WoCs, and the scope for diversification among the WaSCs, careful thought needs to be given to the way in which comparative competition can be used.

There is also scope for comparisons between, for example divisions of WaSCs with a very different operating climate or between similar divisions in different companies. Some companies have found such comparisons valuable in achieving lower costs and higher levels of efficiency.

OWS will encourage comparative competition and will publish the results of its work in this area.

The Office

Let us turn to the Office itself. There are five policy Divisions.

Charges Control are responsible for:
- adjustments to K,
- cost of capital and financial profiles,
- comparative competition, including the preparation of comparative statistics and carrying out efficiency studies,
- policy on mergers and inset appointments,
- tariff structures and methods of charging,
- accounting guidelines.

Engineering Intelligence cover:
- engineering and scientific aspects of capital investment,

- asset management plans and surface investment requirements,
- levels of service,
- performance of capital investment programmes.

Land are responsible for:
- ensuring the core business retains sufficient "interests in land" – ie property, buildings, leases, etc to enable it to continue in the event of a loss of the Licence,
- ensuring customers get half of the net proceeds of disposals of land (through an adjustment to K).

Legal
- give legal advice to the Office,
- monitor and enforce compliance with the Licence.

Consumer Affairs provide:
- approval of Codes of Practice,
- comparisons of "customer care",
- liaison with and support to CSCs,
- investigation of customer complaints and adjudications of any disputes which fall outside the scope of the CSCs.

But clearly many issues involve more than one division and in practice they will work closely together.

Monitoring of Capital Expenditure

One of the biggest challenges facing the water industry is the change to higher quality standards, both in the supply of drinking water and in the level of effluent discharged to the rivers and the sea. The industry will virtually double its capital stock in a decade. The bulk of the large investment programmes now going into operation, which will cost between £25 and £30 billion, at today's prices, over the next 10 years is related to improvements in quality. The understandable desire for environmental improvement may lead to pressures to spend even more.

The public will be paying higher bills, rising by more than 5%

over and above the rate of inflation for the next five years, to finance this programme. They are entitled to see the results.

OWS will monitor investment programmes to ensure that they are achieving their objectives. If they are not doing so, I will need to initiate a downward adjustment of K.

Monitoring should concentrate on where the money is being spent and on the results which are being achieved. I do not propose to do this by looking at individual projects. It would be complex and time consuming to compare each project as it is completed with the original plans. Such an approach would also restrict the flexibility which management need to make changes in the design of the programme that would enable the objectives to be met more effectively or more cheaply. I will expect companies to have their own management system to relate their plans to what they do at the level of projects.

We need to know first how, at a broad level, actual expenditure relates to what was intended in the company's asset management plans. Over the medium term of, say, five years, capital expenditure may vary from what was originally planned as projects are examined in detail. Also priorities may change in response to environmental and other pressures, for example the consequences of the Government's decision to abandon the dumping of sewage sludge in the North Sea. OFWAT will ask the companies to explain such variations in three categories – change of priorities, the use of different solutions to problems, especially where they involve increased current expenditure rather than capital expenditure and where innovative solutions have been developed. We will also want to know where capital plans are being delayed, either because of shortages in the supplying industries or because of shortages of key internal staff.

OFWAT is also developing, in association with the companies themselves, and the quality regulators, a system of "monitoring by performance". The initial criteria which we propose to assess are:

- asset quality
- levels of service
- compliance with drinking water standards (WoCs and WaSCs)
- compliance with discharge consents (WaSCs) only.

This work will require analytic skills and an imaginative approach from my own staff and also from the quality regulators, who are the enforcement agents for drinking water and for waste water. It needs to be done to demonstrate to consumers that their money is being well spent.

Style of Regulation
The following principles will guide our work.

- It is important to distinguish between regulation and management. OWS is concerned with the framework. Companies must have the freedom to manage within that framework.
- OWS will not seek to be confrontational although it will rise to any challenges.
- OWS will adopt an open style. We will not discuss issues that are sub judice. But we will be ready to expose and to discuss the principles we are following and to explain reasons for decision.
- OWS will seek to develop regular flows of information, which can be used for comparative purposes. We will work closely with the industry in doing this. Provided it does not breach commercial confidentiality, we will want to see such information made available to the public.

Conclusion
Natural monopolies need to be regulated in the interests of consumers. Regulation is also required for goods such as drinking water, where issues of health could be concerned and for services,

such as the disposal of sewage, where environmental and public health issues can arise.

The regulation of the industry is, inevitably, complex, and involves a number of different skills. The Government has decided to set up different agencies for different purposes. This has the management advantage that specialist skills can be deployed effectively within single-purpose agencies. But it is essential that the regulatory bodies should work closely together in the interests of consumers. Economic and environmental regulation need to be integrated.

The standards which the industry is asked to meet have to be justified and integrated into existing investment programmes. This will give industry the certainty which it needs to plan and manage its affairs and the customer confidence that the increased costs which they will face are well founded and predictable.

Regulation is necessary, but oppressive regulation is undesirable. The water industry needs to make a leap forward to higher standards of water quality and to meet the challenges of increasingly discriminating customers. On the supply side this involves heavy investment and taking advantage of technological changes and innovations. On the consumer side, it involves innovation in major issues, such as methods of charging. Providing that they operate within the framework set by the public interest, companies must be given the scope for using and developing business skills and exercising their business judgement.

In its turn, OFWAT is ready to meet the challenges it faces. The *Office* is now emerging from its build-up period. Customer Service Committees Chairmen and members have been appointed. We will endeavour to play our part in ensuring that the water industry in England and Wales is the best and most efficient in the world.

2.3 Economic Regulation in a Political Climate: the Case of the Water Industry

Presented 17th November 1992

ROLLING BACK THE FRONTIERS OF THE STATE

In Britain we put a clear dividing line between the public and private sectors of the economy. For example we consolidate the whole of the accounts of the public sector (central government, local government and public corporations) into one entity within the framework of the public accounts. This produces a number of problems, illustrated, for example, by the continuing debate on the private financing of public projects.

Some people, for example many of my professional associates in France, think we take this to extremes in our pursuit of logic. It is not my purpose tonight to go widely into this subject, fascinating though it is. I do, however, want to take it as a point of departure for talking to you about the regulation of the water companies. Some of the most interesting issues in regulating water arise because it hovers on the boundaries of the public and private sectors, where the interface between business and public service becomes almost a day to day concern.

This is not, you may say, the language of rolling back the frontiers of the state – the prime political drive behind the privatisation programme. That there has been checking, and some rolling back, of state power is of significance. But the public sector still plays a major role in the operations of the water companies. In this paper, I propose to consider the position of those frontiers (remembering that these issues are rarely as clear cut in practice as they are in the text books) and the implications for economic regulation of the debate in this area.

This debate covers the public's general attitude to water and sewerage services, environmental and quality pressures, consumer (or customer)ism, and the interface with policy on social benefits. As I have the honour of addressing the Manchester Statistical Society, I shall also have something to say both about the information which we will use in our regulatory tasks and about the dissemination of information to the customer, to the public and to experts in the area. I take some pleasure in doing this because I believe that it is a function of government to provide information to the public as well as to guide its own decisions. This has the salutary – if not always comfortable – effect of exposing the rationale of decision taking to informed challenge. Such information may be misused; but openness helps to prevent the abuse of governmental monopoly in decision taking.

SPECIAL POSITION OF THE WATER COMPANIES

Any utility will be exposed to political pressures. Such pressures will inevitably be strong where most people take the service and where they have limited or no choice about where to buy it. In the case of water, these pressures are particularly strong. There is a widespread belief that water is (or should be) a free good, either because it is a natural resource, or because, like air and unlike coal or natural gas, it has special characteristics as a resource.

Without accepting the logic behind such views, these, we should recognise, are potent elements in the public concern about rising water charges. They are a significant element in a poisonous cocktail which includes rising prices, rising profits, rising dividends and rising Chairmen's salaries.

The objective reality may be rather different. Two simple economic statistics alone may indicate why customers experience problems which then impact on the regulation of the water companies. Water accounts for 1% of consumers' expenditure; it accounts for 3% of gross domestic fixed capital formation. It is not surprising to find large borrowing and rising prices. Add to this the fact that investment will produce long term rather than short term benefits. Customers are paying the bill well before the better quality water comes through the taps and before the rivers and the beaches are unpolluted by sewage.

Water is not simply a utility in the same sense as gas, telecoms and electricity. Water is essential to life and virtually all the population in urban and suburban areas depends on the delivery of water and collection of sewage by water companies. 99% of households are on a public water supply and 95% of households are on mains sewerage. We may expect these percentages to rise as a result of growing regulation of private supplies of water and private disposals of sewage.

There is a health dimension to the quality of drinking water and this drives the debate, even though only a small proportion of the water we use (1-3%) enters our bodies and even though the level of concern is, generally speaking, on the margin of what is measurable in terms of the effect on health. Water services include the collection and disposal of sewage which has a major environmental impact. 28% of pollution incidents in rivers, estuaries and the sea result from disposal of sewage by water and sewerage companies.

This ambivalence about the public and private nature of water and sewerage services extends to the issue of how we pay for our water. There is no national consensus about whether water services should be seen as public services financed from taxation or as utility services financed from revenue. This distinguishes water and sewerage from utilities such as telecoms, gas and electricity, which are seen more directly as commercial services.*

*It must be asked whether private sector bodies should retain the taxation powers they enjoyed whilst in the public sector. In the privatisation statute water companies were denied the power to continue to levy charges on rateable values after the year 2000. But they show a disturbing – if understandable – predilection for switching to the Council Tax, or levying high standing charges of one kind or another. These tendencies may have to be curbed in the public interest.

ENVIRONMENTAL POLITICS

There are very strong environmental pressures on the sector. The environmental pressure groups are capable of exercising considerable leverage on the political climate. The European Commission in Brussels sometimes appears determined to run each country's environmental policy; this is not exclusive to water but has a major effect in that area. At home, the Government has set up powerful agencies such as the National Rivers Authority to improve water quality. There is still a standing Royal Commission (1) on the environment and it has recently reported on water quality.

All too often the public has to rely on information from those with axes to grind. It is often said by the pressure groups that water standards should be raised. But it is not clear how far and how fast customers would like standards to rise, in particular how much they are prepared to pay for this.

These issues would have arisen irrespective of privatisation. But privatisation has both contributed to the debate and changed the incentives on the political agents. Under nationalisation, pressure for higher standards had to be accommodated within the twin pressures of the PSBR and the Government's willingness to raise water charges. Under privatisation, the Department of the Environment is no longer constrained by the Treasury nor by having to announce increased charges. This release from traditional pressures has coincided with the imposition of major quality objectives on the water companies.

At the time of privatisation, all existing obligations – whose pursuit in the past had been constrained by the public finances – were costed and put into a £28 billion ten year investment programme. To finance this prices had to rise significantly over that period. These pressures did not, however, stop in 1989. New price limits were announced for the water companies in August 1989. In March 1990, the Government announced the adoption of the Urban Waste Water Treatment Directive (2). At the time it was said that this would involve capital expenditure of some £1.5 billion;

two years later the cost looks more like £4 to 6 billion and could be considerably more. In 1991, the Drinking Water Inspectorate, following pressure from Brussels to remove every detectable trace of pesticides from drinking water, effectively imposed a capital programme of a further £1 billion on the companies.

Nor is this the end of the story. For example, the World Health Organization is in the process of adopting more stringent guideline standards for lead in drinking water. To meet this standard it would be necessary to remove all lead pipes. This would cost the water companies another £3 billion or so and impose perhaps double that expenditure on the owners of the properties concerned.

Ministers may face rather different incentives than in the days of nationalisation. But the resource consequences are still there. When obligations are imposed, the regulator is obliged to act in a way he considers best calculated to ensure that they can be financed. The capital markets can be relied upon to provide the finance only if the customer has to pay more – not simply to meet the financing cost but in some cases to meet some of the capital costs at the time they are incurred. Our simple ready reckoner suggests that every £1 billion of additional capital investment costs the customer £2 (or just over 1%) a year on the water bill.

CUSTOMERS AND CHARTERS

The eighties were a decade of emerging consumer power, moving away from the producer corporatism of the post-war settlement. The trend seems set to continue during the nineties. The power of consumers is rising relative to that of producers and may be expected to continue to do so as the effects of the considerable liberalisation of the world economy feed through into individual markets. Moreover, consumers are giving place to customers; no-one expects to be called a consumer in the high street shop and those buying utility services do not like to be treated like one.

The scene is shifting from the public service tradition where Platonic Guardians decide what is good for the people, to one of responsiveness to customer wishes and to customer complaints.

The main thrust of the Citizen's Charter seems directed to improving the service provided by public sector bodies. It has had two dimensions when applied to the utilities. On the one hand there has been emphasis on achieving responsiveness to citizen (or customer) wishes, on the measurement of service provision; and where the service is paid for, on the relationship between the quality of the service and the price paid. On the other hand there has been emphasis on the provision of greater competition as an incentive (and a discipline) for better service.

Both aspects have a part to play in the regulation of the water companies. The regulators now have stronger powers, through the Competition and Service (Utilities) Act, 1992 to settle disputes between customers and companies. Settling disputes includes the issue of whether customers are entitled to financial redress for poor quality service. There is a guaranteed standards scheme in the water industry which provides for payments for specified failures, such as not keeping an appointment. We have recently made proposals for strengthening it. We doubt, however, whether it could ever deal with the numerous and complex cases where customers have had poor service. But it was not thought appropriate to give Ofwat powers to force companies to provide compensation. There is a constitutional point at issue here, stemming from the private sector status of the companies.

The Competition and Service (Utilities) Act also widened the scope for competition in the water (as well as the gas) industry. It is now possible for companies to compete across each other's boundaries. This is potentially important where new greenfield development is taking place and for large existing industrial consumers of water (taking more than 250 megalitres of water a year). It is also possible for companies new to the water industry to compete for supply in these areas.

SOCIAL BENEFITS

Water bills may be only 1% of consumers' expenditure, but represent a larger proportion of income for the poorer households.

There are strong general arguments for dealing with problems of low income households through the social benefits system rather than the pricing of a particular commodity. Changes in the social security system have, however, reduced rather than increased the scope for shielding low income water customers from higher prices. The Fowler Reforms of the mid-1980s simplified the system; any suggestion of special arrangements to deal with rising water bills would move in the opposite direction.

The position could be complicated by a switch to metering. Under metering it may prove to be more difficult to deal with the problem of a combination of low income and high consumption. Although there are candidates – for example an addition to (means tested) Family Credit – it is not easy to devise general tests which identify those in this category and provide substantial support, without making widespread payments to others.

There would always remain the problem in meeting any hardship arising from increased water bills from the social benefits system because of the wide range of water bills for customers in different companies. Bills range from £139 to £248 with an interquartile range of £51. A national social security system and local water charges based on local costs do not fit well together.

ECONOMIC REGULATORY REGIME

The regime applied to water, RPI+K, is a different way of expressing the RPI-X system applied to the other utilities. Prices, not profits, are controlled. Price cap regulation, where the price limits are set on a medium term basis, provides important incentives for the companies to reduce their costs.

There are, however, special factors operating in the case of water: the fact that the water K is positive while the gas and telecom (but not electricity) Xs are negative has a significant impact. Because of the public response to price increases above the rate of inflation, there has to be a very clear justification for any particular K factor. The impossibility of financing the industry's capital programmes at current price levels puts emphasis on estimates of the scale of price increases necessitated by the capital costs of investments. The Licence (3,4) within which the companies operate allows them to apply to me for higher prices to finance the expenditure (capital and current) needed to carry out environmental and quality obligations imposed on them. Also, unique among the privatisation statutes, the Water Act requires me to act "in the way I consider best calculated to ... secure ... reasonable returns on ... capital ...".

The regulatory task is complicated not so much by the number of companies (although this imposes a considerable work burden) but by the range of size – from a turnover of £70,000 to £747 million. (The interquartile range is £167million.) A further complication arises because 10 of the companies both supply clean water and take away dirty water, while 23 only supply clean water.

But, on the other hand, the number and variety of companies increases the ability of the regulator to make comparisons between them and use such comparisons in the setting of price limits. Comparative competition may be more important than direct competition.

OBJECTIVES OF THE ECONOMIC REGULATOR

The first question for the regulator is to decide whether to concentrate on balancing the interests of the various groups within the legal framework or adopting a more active approach.

The first generation of utility regulators in the UK have, generally speaking, adopted a relatively active role. This has been my interpretation of the task although it is most important to recognise that regulators operate within a framework of the law and are not part of a law making elected government. I think it is inevitable that a number of choices need to be made; for example:

- is the regulator concerned to balance the interests of shareholders and customers or is he or she supposed to be a champion of customers?
- what profile should the regulator adopt? How much should the regulator raise, or pursue, under issues of public concern? In particular is it the job of the water regulator to try to keep down prices rather than simply administer the rate at which they increase?
- how active should the regulator be in seeking reform of aspects of the regime under which he operates?

RULES AND DISCRETION

Inevitably there is more discretion in a regime in its early days. It would scarcely be possible to formulate a whole regulatory regime on paper before it began, let alone breathe life into it before putting it into operation. It is not, as Arthur Young said in 1789, as though a constitution were "a pudding to be made out of a recipe".

Anyone operating within any set of arrangements will naturally take account of the emphasis placed on certain factors by the other actors on the scene. The water regulator is given the task of operating a system of customer representation and individual customer redress through the statutory Customer Service Committees (CSC's) whose chairmen and members he is to appoint and resource; this will inevitably influence what he or she does.

I have emphasised my position in safeguarding the interests of customers. This is not because I think the interest of customers should be placed above those of shareholders. Indeed, there is no necessary conflict between the two; customers want the investment which can only be financed by shareholders and creditors. But, while shareholders could earn reasonable returns without the existence of an economic regulator, customers could not be safeguarded against monopolistic exploitation without one.

I have seen it as one of the tasks of the economic regulator to exercise general restraint in increases in customers' bills. As the main driving force behind higher bills is not excess profits and dividends but the scale of environmental obligations, I have put a good deal of effort into arguing the importance of costing obligations before they are adopted. That such a procedure makes such obvious common sense to a large body of social scientists does not guarantee its acceptance.

Linked to the specification of costs and benefits, I have also suggested that customers might challenge the worthwhileness of the quality obligations being imposed on water companies. It is not, of course, a question of being against environmental and quality improvements. It is a question of the scale of the benefit and the timing of the imposition of the new obligation compared with the cost of achieving it.

STABILITY AND OUTPUTS

At a more technical level, I have emphasised the importance of stability and the prime importance of looking at outputs (results for customers) rather than inputs (expenditure and work carried out). Inputs follow from a correct specification of outputs, not the other way round.

The water industry has not enjoyed a stable environment. Investment, for example, has been subject to great fluctuations. Rather like the 10,000 men of the noble Duke of York, it was marched up the hill in the early 70s and down again in the late 70s to be marched up the hill again in the early 1990s. It would help the companies to plan and to deliver greater efficiency and lower costs, if investment were to continue in a rather more stable way than has been the case in the past. Such stability would also help customers by moderating the divergence of increases in water prices from the RPI.

I have, therefore, stressed the importance of a medium term approach. Most major decisions should, in my view, be made at quinquennial Periodic Reviews, leaving adjustments between such reviews to a minimum. At such reviews, regulators need to take a thorough look at obligations placed on the companies, at their investment implications, at the appropriate return on capital and at the levels of customer service to be achieved. Between reviews, adjustments should only be made to keep on a sensible medium term track. The difficulty with this approach, however, arises not from the companies, but from the disjunction which can arise between the objectives of the companies and the economic regulator on the one hand and the objectives of the quality and environmental regulators on the other hand. But sensible reconciliation should be possible, and this is now being pursued on both sides.

REGULATORY PROFILE AND PUBLIC CONSULTATION

The question of the profile of the economic regulator raises some delicate questions. Many of the issues – water quality, metering and "water poverty" – are political. While leadership may be necessary, a non-elected public official must avoid making overt political judgements or usurping the proper role of the elected government of the day.

The route I have chosen is that of consultation, where consultation is based on the provision of information. The two go hand in hand; they have to be developed in a balanced way.

REGULATORY INFORMATION

The information base in the water industry is modest both in quantity and quality. If the task of setting prices is to be done well, systematic information must be collected on a regular basis. We have taken initiatives in a number of areas.

- The specification and analysis of good regulatory accounts for the appointed water and sewerage business. In consultation with the industry, Ofwat has laid down guidelines for current cost accounts (5) (dealing with the issue of accounting for inflation).

- The specification of information on the progress of the investment programme – monitoring (real) financial outturns against plans, looking at activity measures (such as miles of pipes laid and the cost of achieving them), and at the level of investment in achieving compliance with water quality standards.
- Specification, for the first time, of the main outputs of the industry (water delivered to customers and sewage collected and disposed of) and the measurement of the costs per unit of carrying out these activities.
- Specification and measurement of the quality of service received by customers – adequacy of water resources to meet demand, adequacy of response to customer complaints and queries and adequacy of service standards in relation to pressure, interruptions in supply and flooding from sewers.
- Integration of engineering, accounting, economic and financial information in a quinquennial strategic business plan looking at least ten years ahead. This has developed a long way from the asset management plans specified for underground assets in the Licence.

These various developments are, of course, of limited value unless the information is of sufficient quality. We have, therefore, sought to develop the role of independent certifiers (engineers, auditors, etc) appointed by the companies, but whose appointments must be approved by us, and who owe the regulator a duty of care.

The use of independent certifiers may be necessary to secure good information, but they are not sufficient. We need to concentrate on ensuring the broad accuracy of the information base concentrating on a relatively small number of key figures. In time, the spread and depth of the information can be improved. But it would be foolish of us to risk getting lost in detail at an early stage of the venture. We must also be careful to concentrate on outputs (results) and not risk getting sucked into inputs and therefore into the resource decisions which companies should make. If we allowed this to happen we would risk weakening incentives to efficient behaviour.

Handling of data is also important. We have developed software systems to enable us to collect from, and share with, the companies information on performance and on tariff structures. This information can be analysed quickly; this year the first analyses of the main return, which comes to us each July, were being circulated within Ofwat within a few days.

Some of this information is provided to us on a Commercial-in-Confidence basis. But, if the regime is to be transparent, much of this information should be in the public domain. We have therefore instituted Annual Reports on:

- company financial performance (revenue, costs, return on capital, etc) and progress on capital expenditure (6)
- costs of water delivered, and amount of water not delivered (leakage from company distribution systems) (7)
- levels of service received by customers (8)

As the information improves we will develop comparisons between the performance of the companies as well as tracking their performance over time.

We aim to set out the main facts in an accessible way; we are also ready to provide more detailed information on request. In addition to what we publish ourselves, we provide information (and sponsorship) to the Centre for the Study of Regulated Industries, who publish financial information, and information on tariffs (9,10), in more detail, following on the statistical series established some years ago by CIPFA.

We have also paid considerable attention to the communication of information on water regulation to customers generally. We attempt, in our Annual Report (11), to set out a clear and accessible account of our activities. (The Annual Report also provides a reference document setting out basic facts and listing our publications during the year.) Each of the customer service committees also produce an Annual Report (12). We have instituted a series of information notes (13), setting out simply and briefly the key elements in the regulatory regime. We have also produced a series of leaflets (14-16), some telling customers about our services – including those of our CSC's – and some publicising useful information, often not available before, on for example, the cost of undertaking water using activities, such as taking a bath, watering the garden, or flushing the lavatory. We have also produced two videos (13,18) and an audiotape (19).

RESEARCH

We are also committed to a programme of (modest) research. In particular:

- We commissioned a study (20) of customer preference so that we would know the main outputs, things which customers wanted. This is fundamental to any measures of company performance. We are continuing this work to explore the possibility of achieving better measures of willingness to pay for improvement in water quality.

- We commissioned from OPCS (21) a study on charging methods (metering, banding or flat rate charging). This was an essential input into our strategy on Paying for Water.

- We commissioned a study of customer views on meter location (22) and on the social and financial impact of water metering (23).

- We have commissioned research from the Institute for Fiscal Studies (not yet completed) which will integrate data on water consumption into a household model and enable us to relate developments in water bills – on different bases of charging – to the social and economic characteristics of households.

- We have carried out some internal research (subject to tight resource constraints). We have analysed water company costs and the contribution made by factors outside a company's control (geology, geography, etc) and will publish a research paper on this important subject in the spring.

CONSULTATION

In parallel with the specification, gathering and publication of information, and our research work, we have engaged on a number of public consultations, and encouraged the companies to consult with their customers. The main examples are:

- Paying for Water 1990 (24). We set out options in the form of a consultation paper, leaflets, and video and public meetings. This included both charging methods (metering etc) and the structure of tariffs (size of standing charge, etc). As I have mentioned, we commissioned a structured survey of 4,000 households. Questionnaires were also issued to nearly 18 million households with their water bills, not to get a statistically valid set of answers, but to give everyone the opportunity to respond. We used this consultation in the preparation of a strategy for paying for water and also in our continuing work on the balance between the measured and unmeasured tariffs used by water companies.

- Cost of Capital 1991 (25). We issued a two volume paper aimed at the City, setting out our approach and assembling such information as was available on the costs of borrowing and of equity. We received a large number of responses from investors and their advisers and a three volume riposte from the two trade associations. We will take account of this when we come to set price limits at the Periodic Review in 1994.

- Cost of Quality 1992 (26). We issued a paper which analysed the costs of existing and potential quality and environmental obligations and their implications for customer bills. We will take account of the responses to this paper when talking to the companies about their market plans, before these are translated into their strategic business plans. We will also use these responses in our dialogue with the quality regulators.

- Assessing Capital Values, 1992 (27). We recently issued a consultation paper on a framework for incorporating the "reasonable rate of return" into price limits. This is essentially concerned with translating Cost of Capital numbers into an accounting framework. We hope this will achieve a better articulated and a more transparent approach.
- Guaranteed Standards Scheme, 1992 (28). We published our proposals and amended them in the light of comments before submitting recommendations to the Secretaries of State.
- Debt and Disconnection, 1992 (29); Services to Disabled and Elderly Customers, 1991 (30). We consulted on guidelines before issuing them to companies.
- Disputes resolution, (1992) (31). We consulted on the criteria we proposed to follow in using the new powers given to us in the Competition and Services (Utilities) Act, 1992.
- Guidelines for Optional Metering, 1992 (32). We have been very concerned to stimulate the companies to improve their optional metering schemes in order to promote customer choice. These issues cover the provision of information for customers, reasonable charges for installation and meter location, as well as the crucial issue of a fair tariff for measured customers in comparison with that for unmeasured customers.

In addition we have developed a "due process" consultation in respect of changes in the Licences under which the companies operate. This has included public consultation on amendments concerned to regulate transactions between the Appointed Business and other parts of the Group company and so to safeguard the interests of the customers of the core water and sewerage businesses. This involved steps to protect the capital of the core business (in 1991) and further amendments to protect its income following the 1992 Utilities Act.

COMPANY MARKET PLANS

I am determined to involve customers as much as possible. I have, therefore, asked the companies to produce, by next spring, their own market plans after consultation with their customers. These market plans would be their first approach to the strategic business plans which they will submit to me in the spring of 1994 for determination of their K factors for the next ten years. I have encouraged the companies to engage in various forms of consultation with customers, starting with the provision of a sound information base. I hope that consultation will mobilise the views of more than an articulate minority of customers. But if it does no more than alert people to the position in which they will find themselves as a result of the external pressures operating on the companies, it will have served a useful purpose. How far we should go in opening up these processes of government and regulation to the public, poses some very interesting questions. British governmental processes may have been too inward looking and greater exposure may be in the public interest. Here again I find myself taking a position which may be said to go wider than what I am required to do under the Act. But I argue that one of the merits of privatisation was to create a more transparent regime. For this greater transparency to work well, it needs adequate information.

CUSTOMER SERVICE COMMITTEES

I have referred to CSCs earlier, but left a substantive discussion until late in the paper.

For me, there are two major aspects of the CSCs. First they are the part of the office primarily concerned with the individual customer as opposed to the generality of customers who are protected by our general regulatory powers and policies. Secondly, they are a key aspect of the contact with customers and hence with the political rather than technical part of our work.

I hasten to add that there is no sharp division between political and technical matters. The CSCs, for example, have taken a close interest in the structure of tariffs and tariff policies – notably in relation to standing charges and the balance of measured and unmeasured changes. In this, they have worked closely with our Charges Control Division in Birmingham. This joint working has had a powerful influence on some of the companies.

I will mention two aspects of the work which CSCs have pursued in protecting the interest of individual customers. One concerns the complaints systems operated by individual companies. The water companies get ten times as many complaints as Ofwat. We could not possibly handle all of them, nor would it be sensible public policy to expand the office to do this. The prime responsibility for dealing with complaints rests with companies and our role should be limited to ensuring that companies have good systems for handling complaints and remedying those not properly dealt with by the company concerned.

CSCs have sought to ensure that where customers have not been properly dealt with, they should get proper redress – often financial compensation or the payment of a rebate. The CSCs have been quite successful in this area. We did not collect such information centrally before April 1991. In 1991–92, however, CSCs obtained financial redress amounting to £840,000. In the first 6 months of 1992–93, the figure amounted to £700,000. (This is as much as the Gas Consumer Council achieved over a period of six years.) Some CSCs have pressed for extension of Ofwat powers to award compensation. They have argued that the Director General should have powers to award compensation in cases of disputes.

Secondly, the CSC network, acting through the Chairmen's Group (the Chairmen of the ten regional CSCs who meet regularly with me), provides a sounding board and a source of advice and information for the Director General on the way in which he should develop the regime. I found their advice of great value and would be hard put to rehearse all the occasions when it has had a material influence on what I have done.

The success of the Chairmen's Group in influencing the direction of the regulatory regime has owed much to the calibre of the Chairmen who have been willing to serve and also to their diverse backgrounds and experience.

I have various moves in hand for strengthening the position of the Chairmen's Group and for raising its public profile.

CONCLUSION

Rather than take a narrow focus, I thought I should talk about the broad thrust we have developed in putting flesh on the bones of the regulatory regime laid down by Parliament in the Water Act and by the Secretaries of State in the Licence under which the companies were appointed to carry out their statutory roles.

I have emphasised the interplay between policies and information and the need to manage wider political issues as well as the technical aspects of tariffs, corporate finance or investment planning. I have not tried to cover everything; the Cook's tour would have some extra excursions looking, for example, at the whole issue of the diversification of the water companies into other activities and the work of the regulator in ensuring that the interests of the core water customers are adequately protected.

REFERENCES

1. Freshwater quality. Royal Commission on Environmental Pollution. Cm 1966. HMSO, 1992. 0 10 119662 8
2. Council directive of 21 May 1991 concerning urban waste water treatment (91/271/EEC). Official Journal of the European Communities, 30 May 1991, L 135/40 – L 135/52
3. Instrument of appointment of the water and sewerage undertakers. Department of the Environment and Welsh Office. HMSO, 1989. ISBN 0 11 752228 7

4. Instrument of appointment of the water undertakers. Department of the Environment and Welsh Office. HMSO, 1989. ISBN 0 11 752257 0
5. Guideline for accounting for current costs. (RAG 1). OFWAT, May 1992.
6. Capital investment and financial performance of the water companies in England and Wales 1991-92. OFWAT, October 1992. (published annually)
7. Water delivered. Due for publication late 1992. (published annually)
8. Levels of service for the water industry in England and Wales 1990–91. OFWAT, December 1992. (1991–92 edition due late 1992, published annually)
9. The UK water industry: charges for water services 1992–93. Centre for the Study of Regulated Industries, May 1992. (published annually)
10. The UK water industry: water services and costs 1990–91. Centre for the Study of Regulated Industries, March 1992. (published annually)
11. OFWAT annual report 1991. HC 31. HMSO, June 1992. ISBN 0 10 203193 2 (published annually)
12. Customer Service Committees. Annual reports 1991-92. OFWAT, June 1992.
    Central Customer Service Committee
    Eastern Customer Service Committee
    Northumbria Customer Service Committee
    North West Customer Service Committee
    Southern Customer Service Committee
    South West Customer Service Committee
    Thames Customer Service Committee
    Customer Service Committee for Wales
    Wessex Customer Service Committee
    Yorkshire Customer Service Committee

13. Information notes. OFWAT.
    1. Monitoring company performance: the July return. Revised. January 1992.
    2. Financing of major environmental improvements. April 1991.
    3. Why water bills are rising and how they are controlled. Revised. March 1992.

4. Guaranteed standards scheme. May 1991.
5. Comparative competition. May 1991.
6. Controls on land disposal. Revised. February 1992.
7. Charges for a new connection to the mains or sewer. October 1991.
8. The K factor – what it is and how it can be changed. October 1991.
9. Diversification by water companies. Revised. April 1992.
10. Increasing competition in the water industry. April 1992.
11. First time rural sewerage. August 1992.
12. Water pressure. May 1992.
13. Water delivered. May 1992.
14. Responsibility for water and sewerage pipes. June 1992.
15. Optional metering. July 1992.
16. Water charges and company profits. July 1992.

14. Water and sewerage bills 1992–93. OFWAT, March 1992.
15. Water and you. OFWAT, May 1992.
16. Protecting the interests of water customers. OFWAT, October 1992.
17. Paying for water: a time for decisions. OFWAT video tape, November 1990.
18. The visit: OFWAT and a forceful mother-in-law help solve a young couple's problem with their water bill. OFWAT video tape, November 1991.
19. All about OFWAT: audio cassette tape produced for the visually disadvantaged and caring and advice agencies. OFWAT, September 1992.
20. Paying for water: customer questionnaire. OFWAT, July 1991.
21. Paying for water: OPCS omnibus survey. OFWAT, June 1991.
22. The customer viewpoint: a quantitative survey (MORI report). OFWAT, May 1992.
23. The social impact of water metering. OFWAT, August 1992.
24. Paying for water: a time for decisions. OFWAT, November 1990. Consultation paper, statement, leaflet.
25. Cost of capital: a consultation paper. OFWAT, July 1991.
26. Cost of quality: a strategic assessment of the prospects for future water bills. OFWAT, August 1992.
27. Assessing capital values at the periodic review: a consultation paper

on the framework for reflecting reasonable returns on capital in price limits . OFWAT, November 1992.

28. Compensation for customers: a consultation paper. OFWAT, May 1992.
29. Guidelines on debt and disconnection. OFWAT, April 1992.
30. Guidelines on services for disabled and elderly customers. OFWAT, September 1991.
31. Competition and Service (Utilities) Act 1992: determination of disputes. MD 83. OFWAT, August 1992.
32. Guidelines on optional metering. OFWAT, May 1992.

2.4   The impact of EC Directives on water customers in England and Wales

Journal of European Public policy, 3: 4 December 1996

ABSTRACT

Since 1989, customers' bills for water and sewerage services in England and Wales have risen in real terms. A large proportion of the increase has been required to fund compliance with the standards and timescales laid out in legislation transposing EC Directives. This article explains the process used to set the limits on customers' bills and reflects on the further impact of proposed new legislation.

Keywords
Affordability; consumers; EU environmental policy; implementation costs; water bills; water industry.

REGULATION OF THE WATER INDUSTRY IN ENGLAND AND WALES

Legislation introduced in 1989, and consolidated in 1991, established a new system of economic regulation and the appointment of the Director General of Water Services (and the creation of the Director's Office of Water Services – Ofwat). The Water Industry Act 1991 sets out the primary duty of the Director – to ensure that the water and sewerage undertakers for England and Wales properly carry out their functions and can finance them. The Director also has a duty to protect the interests of customers in respect of the charges that they pay and the quality of the services that they receive.

Responsibility for setting the drinking water quality and environmental standards, with which the undertakers must comply, lies with the Secretary of State for the Environment (or Wales where appropriate). Many of these standards are included in legislation agreed by the European Community. Enforcement of these standards is carried out by the Drinking Water Inspectorate (DWI) and the Environment Agency (EA) – formerly the National Rivers Authority (NRA). Ofwat works closely with the quality regulators to ensure that customers receive the improved standards for which they are paying.

THE IMPACT OF QUALITY

In 1989, at the privatization of the ten water and sewerage companies, the Secretaries of State for the Environment and Wales set price limits which allowed companies to carry out an extensive programme of capital work, to maintain and improve services, and to raise quality standards relating to the environment and drinking water. During the first ten years a capital spending programme of £28 billion in 1989 prices was planned, requiring prices to customers' bills to rise on average 5 per cent per year in real terms during the first five years to 1995.

The Water Act 1989 placed a duty on water companies to supply water that is wholesome at the time of supply. Wholesomeness is defined by the standards and other require-ments set out in the Water Supply (Water Quality) Regulations 1989 and subsequent amendments. These regulations incorporate the relevant requirements of the EC Drinking Water Directive (80/778/EEC) as well as some national standards. The companies were already supplying very good quality water. The Chief Inspector of the DWI reported that, in 1991, 98.7 per cent of the 3.6 million analytical tests carried out complied with the regulations (DWI 1992). A detailed work programme was defined to improve compliance towards 100 per cent. Extensive compliance programmes were undertaken for nitrates and pesticides as well as for quality problems attributable to the condition of the water distribution system. The Chief Inspector reported improvements in company performance in 1995 compared with 1990 for these parameters and for compliance with microbiological standards (DWI 1996).

For the sewerage service, funding was arranged in 1989 to continue improvements to the quality of designated bathing waters, as set out in the EC Directive on the Quality of Bathing Water 1976 (76/160/EEC). The NRA reported that 89 per cent of 425 designated bathing waters complied with the mandatory quality standards in 1995 compared with 78 per cent of 407 in 1990. A large capital programme to deal with pollution to inland waters, such as rivers, required by the national Control of Pollution Act 1974, also continued after privatization.

During the first two years of the new regime, there was a review of the pesticide compliance programme and this was brought forward to achieve drinking water compliance well before the year 2000. An advancement of the bathing waters compliance programme was also announced with the majority of schemes to be completed by 1995. These changes placed extra burdens on a number of the companies. The extra obligations were eligible for consideration as a relevant change of circumstances under Condition B of the licence under which companies operate. Undertakers are allowed to ask the Director to review price limits to allow the cost of these additional obligations to be passed on to customers. Two companies asked for a review of price limits – South West Water Services Ltd and North West Water Ltd.

The major impact was for customers of South West Water Ltd. To make provisions for the accelerated bathing water compliance programme and the ending of sewage sludge disposal at sea, prices had to be allowed to rise to 11.5 per cent above inflation for each of the three years 1992–3, 1993–4 and 1994–5, instead of the earlier 6.5 per cent. This gave an average household bill of £185 for unmeasured sewerage in the region, compared with the national average of £105 and the lowest in the country of £83.

It was apparent that the economic and regulatory climate in which the companies were operating was evolving and that a review of prices would be necessary after five years, rather than allowing the price limits set by the Secretaries of State at the time of privatization to run for the full ten years.

COST OF QUALITY DEBATE

The Director has a duty to ensure that companies can finance their functions, and when preparing for the Periodic Review of prices in 1994, he needed to take account of the cost to the companies of implementing Directives already agreed and any new obligations which were likely to be placed on companies during the ten years of the price limits.

As a first step it was necessary to have estimates of the possible scale of costs which might be required. In August 1992, Ofwat published *The Cost of Quality: A Strategic Assessment*, which provided an assessment of the prospects for future water bills (Ofwat 1992). This was based on outline and preliminary costing information provided by the companies on the contemporary interpretation of the potential obligations and their implications for the companies. The costings submitted were reviewed by a firm of engineering consultants.

The publication of *The Cost of Quality* widened the debate over the possible cost of meeting quality standards. A wide range of possible bill increases was forecast, depending on the obligations which might be required and the timescale for implementation. Two scenarios were explored which indicated that the impact on customers' bills could be significantly affected by the range of legislation dealing with quality standards enacted within the ten years of the price limits.

A year before prices were set, it was apparent that the continuation of the quality compliance programmes and the introduction of other legislation, particularly the Urban Waste Water Treatment Directive (UWWTD) (91/271/EEC), would have a major impact on the process of setting the new price limits.

Before setting prices it was necessary for the obligations, both existing and potential, to be identified and for there to be a clear view on how they were to be introduced and enforced. Ofwat, the DWI, the NRA and the industry jointly developed guidelines based on guidance from the Department of the Environment (DoE). Individual companies costed out the implications of various options, including the cost of dealing with a number of EC Directives, particularly the UWWTD, and possible changes to the requirements for supplying water which might be included in a revised Directive or pre-empted nationally.

On the basis of these costings, average national household bills would have needed to rise by over a quarter by the year 2000 to meet all the potential new quality obligations. This was in addition to the increases estimated by some companies to improve the standard of the service offered to customers; for example, improving water pressure and reducing the risk of flooding from sewers.

This worrying information was included in *Paying for Quality: The Political Perspective* published in July 1993, in which the Secretaries of State for the Environment and for Wales were asked to confirm the new obligations which companies were likely to face and the timescales for achieving them (Ofwat 1993). Two possible scenarios were costed – first, that of continuing with both current obligations and those confirmed for the future, and, second, possible additions where there might be some discretion, particularly in the involvement and timescale of national initiatives.

The Secretaries of State gave their guidance in a public document *Water Charges: The Quality Framework* (DoE and WO 1993). The clear message was that the requirements of existing EC legislation must be met, as well as those of existing domestic legislation. Also, for the purposes of price setting for the period 1995–2000, allowance should not be made for further tightening of standards. If standards were introduced in the years between price reviews, there were hiechanisms for companies to ask for an interim price review, or have the extra costs taken into consideration at the next price setting.

There were further detailed discussions with the quality regulators, the companies and the DoE on the procedure and details of the obligations that were eligible for specific funding in price limits. Companies submitted their Strategic Business Plans to Ofwat in March 1994 and, after consideration of the scale of their obligations in quality and other areas, the new price caps were set in July 1994.

OUTCOME OF PERIODIC REVIEW

During the ten years to 2005, household bills may rise on average by £23 in real terms (1994-5 prices). The increase in bills needed to pay for new quality standards would have been £44, but decreases to take into account efficiency and a reduction in the return on existing assets bring this down to £23 (Ofwat 1994). For those companies which only supply water, bills are generally falling in real terms as the drinking water compliance programmes are completed. Without the new quality demands, in particular on the sewerage service, household bills would be going down. It is the demands of these quality standards that set the water industry apart from the other utilities and account for the increases in bills in real terms.

These average figures mask considerable regional variations. The regional pattern is dominated by the consequences of legally enforceable waste water obligations, such as the UWWTD. In those areas where companies have a long coastline in relation to the resident population, such as Southern, North West and South West, price increases are higher than for inland companies such as Thames and Severn Trent. Inland, the long-standing practice of providing secondary treatment largely satisfied the requirements of the UWWTD, and improvements rather than complete new works were required.

Ofwat allowed in price limits for a capital expenditure programme for the water service of £3.9 billion over ten years. This included the construction of over 120 pesticide and thirty nitrate removal plants to complete the compliance programmes, fitting of treatment plant at a hundred additional water sources to reduce lead being dissolved by tap water, and the renovation of 25,000 km of water distribution mains (8 per cent of the system) to comply with standards set out in the EC Drinking Water Directive.

The £7.3 billion capital programme for the sewerage service includes £6.8 billion to meet the requirements of European legislation, including completion of the Bathing Waters programme, the ending of sewage sludge dumping in the sea, and the implementation of the other UWWTD requirements by the due dates. This means that primary sewage treatment facilities for discharges to coastal water arising from a population equivalent of 7 million will be constructed. A minimum of secondary sewage treatment for a population equivalent of 15 million to estuarial waters will be provided, while improvements to sewage treatment works discharging to fresh waters and serving a population equivalent of 19 million will be undertaken. Overall, sewage treatment facilities serving more than two-thirds of the population equivalent of England and Wales will be improved.

Since the Periodic Review there have been further changes in legislation and interpretation which may have an effect on the costs being incurred by companies. For example, the Judicial Review on the definition of the Humber and Severn estuary boundaries may mean that secondary sewage treatment will have to be installed at discharges to these areas, at an estimated cost of £115-150 million. It is not only European legislation which has an impact on bills; the interpretation of the Directives and national legal decisions are also important.

THE IMPORTANCE OF SOUNDLY BASED COST ESTIMATES

Article 130r of the Treaty on European Union sets out the principles for EC environmental policy.

Community policies should aim at a high level of protection, and be based on the precautionary principle – the principle that preventive action should be taken, and that the polluter should pay. The Community should also take account of the available scientific and technical data, the potential benefits, and the cost of action or lack of it.

This is the legal requirement, but there are many cases in which these principles do not appear to have been applied by the EC in a consistent manner, and customers are paying considerable amounts in increased water bills, without corresponding improvements to the service they receive.

It is essential that the costs of meeting new quality standards are available at the time the decision is made on the standards to be set. The costs should be derived from well-specified projects, and should be attributable and auditable. For example, in 1990 the DoE commissioned consultants to estimate the cost associated with the introduction of the UWWTD. It was estimated that the additional costs of meeting its provisions would be about £1.5 billion. Estimated costs rose sharply after the Directive was agreed by the member states in May 1991. In *Paying for Quality* companies estimated that the capital cost would be around £10 billion. Eventually, an allowance of £6.8 billion, including money to be spent on some bathing waters, was made. Decisions on standards were made with the assistance of cost estimates that were, in retrospect, much too low, and the provision of closely defined cost estimates by all parties may well have changed the timescale for implementation, if not the actual standards. It is necessary to devise a procedure to ensure that reasonable cost estimates are available for standard setters, including a range of options. Only then will it be possible to assess the costs alongside the benefits. This could be encouraged by requiring water and sewerage companies in England and Wales to be directly involved in the estimation of costs and placing a ceiling on the allowance made in price limits based on these estimates.

SOUND SCIENTIFIC INFORMATION

It is essential that future standards should be set on the basis of sound scientifically based judgements. In the past this has been applied to varying degrees. When there have been recommendations for tightening standards, these are considered or adopted. There is less likelihood of the opposite. The key example is the pesticides parameter. The standard for individual pesticides in the EC Drinking Water Directive is a maximum permitted level for individual pesticides of 0.1 µg/l, a surrogate zero. The precautionary principle was employed. Until sufficient scientific, toxicological and medical evidence was available, the permitted level of pesticides and pesticide residues in drinking water was to be set at this very low level.

Pesticides are a chemically heterogeneous group of products and the data are now available to investigate the setting of individual standards. The new edition of the WHO *Guidelines for Drinking Water Quality* (WHO 1993) has set guideline values for thirty-four pesticides. A guideline value represents the concentration of a constituent that does not result in any significant risk to the health of the consumer over a lifetime of consumption. The WHO set out a range of these guideline values from below 0.1 µg/l to 100 µg/l. However, the proposed revision to the EC Drinking Water Directive does not incorporate a change to the 0.1 µg/l maximum permitted level. In England and Wales it is permitted for some foods to contain up to 5mg/kg of specified pesticides. It is acceptable for potatoes to contain 3mg/kg of carbendazim and yet it would not be permitted for them to be prepared with water that contains more than 0.1 µg/l of the same pesticide: a standard 30,000 times stricter (SI 1985 (1994)).

The adherence to the precautionary principle does have associated costs. In this case, water companies in England and

Wales have now spent, or are planning to spend, more than £1 billion on capital plant to attain the standards for pesticides. Operating these plants is also expensive. If the WHO guideline levels were adopted, only a small proportion of this plant would be needed. This would not lead to a significant increase in the risk to consumers. In *Drinking Water 1994*, the Chief Inspector reported that only one pesticide sample breached the WHO guideline level in over 1.1 million samples analysed in that year.

BALANCING OF COSTS AND BENEFITS – THE LEAD PARAMETER

The proposals in the draft revised Drinking Water Directive do take note of a tightened guideline level by WHO for lead. The WHO guideline level for lead in drinking water has been lowered from the current level of 50 µg/l to 10 µg/l, and this is reflected in the revised Directive. The process of interpreting this standard will have a considerable impact on customers of the water industry. For example, the current European Directive standard of 50 µg/l on a flushed sample is much less strict than the UK regulation of 50 µg/l on a "first draw' sample.

If all lead plumbing needs to be replaced, this will be expensive. From information submitted by companies to Ofwat in 1993, it would cost about £2 billion to replace pipework owned by the water companies. The costs of replacement would be passed to all customers. The remaining replacement of lead pipework, estimated to cost over £7 billion, is the responsibility of property owners (KIWA/DVGW/WRc 1995). If the water companies were required to replace all communication pipes, this would have a significant effect on bills and little impact on the amount of lead ingested by vulnerable groups. Lead will still be dissolved from other pipework in the property. If £2 billion is available to spend on protecting vulnerable groups from the effects of high lead levels, would the replacement of all company lead communication pipes be the most effective way?

It may be more sensible to consider the use of selective standards and policies. Some of these issues have been explored in an occasional paper published by the Ofwat National Customer Council (ONCC 1995). This argues that those drafting legislation and setting standards should take an integrated approach, rather than tackling each standard separately. Looking at the total exposure of populations to, for example, pesticides and lead, and the costs involved in control, may provide a different perspective on the most cost-effective application of an all too finite resource – finance. The ability of customers to pay increasing water bills is limited and instead of all the new obligations being placed on them in a piecemeal fashion, steadily increasing the burden, they should be examined as a whole. There is the irony that the ozonation process being used by some water companies to attain pesticide standards may produce, as a by-product, bromate which is a known genotoxin and carcinogen. The so-called solution may produce more health risks than the original problem.

THE POLLUTER PAYS PRINCIPLE

The enforcement of the pesticides parameter requires customers to pay for the removal of pesticides. The principle of the polluter pays has yet to be applied to the contamination of water resources by pesticides or nitrates. This means that customers are paying at both ends, paying for the removal of contaminants from drinking water, and also paying the full costs of the purification of waste water. There is a basic anomaly, which is having a significant impact on customers' bills.

FUTURE QUALITY STANDARDS

The last Periodic Review only made provision for obligations for which legislation had been passed, or on the basis of guidance given by the Secretaries of State. Even when the current compliance programmes have been completed, the demands on customers will not cease. Bills will have to remain at a higher level to reflect the higher operating costs and the return for the companies on new assets and their replacement in due course.

Three forthcoming major pieces of legislation at European level will have repercussions for water customers:

1   the proposed revision to the Drinking Water Directive;
2   the proposed revision to the Bathing Water Directive;
3   the Framework Directive on Water Resources, which the Commission is drafting.

If all the proposed forthcoming quality standards at European and national level are implemented, alongside the current programme, there will be a heavy burden of costs for the customers. The speed of any implementation is uncertain. However, the average unmeasured (unmetered) household bill could rise by up to £15-30 in real terms by the year 2005, in addition to the increases already in price limits to the year 2005. This average bill again masks considerable regional variations, depending on the particular Directive and quality standards.

It is essential for decisions to be taken on new Directives with proper regard for the interests of the single largest, and generally most ignored, interest group of all – the customers. Customers pay for higher standards in their water and sewerage bills. Directives must be drafted, more so than in the past, on the basis of a full and proper analysis of costs and benefits, and take account of the latest scientific evidence. The affordability of higher standards must also feature strongly in the decision-making process. Unless the standard setters and decision-takers in Brussels do take this into account, and prioritize proposals for higher water quality standards and develop sensible and affordable programmes, there is a real risk that water customers' bills will rise to unacceptable levels. In the longer term this could be damaging to the achievement of higher standards.

The regulatory regime in England and Wales has included a strong role for customer representatives. The ten regional Ofwat

Customer Service Committees (CSCs) have the statutory duty to represent the interests of water customers both to the companies and to the Director. The Ofwat National Customer Council (ONCC) brings together the ten CSC Chairmen and the Director. ONCC advises and assists the Director in carrying out his statutory duty to protect the interests of customers. The Chairmen were involved to an extent unprecedented in utility regulation in the re-setting of price limits in 1994, representing the interests of customers.

ONCC also has a key role to play in representing the interests of water customers in Europe. Britain is believed to be alone among EC member states in having consumer representation arrangements which are utility specific. The customer voice has hitherto gone largely unheard in Brussels in contrast to the voices of the industry, environmental groups and other bodies, which have been heard loudly and clearly. The costs and affordability to the customers must be considered. Water customers must be consulted and their views must be given appropriate weight before decisions are taken at European level on future water policy.

REFERENCES

Department of the Environment and Welsh Office (DoE and WO) (1993) *Water Charges: The Quality Framework*, London: Department of the Environment and Welsh Office.

Drinking Water Inspectorate (DWI) (1992) *Drinking Water 1991: A Report by the Chief Inspector, Drinking Water Inspectorate*, London: HMSO.

Drinking Water Inspectorate (DWI) (1995) *Drinking Water 1994: A Report by the Chief Inspector, Drinking Water Inspectorate*, London: HMSO.

Drinking Water Inspectorate (DWI) (1996) *Drinking Water 1995: A Report by the Chief Inspector, Drinking Water Inspectorate*, London: HMSO.

KIWA/DVGW/WRc (1995) *The Financial and Economic Implications of a Change of the MAC for Lead*. EC3818, Brussels: EC.

Office of Water Services (Ofwat) (1992) *The Cost of Quality: A Strategic Assessment of the Prospects for Future Water Bills*, Birmingham: Ofwat.

Office of Water Services (Ofwat) (1993) *Paying for Quality: The Political Perspective*, Birmingham: Ofwat.

Office of Water Services (Ofwat) (1994) *Future Changes for Water and Sewerage Companies: The Outcome of the Periodic Review*, Birmingham: Ofwat.

Ofwat National Consumer Council (ONCC) (1995) *Achieving a Higher Standard for Lead in Drinking Water in England and Wales*, Birmingham: Ofwat.

SI 1985 (1994) *Agriculture, Pesticides. The Pesticides (Maximum Residue Levels in Crops, Food and Feeding Stuffs) Regulations 1994*, London: HMSO.

SI 1147 (1989) *Water, England and Wales. The Water Supply (Water Quality) Regulations 1989*, London: HMSO.

World Health Organization (WHO) (1993) *Guidelines for Drinking Water Quality. Volume 1 Recommendations*, 2nd edn, Geneva: WHO.

2.5 Taking a View on Price Review. A Perspective on Economic Regulation in the Water Industry

Ian Byatt, Director General of Water Services, looks at some of the recent issues and achievements of regulation in the water and sewerage industry. And against the background of the price limits he set in 1994, he looks ahead to his second price review which will set price limits from the year 2000.

The end of 1996 was an important milestone in water regulation. We were able to document the water companies' performance during the first year of the price limits set in 1994. This article provides an opportunity to look back at those price limits and, in doing so, to put them into the context of the second Periodic Review to take place in 1999.

ECONOMIC AND SOCIAL OBJECTIVES

As Ofwat's latest reports show, environmental quality is improving and levels of service to customers are rising. Regulation has delivered on the economic virtues.

The price limits set in 1994 allowed, on average, for a modest increase in prices over the next ten years. This increase resulted mainly from the cost of implementing the EC Waste Water Directive. Without new quality obligations, bills would now be falling in real terms.

This is in marked contrast to the experience of the first five years following privatisation. The price limits set by the Secretaries of

State in 1989 envisaged an increase in the average annual household bill of £43 in today's prices. This was made up of an increase of £32 to finance quality obligations, £16 to finance enhanced service levels and growth in the capacity of the system, less an efficiency factor of – £5.

In 1994, the new price limits envisaged an increase in the average annual household bill in the next ten years of £23. This was made up of a larger quality factor of +£44, a more modest factor of +£3 to allow for enhanced levels of service and growth in the capacity of the system and a much bigger efficiency factor of – £24 to allow for both reduced profitability and greater efficiency.

The benefit to customers in the form of lower bills from the 1994 price limits, compared with those set in 1989, was nearly £2 billion. With the exception of sewerage customers in some coastal areas, bills are now relatively stable, and in some cases they are falling in real terms despite the fact that the price limits allow for more capital expenditure than in 1989 to improve the quality of water (both drinking water and waste water discharged to rivers and the sea).

Of the regulated utilities, water is the exception to falling bills because of the need to finance investment programmes which have amounted to some 2.5 per cent of total national GDCF – for an industry accounting for only 1 per cent of consumers' expenditure. Investment in the water industry, at £2.6bn in 1995-96, is much higher than before privatisation.

Costs are now showing more benign trends. The figures for operating costs in 1995-96 show a reduction, in real terms, compared with recent years. As companies respond to incentives, costs are now running below what was allowed for in price limits in 1994 – the amount varying with the company – and the expectation is already building up that price limits can be lowered at the next Review. Last year the cost of delivering water to customers fell in real terms for the first time since privatisation. And sewerage unit costs rose only modestly.

This parallels what happened at the 1994 Review as incentive regulation continues to work. Operating expenditure in 1992–93 was, on average, some 6% below what was anticipated by the Secretary of State in 1989, after adjusting for inflation. This contributed to the negative efficiency factor at the 1994 Review, but was then outweighed by the large positive quality factor.

The companies, rather than concentrating on garnering ever more resources, have used those they have more effectively. Costs have been reduced as a result. This will lead to lower prices at subsequent reviews. It does, however, not preclude additional sharing of benefits between formal price reviews, as some companies have already done. While regulation has clearly delivered in economic terms, there are a number of social issues which have met with varying degrees of success.

Disconnections

The number of households which had their water supply disconnected for non-payment of their bills initially rose sharply following privatisation. But, since 1992, when new guidelines were issued to the companies, the number has fallen to pre-privatisation levels. It was necessary to push the companies into much better procedures and better payment methods for customers who have difficulty in budgeting. The fact remains, however, that there are some customers who cannot afford to pay their bills – and they need a sympathetic approach by the water companies.

Pre-payment devices

One option which has helped customers budget – and which offers an alternative to disconnection – is Budget Payment Units. The number of customers choosing to use these units rose by some 43% in the first six months of 1996. Over 21,000 are now in use. Critics suggest the reduction in disconnections is solely linked to the increased take-up of these units. This is not so. From a social point of view, if customers find the units helpful in paying bills, their choice should not be restricted. But the legality of these units has been challenged and it is now for the High Court to clarify the legal position.

Social issues of metering

The sharp increase in bills was not cushioned by any changes in social security. Some groups – such as low income households with children, who have not enjoyed the general increase in prosperity – have lost out. Where these households were moved into new or refurbished local authority or housing association housing, with compulsory meters, it has led to adverse publicity for metering if their bills subsequently rose. Without supporting universal metering, there is a strong case for the spread of selective metering where it is cheap and economic to do so. The issues make it even more important that companies should offer customers in debt a wide range of easy payment options – and advertise them – to help them budget. Budget Payment Units can play an important role here.

Regional disparity

The price limits set in 1989 led to greater regional disparity in water bills. This was exacerbated by the Government's acceleration of quality improvements to bathing beaches in the South West in 1990. Some of these factors are only now working themselves through, such as the significant price increases on the South Coast as a result of the EC Waste Water Directive.

Fat cats, dividends and share options

There has been constant criticism of salaries, dividends and share options. This is not an area for regulators – it is for shareholders to ensure their executives do a good job and give value for money. Share options have probably made the biggest headlines, although it is worth remembering that for the last four years the water sector has performed in line with the market; the big gains were in the years 1989-92. The salaries point may have been overdone – but it has stuck. This is not an area for regulators. The regulatory cure may be worse than the disease. It is for shareholders to ensure that they get value for money from their managers, looking at the long-run position of the company, not simply at present profitability. Shareholders, including institutional investors, are encouraged to consider the special position of regulated water utilities. Like all companies, they will only thrive if they look after their customers, albeit in the absence of short-term financial advantage. Some of them are in danger of appearing *'plus capitaliste que les capitalistes.'*

Where the sphere of activity in the regulated water business is very different from that of the plc, as in the case of the multi-utilities (United Utilities/North West Water, Hyder/Dwr Cymru and Scottish Power/Southern Water) there is a strong case for separate listing of the water business, or for the issue of targetted stock. This would institutionalise them as free standing bodies and would ensure independence for the Board, as well as providing stock market information for the regulator. We intend to pursue this issue at an industry level.

Stopping the price escalator
We have been living with rising prices for a long time. At one stage it looked like an endless escalator. This was slowed down at the last price review, with help from the government in reining back on new quality obligations. There needs to be continuing co-operation in this area, where co-operation means controlling environmental and quality ambitions.

An important lesson – for companies as well as governments – is that these social matters do not go away on privatisation. For the companies, they are not just another plc; they have to learn to accept social responsibilities and to present themselves as responsible bodies. For governments, they have to be clear and explicit about non-economic factors – such as quality obligations in water. Otherwise the responsibility placed on regulators, who have largely economic objectives, is too great.

Unless government is explicit about social responsibilities and is to be accountable for them, the independence of regulators can be compromised. As far as water quality and environmental obligations are concerned, the division of responsibility has worked well. Ofwat asked Ministers to address the cost of quality in 1993. This was done and decisions made which enabled us to do the economic and financial analysis to set price limits in 1994.

Independent regulators

This independence is at the heart of arrangements. Regulators are accountable for carrying out their statutory duties. These are mainly about economic efficiency (return on capital, productivity assessments, undue discrimination, competition, etc) the elements of the situation where, to quote Nigel Lawson, 'the government of business is not the business of government'.

THE NEXT PERIODIC REVIEW

In October 1996 Ofwat announced that all price limits would be reviewed in 1999. The new price limits will take effect from 1 April 2000.

Trends over the last five years in all aspects of company performance will be looked at and full account will be taken of the very encouraging efficiency savings made by the companies, which will then be shared with customers. The evidence is that price limits could come down.

Five years is a reasonable time period for a review of price limits. The companies' licence allows for this to happen. While there are new obligations on the horizon, a ten year review is too long. At the same time more frequent adjustments would have considerable disadvantages in this long-term industry, and would damage the incentive of price cap regulation to reduce costs and bring about efficiency savings.

The companies must deliver the legal obligations allowed for in existing price limits, and the levels of service their customers expect. If any company fails to deliver, then it will be penalised. Ofwat will be working closely with the quality regulators, whose job it is to police the companies' progress against their obligations, to address the issues. During the 1995 drought one company came very close to failing in its duty to supply customers with water, and many failed adequately to manage the demand upon their resources. This influenced the decision to take the earliest opportunity to review price limits.

The announcement of the next review was timed to allow for full and effective planning of the process of the review, including full consultation with the public and to remove speculation and regulatory uncertainty relating to it. We want to stimulate informed debate on the issues.

Ofwat will publish a periodic review schedule, including plans for consultation, early in 1997. In the meantime, in the context of the 1999 review, it is useful to look again at some of the economic issues handled at the last review.

Economic factors

In a capital intensive industry, where the regulator is statutorily enjoined to secure that companies get a reasonable return on capital, there are issues relating to the capital base and the real rate of return on that base. Quantitatively, the first is more important than the second.

On the capital base, Ofwat rejected the replacement costs of assets (£120bn) and indicative value calculated by the Secretary of State at privatisation (£16bn). We opted instead for the market value at flotation, less the cash injection (Green Dowry) to the former authorities and plus an estimate of a comparable valuation for the water only companies (the statutory water companies) (£7bn). To this we added subsequent net investment – gross investment less depreciation charges.

For the rate of return, it seemed that companies could finance their functions at a lower rate of return. There was scope for a reduction in prices as a result of the convergence of the return on new capital to 5-6% post business taxes, and interest cover (on unfavourable scenarios) of no lower than two.

So, on both rate of return and capital base there was a considerable tightening – resulting in substantial reductions in prices by the end of the ten year price setting period. As returns in 1992-3, measured in this way, were well above 5-6%, Ofwat applied the 5-6% to new assets and phased out the 'excess' return on capital over ten years (although most of the convergence took place in the first five years). The judgement on the speed of this transfer from shareholders to customers was taken both to preserve incentives, which might be damaged by an instant movement to a lower rate of return, and to respect some privatisation expectations. In the cases of South West Water and Portsmouth Water, which appealed against Ofwat's decisions, the Monopolies and Mergers Commission used a five year phase out – which, on reflection, is a better solution. But they allowed for rather more capital expenditure than Ofwat had done, resulting in virtually the same price limits as Ofwat had set.

Levels of expenditure to be allowed for in price limits were dealt with

- by dividing expenditure into purpose categories, provision of base service levels (existing outputs, including maintenance of existing capital stock), enhanced levels of service to customers (better pressure, quicker response to complaints, etc), additions to the stock or other policies to achieve the right supply/demand balance and enhanced quantity (to deal with new EC and national obligations);
- by looking at different levels of operating expenditure in different companies, relating them to differences in operating environment and assuming efficiency targets based in part on general improvements in efficiency and in part in convergence towards the more efficient companies;
- by allowing for capital expenditure on new quality obligations after going through a rigorous process with Government (involving the Treasury) and not allowing in price limits for most claims for other capital expenditure said to be necessary to improve services for customers;

- allowing for continued expenditure on capital maintenance, to maintain the serviceability trends of the past – after adjusting for efficiency assumptions. Companies should link measures of serviceability to customers with the condition of their assets. The companies' Strategic Business Plans at the last Periodic Review indicated that 91% of the potable water pipes and between 88 and 90% of the sewers were in satisfactory condition. It is scarcely necessary to replace assets that are working satisfactorily;
- allowing for increased demand by a combination of finance for meters and a relatively low national yardstick for expansion of capacity.

Increases in demand can be met by reducing leakage and installing meters, with expensive reservoir construction as the last measure. Selective metering is an essential element in developing a proper relationship between supply and demand. There are economic and political constraints on how rapidly it will develop. But without progress towards a greater penetration of metering it will prove increasingly difficult to meet economic and environmental objectives.

Elements in the K Factor

At the 1994 Review, Ofwat decomposed decisions on the price limits, breaking down the price limit, or K factor into –X (the efficiency factor) and +Q (the quality factor). In 1999, additional elements need to go into the picture.

It is useful to distinguish between an element in the K factor to allow for past achievements in reducing costs below what the regulator had allowed for at the previous Review. Some commentators assume that this P_o adjustment would take place quickly.

That would leave a separate element – perhaps best described as a grouping of elements – in the K factor which is addressing the future rather than the past – setting out expectations for the subsequent years of the price limits rather than correcting the past difference between expectations and outcomes.

This grouping of elements in the forward looking K factor could comprise:

X The efficiency/resource allocation factor which relates to efficiency and return on capital.

Q The quality of water factor – drinking water and waste water.

S The levels of service factor which governs the extent to which improved levels of service are reflected in price levels as opposed to being financed through greater efficiency. Last time the S factor was quite small.

V A factor relating to supply and demand for the quantity of water. This may be negative if a company has water to sell, or zero if new resources or, more generally expansion in the capacity of the system, are financed out of higher payments for additional supplies of water, ie through metering, or positive, if bills have to rise in advance of new supplies becoming available.

It is important to think of the elements as components in a group. We do not intend to determine separate price limits for each. Customers may feel that if the P_o adjustment is negative – reducing bills in real terms – it would be perverse for the combination of the X, S, V and Q factors to reverse this. Trade-offs between those factors would need to be considered, while maintaining an overall limit on prices.

The output principle

Although price limits must allow for the justifiable costs of the necessary inputs, the regime should focus on outputs – what customers and the environment are receiving. This starts by discovering what customers want – and are prepared to pay for – and establishing environmental obligations. When price limits are set, the regulator is then concerned to ensure that companies deliver their outputs.

This involves continuing work with the quality regulators (the Environment Agency and the Drinking Water Inspectorate) to ensure that legally enforceable quality obligations are met and collecting company information on customer service – both measured indicators such as water pressure and qualitative information on customer care. Ofwat has worked with the quality regulators to develop milestones for the delivery of the major compliance programmes and with the companies and the Drinking Water Inspectorate on an audit of distribution undertakings. Ofwat has developed measures of serviceability to customers to ensure that the infrastructure of the companies is kept in reasonable condition. The results are published annually and, if companies are not performing adequately, we will investigate and, if necessary, take enforcement action at the review or earlier.

Our approach is to develop a framework of rewards and penalties. There should not be large unexplained differences between bids for expenditure allowed for in price limits and outturns.

Communication is the key
The regulatory process is critical. There are several key elements in the process of communications which will be taken forward to the next review. For the 1994 review we consulted widely – and not only with experts – on technical matters (such as the return on capital, financing of growth and financing of quality) and on customers' wishes and expectations. Ofwat's own organisation which, we are glad to say, includes the Customer Service Committees, provided the channel for the latter. The companies were also encouraged to produce market plans in advance of the price review where they set out options for customers, the services which they thought they should supply and the price tags which they thought should be attached to them.

A second important element is the need to be ready to explain the situation to politicians of all parties and the media (as a means of reaching the public), and to lay out the options and the way ahead recommended by the regulator. There is bound to be scope for more, but the contrast with the nationalised days is very striking.

Thirdly, it is necessary to establish a system of communication with the companies aimed at action rather than confrontation. This does not avoid disagreement, but emphasises progress towards defined objectives and, wherever possible, agreement. This is often done quite openly – through MD letters (formal letters from Ofwat to managing directors of water companies) which are publicly available, consultation papers, and through public conferences. There are also privileged discussions in working parties, and one to one meetings with individual companies. Finally a timetable, information requirements and all the proposed processes to be followed in the price review will be set out in advance, involving fairness to companies and participation (usually through representatives) for customers.

All of these processes are designed to produce greater openness and understanding and greater opportunity for all the participants to express their views – taking account of information as well as preferences. It could well involve public hearings. But exercises in consultation must be kept relatively simple if they are to reach the people concerned. The UK should not import US style openness, with endless rate hearings, armies of lawyers and stacks of computer paper without thinking very carefully what we want the participatory process to achieve. In using this we should take full account of our own style and institutions.

WHAT OF REGULATORY REFORM?

There is much discussion of the differences between regulators and the importance of the personalities and policies of individual regulators. There are large costs to change – many of which will be visited on regulators through loss of expertise and information. Reform should be based on a very careful consideration of objectives – not driven by one perceived problem – and must recognise that alternative arrangements will also have disadvantages as well as advantages. This is all very obvious, but worth repeating. As far as water is concerned, we are dealing with a very different industry and legislation from the other utilities. The existing arrangements have great merits and, not surprisingly, evolutionary changes are to be preferred to revolutionary ones. Many of the problems arose from the original privatisation.

There was great uncertainty about prospects for efficiency in operating costs and, more importantly, in the use of the capital stock, when companies left the traditional public sector environment. And there was uncertainty about how quickly this efficiency would become evident. Hence the importance of a regulatory regime which preserves incentives rather than trying to get everything precisely right.

The low gearing of privatised companies had a number of consequences. Stock market prices have been more volatile, disturbing the public and exacerbating the share option issue. It has led to dividends well above what is justified to meet the cost of capital and reward efficiency. It has led to takeovers whose operating benefits are no more than modest. There is the obvious difficulty in judging 'optimal' gearing. But it makes a lot of sense to inject debt at privatisation – and may not affect the share price as much as the City advisers often claim. Some problems have been easier to handle. At all privatisations the X factors have been too small. But they have successively tightened as evidence of greater efficiency, resulting from incentives, has provided the evidence for this.

There are three modest reforms which seem desirable. First, experimentation with informal benefit sharing mechanisms when companies significantly outperform the expectations of regulators when they set price limits. Second, tighter ring fencing of the regulated utility – linked by changes in corporate governance to keep it close to its customers and require it to act as if it were a separate plc, and, possibly, to develop these characteristics which are not simply these of 'another plc'. The idea of a customer corporation, development of mutuality, some elements of US 'private not for profit' all need to be discussed – although they may pose some threats to incentives and efficiency. Finally, on organisational matters, we are in favour of retaining sectoral regulators, strengthening the links, perhaps bringing them together as a college, with the Director General of Fair Trading in the Chair, to ensure consistency on process and common issues such as the cost of capital and developments of RPI-X.

In conclusion, the regulatory system is a good one and has worked well. Our companies deliver very high quality drinking water with 99.5 per cent of tests showing compliance with standards. At the same time price rises have been reined back. The incentives of price cap regulation are working and we must be cautious about damaging those incentives. But, looking ahead, the system will and must evolve.

CHAPTER 3

Recollections and Appraisal

3.1 The Water Regulation Regime in England and Wales

in *Regulation of Network Utilities: the European Experience; ed: Cluade Henry, Michel Matheu and Alain Jeunemaitre, Oxford University Press, 2001*

THE ECONOMIC AND POLITICAL CONTEXT

Privatization arose from the economic and political difficulties of Britain in the 1970s. Solutions had to be found to high inflation, growing microeconomic inflexibility, and ineffective attempts by government to manage the economy. Macroeconomic policy seemed unable to control inflation and to generate employment. Microeconomic intervention was propping up inefficient companies and reducing the ability of the economy to adjust to new challenges.

Privatization was only one element in the reforms of the 1980s. The control of inflation, the reform of the tax system, the greater flexibility of the labour market, including a shift of power away from the unions, and tighter control of public spending were all necessary to restore the health of the economy and to revive the liberal basis of economic life essential to economic success. But privatization was a crucial element.

For the utilities, privatization started in a hesitant way. The initial approach of the government that came to power in 1979 was to seek a more liberal approach to the financing of nationalized industry investment, especially in telecommunications. It proved, however, impossible to do this within the constraints necessarily put on public borrowing to deliver the government's anti-inflation policy.

Following the failure of the 'Busby Bonds',[1] the government then made the bold decision to privatize British Telecom. As it was at that time a monopoly, a regulatory regime was set up to control its prices. Following the pioneering work of Professor Stephen Littlechild[2] (1986), the government decided on arm's-length control by a specialist regulator on an RPI – X basis. Price control was seen as temporary, pending the development of competition.

THE WATER INDUSTRY AND THE NEED FOR REGULATION

Plans for further privatization of other utilities followed the success of the flotation of British Telecom. Of the privatizations in the 1980s, the water industry was the most controversial. How could public service be provided by a private monopoly, and, moreover, one where the prospects for competition seemed remote?

On the other hand, the water industry was in need of capital to meet the European Community obligations resulting from previous and new directives. It was also argued by the water authorities that their assets needed substantial renewal as a result of constraints on public expenditure, especially those resulting from the conditions imposed on the UK in 1976 for support by the International Monetary Fund.

A first, and major, step towards privatization was taken by the then secretary of state, Nicholas Ridley, when in 1988 he began to separate out the regulatory functions of the regional water authorities from their service functions. The management of river basins, in particular the policing of the discharge of waste water to rivers, estuaries, and coastal water, was put into the hands of a new National Rivers Authority (NRA). (Subsequently the

---

[1] The government spent some time considering how BT might be able to borrow on specific bonds while remaining a public corporation.
[2] S.C. Littlechild, *Economic Regulation of Privatised Water Authorities: A Report Submitted to the Department of the Environment*, London: HMSO, January 1986.

NRA was incorporated into the Environment Agency, EA.) This removed from the water authorities their ability to set their own environmental objectives and standards. These objectives could now be set by a body remaining in the public sector, so that privatized water companies would have clear, externally imposed, environmental objectives.

The process went a step further with the establishment of the Drinking Water Inspectorate (DWI), initially within the Department of the Environment, to police standards of drinking water. In due course the DWI would become a free-standing body, within the public sector.

ECONOMIC REGULATION

The architecture for regulation was completed by establishing an economic regulator to control the prices that the privatized companies could charge. This price control was to be of the form RPI ± K, where K was a factor that would take account of a company's capital investment programme as well as its prospective increase in efficiency.

It was expected, at privatization, that RPI ± K would protect customers, yet give companies scope to use business methods to increase efficiency. The K factor would be set only periodically – in the case of water, every five or ten years.

The new regime was intended:

1. to improve water quality (both supplies of drinking water and discharge of waste water) to meet EU, and national, objectives;
2. to protect customers by limiting the prices they could be charged (and to avoid deterioration in customer service);
3. to mobilize business skills to provide services to customers and to the environment efficiently and economically;
4. to develop a framework that utilized comparative competition to the benefit of customers; and
5. to enable market competition to develop.

In setting price limits, the regulator has to act in the manner that he considers is best calculated to ensure that the companies properly carry out their functions and can finance them. Subject to that he must protect customers, promote efficiency and economy, and facilitate competition between existing and potential suppliers.

It was originally envisaged that price reviews would take place every ten years to reflect the long-term nature of the industry. Meanwhile, companies would be able to apply for adjustments to their price limits to reflect specified changes in circumstances such as a new legally enforceable water quality obligation. Provision was made also for five-year reviews; in practice, five-year reviews have become the norm.

The regulator, the Director General of Water Services (DGWS), is appointed by ministers but acts independently from them in carrying out his statutory duties. He is appointed for a term of up to five years and thus has sufficient security of tenure to take an independent position. He remains, however, subject to challenge in the courts if he exceeds his powers. His decisions on price limits are subject to appeal to the Competition Commission (previously the Monopolies & Mergers Commission).

The DGWS is financed, through licence fees paid by the companies, to appoint an office (OFWAT) to assist him in the discharge of his statutory duties. To help him in his task of protecting customers, he appoints customer service committees (CSCs). Each company is allocated to a CSC, which acts as an informed customer champion. The chairmen of the CSCs come together in the OFWAT National Customer Council.

THE BIRTH PANGS AND THE HEALTHY BABY

The privatization itself was risky. Nowhere in the world did a fully privatized water and sewerage business exist. Many were sceptical, particularly about one of the water authorities which had a record of weakness. Political uncertainty about the result of the impending General Election in 1992 added to the risks.

Inevitably, the flotation price was low. While initially the taxpayer may have lost, the customer has gained, as the asset valuation used for regulating purposes is based on the flotation price plus subsequent net investment, all indexed to today's price level. The taxpayer's losses were recouped by the windfall (utility) tax levied in 1997 by the incoming Labour government.

Shareholders have had a good return, amounting to between 11 and 16 per cent annually in real terms, over the period since privatization before payment of the utility tax. They have been compensated for the risks involved in the flotation of the water companies.

ACHIEVEMENTS OF THE LAST TEN YEARS

What has been achieved over the last ten years? What has gone well?

There have been spectacular successes, stemming from two factors:

1. privatization of the companies, i.e. those ultimately responsible for delivery of services to customers and to the environment;
2. a system of incentive regulation managed by an appointed regulator who acts at arm's length from ministers.

This success has shown itself in a number of ways.

- Prices to customers, after rising considerably in the five years after privatization, have now fallen, back towards the pre-privatization level.
- There is much greater efficiency. This is well documented and covers operations, capital maintenance, quality enhancement, and the raising of finance. Moreover, the companies have indicated that they can increase their efficiency even further.
- As a result of a doubling of investment, compared with the days of nationalization, the delivery of service to customers and to the environment has improved dramatically. This is

also well documented. There are, however, issues about the cost effectiveness of some of the expenditure involved.

DRIVERS OF THE BILLS

In the early years of privatization, bills were driven upwards by obligations, mainly for higher standards of drinking water quality and for better protection of the environment. Higher efficiency has been a growing countervailing force. As Table 4.1 shows, over the fifteen years since privatization the annual average household bill will have risen by some €61. Quality improvements will have accounted for an increase of €158, while other improvements and the growth of supply will have accounted for an increase of €35. Offsetting these increases, efficiency improvements will have accounted for a decrease of €133.

The position has varied in each of the three five-year periods. The increase driven by quality improvements is much the same for all three – around €48 per household customer. These figures do not, however, take account of the growing efficiency achieved by the companies in delivering the quality improvements. Allowing for this, the quality programmes have become bigger; that is, outputs have increased in each of the five-year periods.

Table 4.1. Changes in Annual Household Water Rates, 1990–2005

	Constant prices (€)			
	1990–5	1995–2000	2000–5	1990–2005
Quality improvements	58	54	46	158
Other improvements and growth in supply	29	5	2	35
Greater efficiency	-8	-29	-96	-133
Total change	78	30	-48	61

The effect on the bills of other improvements and the growth of supply has become smaller, period by period. This reflects the slower growth in demand for water, the regulator's view that such growth should be self-financing, and the ability of the companies to improve customer service without explicit allowance in price limits.

The changes in efficiency are dramatic. At privatization in 1989, ministers assumed that companies could become more efficient, but, following the experience of nationalization, not by very much. In practice, the companies did better than was assumed. In *Future Charges for Water and Sewerage Services*[3] OFWAT set price limits on the basis that efficiency could improve at a faster rate. Again the companies out-performed. In *Final Determinations*[4] OFWAT was able to assume a much bigger increase in efficiency, taking account of past out-performance as well as assuming further efficiency savings in the future.

In 1989 it was assumed that quality improvements would push the bill up much more than efficiency improvements would pull it down. By 1994 the gap was much smaller. Bills would have gone down significantly had it not been for the scale of improvements to water quality and to the environment. By 1999, the scale of the efficiency achieved by the water companies was such that a large quality programme could be carried out and bills could still fall.

It might be more difficult in the future to combine reductions in bills with a large quality programme. The growth in efficiency may slow down. (In setting price limits, we assumed a slower growth in efficiency in 2000–5 than took place in 1995–2000.) The cost of capital has fallen, but by 2005 companies may have limited scope to increase gearing further. The scale of quality investment may, however, be smaller to reflect the view of the Chairman of the EA

---

[3] Office of Water Services, *Future Charges for Water and Sewerage Services: The Outcome of the Periodic Review*, Birmingham, July 1994.
[4] Office of Water Services, *Final Determinations: Future Water and Sewerage Charges 2000–05*, Birmingham, November 1999.

that 'by 2005 most of the environmental damage of the past 200 years will have been repaired'.

It is crucial to make rational decisions about the scale of new quality obligations. The EA should develop environmental trade-offs – e.g. between air and water pollution – as well as progressing its analysis in water. Some of the quality projects have shown poor value for money. Customers increasingly expect more careful attention to be given to assessments of benefit as set against costs.

DELIVERY OF OUTCOMES

The regulators will monitor the delivery of the service provided by the water companies to customers and to the environment. The quality regulators will act if timed obligations are not met. OFWAT will ensure that there is no deterioration in standards of service.

Exactly how companies meet their obligations should depend on how efficient and innovative they can be. We allow for what we regard as reasonable levels of expenditure in setting price limits. But no one in OFWAT insists that any particular levels of expenditure be met. If companies can do the job more economically, their shareholders deserve a reward. Equally, if companies spend more than is allowed for in price limits, this should be at the expense of shareholders.

THE QUALITY DEBATE

Because of the importance, to the investment programme and to prices to customers, of improvements in water and environmental quality, I sought to stage a debate on those matters in *The cost of quality*,[5] which set out two quality scenarios and showed how they would affect customers' bills. This exercise in transparency

[5]Office of Water Services, *The Cost of Quality: A Strategic Assessment of the Prospects for Future Water Bills*, Birmingham, August 1992.

has led to the publication of much more information in the cost of improving quality. Unfortunately, work on estimating benefits has lagged behind.

Nevertheless, we have, at both the 1994 and 1999 price reviews, sent an open letter to ministers,[6] setting out our views of the costs of the water quality and environmental programmes being considered. In both reviews, ministers have replied in public,[7] setting out their position on the water quality and environmental obligations which, knowing the costs, they wish to impose on water companies during the period of the price limits.

As meeting these obligations will be part of the functions of a water company, the regulator can allow for the costs of (economical) discharge of these obligations in price limits.

THE STRUCTURE OF THE WATER COMPANIES

The water industry is highly capital-intensive with high investment relative to turnover. There are ten water and sewerage companies

[6]Office of Water Services, *Paying for Quality: The Political Perspective*, Birmingham, July 1993; *Setting the Quality Framework: An Open Letter to the Secretary of State for the Environment, Transport and the Regions and the Secretary of State for Wales*, Birmingham, April 1998; *informing the Final Decisions on 'Raising the Quality': An Open Letter to the Secretary of State for the Environment, Transport and the Regions and the Secretary of State for Wales*, Birmingham, January 1999.

[7]Department of the Environment, Welsh Office, *Water Charges: The Quality Framework*, London: Department of the Environment, October 1993; Department of the Environment, Transport and the Regions, Welsh Office, *Raising the Quality: Guidance to the Director General of Water Services on the Environmental and Quality Objectives to be Achieved by the Water Industry in England and Wales 2000–05*, London: Department of the Environment, Transport and the Regions, September 1998; *Maintaining Public Water Supplies: Ministerial Guidance to the Director General of Water Services on Issues Arising in Preparation of Water Resources Plans by the Water Companies of England and Wales*, London: Department of the Environment, Transport and the Regions, January 1999.

(WaSCs) and fourteen water-only companies (WoCs). The WoCs had never been nationalized, but had been subject to dividend control for many years.

There are 22 million water customers and 21 million sewerage customers.[8] Household customers account for 80 per cent of customers: 99.6 per cent of households are connected to the public water supply and 95.5 per cent to the public sewerage system. Water companies also serve business customers and are major contributors to draining highways and other surface areas.

While the water companies are regional monopolies, they must provide services to all customers and they must also comply with rising quality obligations. If companies fail to meet their obligations they face prosecution and enforcement action by regulators, which ultimately could lead to the loss of a company's licence.

The demand for water is broadly constant. Household demand accounts for 70 per cent of water delivered.[9] This continues to rise as the number of households increase. Water delivered to business customers, on the other hand, especially to large customers, is falling.

The combined turnover of the companies is €11 billion.[10] They have a regulatory capital value of €42 billion. Since privatization they have invested about €52 billion; annual investment is expected to continue to run at €5 billion.

The companies vary greatly in size. The turnover of the WaSCs varies from €2 billion (Thames Water Utilities) to €0.4 billion (Wessex Water Services). The turnover of the WoCs varies from €224 million (Three Valleys) to €24 million (Cambridge).

---

[8]Office of Water Services, *Report on Tariff Structure and Charges*, published annually since 1995.
[9]Office of Water Services, *Report on Leakage and Water Efficiency*, published annually since 1997.
[10]Office of Water Services, *Report on Financial Performance and Expenditure of the Water Companies in England and Wales*, published annually since 1991; *Report on Company Performance*, published annually since 1992.

The water industry is part of the global market. French companies (Vivendi, Suez Lyonnaise des Eaux, and Saur) own one WaSC (Northumbrian) and six WoCs. The US Enron Corporation owns a WaSC (Wessex). Scottish Power owns another WaSC (Southern Water). Union Fenosa (Spain) recently bought Cambridge Water Company. Towards the end of 2000, RWE (Germany) took over Thames Water. All companies are subject to takeover. If overseas companies can improve the effectiveness and efficiency of the water industry in England and Wales, they are welcomed. The playing field is level, irrespective of nationality.

THE SCOPE FOR COMPARATIVE COMPETITION

The scope for market competition has been limited, but the water industry has offered more scope for comparative competition than perhaps any of the other utilities.

Not only did we inherit a range of companies operating in different parts of the country, but Parliament decided that, in order to protect the regulator's ability to compare the costs and performance of water companies, any merger above a relatively small scale should be referred to the Competition Commission.[11] The Commission has to decide on the scale of any detriment to the regulator's ability to make comparisons, judge whether any other benefit that could arise only from the merger might outweigh any such detriment, and make a recommendation to ministers who make the final decisions on whether or not the merger can proceed. The Commission might recommend that the merger is not against the public interest, that it should proceed only subject to a remedy to counter any detriment, or that it is against the public interest and should not be allowed to proceed.

---

[11]SI 1994/73, *The Water Enterprises (Merger) (Modification) Regulations, 1994*, London: HMSO, 1994.

The Commission has heard several cases, notably the formation of the Three Valleys Company (Vivendi) in North London,[12] the takeover of Northumbrian Water by Suez Lyonnaise,[13] the proposed takeover of South West Water by either Wessex Water or Severn Trent Water,[14] and the takeover of Mid Kent Water by a joint venture consisting of Vivendi and Saur.[15] The first of these cases (Three Valleys) was allowed to proceed subject to a 10 per cent reduction in prices over a period of six years. The second (Northumbrian) was allowed to proceed subject to a price reduction (for water only) of 15 per cent over a period of six years. The other two proposals were blocked.

I have consistently argued that loss of comparators[16] constitutes a detriment to all customers nationally, because the existence of comparators helps the regulator to set tight price limits and encourages companies to improve customer service. But I have not taken a rigid position. There have been a number of small mergers; the number of licences has fallen from thirty-nine to twenty-four. Where a merger could provide benefits to customers, as in the case of Three Valleys and Northumbrian, it has been allowed to proceed subject to price reductions.

---

[12]Monopolies and Mergers Commission, *General Utilities, The Colne Valley Company and Rickmansworth Water Company: A Report on the Proposed Merger*, Cm. 1029, London: HMSO, April 1990.

[13]Monopolies and Mergers Commission, *Lyonnaise des Eaux SA and Northumbria Water Group plc: A Report on the Merger Situation*, Cm. 2936, London: HMSO, July 1995.

[14]Monopolies and Mergers Commission, *Wessex Water plc and South West Water plc: A Report on the Proposed Merger*, Cm. 3430, London: Stationery Office, October 1996; *Severn Trent Water plc and South West Water plc: A Report on the Proposed Merger*, Cm. 3429, London: Stationery Office, October 1996.

[15]Monopolies and Mergers Commission, *Mid Kent Holdings plc and General Utilities plc and Saur plc: A Report on the Proposed Merger*, Cm. 3514, London: Stationery Office, January 1997.

THE POLITICAL DIMENSION

The regime was put in place by a Conservative government whose objective was to roll back the frontiers of the state. It believed that the government of business was not the business of government. It also believed that, where markets were not able to achieve a good solution on their own, for example because there was significant monopoly power, privatization plus regulation was preferable to state ownership.

The New Labour government elected in 1997 has a different philosophical approach to further privatization. It has, however, set its face against any renationalization and affirmed its commitment to arm's-length regulation. It believes that RPI – X should be retained as the fundamental system of price regulation, so long as regulators continue to judge that this is best for customers. It has gone further than its Conservative predecessor in pushing for more competition in the UK economy. The Chancellor of the Exchequer has emphasized the importance of competition to benefit customers, especially by reducing prices. In 1998 Parliament passed the Competition Act.[17] This Act gives considerable power to sector regulators acting concurrently with the Director General of Fair Trading to punish abuse of a dominant market position within the UK.

Despite this clear position, there remain siren calls for more involvement by ministers in matters that are the province of regulators. Taken to extremes, they could involve the nationalization of regulation while the companies remained privatized. I advise ministers to read Homer and follow the example of Odysseus, who asked his crew to plug his ears and tie him to the mast. While the interest of ministers in social and environmental matters is to be welcomed, they should not blur responsibilities, or, worse still, the arm's length relationship, by using social and environmental concerns to intrude into economic regulation.

[16]Ibid.
[17]*Competition Act* 1998, London: Stationery Office, November 1998.

Our liberal civil society, a community of citizens, benefits from a plurality of institutions. Utility regulators are a recent but a significant addition. They can take their place alongside other non-ministerial decision-making bodies. They take their authority from their statutory duties, establishing their credibility through openness, integrity, and fairness.

THE REGULATORY AGENDA

As the first director general, I have had considerable scope in setting the agenda and responding to events.

I made my first statement, published in the privatization prospectus,[18] shortly after my appointment in August 1989. Most of it has been put into operation. But the agenda has developed; we have been part of an historical process. Adapting to this, and seizing opportunities when they arise, is a major part of the regulator's trade.

The position of the regulator has been even more exposed than I had expected. I knew utilities would always be in the public eye, and that greater transparency would expose issues previously kept under wraps. I could see the conflicts inherent in concerns for the environment and concerns for bills. But I had not expected the scale of the conflicts and degree of the antagonisms.

Paradoxically, perhaps, the independence of the regulator from ministers has made it easier to chart a steady course and to balance conflicting interests. Government ministers usually have a short term of office and are subject to constant pressures to satisfy interest groups. Their turnover is rapid; in eleven years I have worked with twelve different secretaries of state (six English and six Welsh)[19] and six different ministers for the environment.

---

[18]*The Water Shares Offer: Prospectus. Offers for Sale on Behalf of the Secretary of State for the Environment and the Secretary of State for Wales*, London: Schroders, 1989.

[19]I include, since the establishment of a Welsh Assembly, two first secretaries.

I needed regulatory stability to establish good systems for regulating monopoly utilities:

- *good process,* allowing wide consultation with interested parties, proper relationships with companies, and opportunities for the paying customers to register their views. We needed to devise practical ways of establishing our integrity and building up the confidence of diverse groups;
- *an accepted methodology.* We started with RPI – X as the brain-child of Stephen Littlechild. It has evolved over the years into a sophisticated mediumterm approach, increasingly finely tuned but retaining powerful incentives to greater efficiency. This has involved careful analysis of costs and performance across all the companies and extensive work on the cost of capital;
- *sound information,* collected on a comparative basis, on the costs, levels of service, environmental improvements, and efficiency of water companies. This information has been widely disseminated, in accessible form,[20] to reach a wide range of interested parties. The basic data July Returns[21] is available through our Library.

Transparency of process and content are desirable in order to develop good policy. Experience has taught me that it is a great strength to independent regulators. It is not possible to please everyone, but in a mature society, wide knowledge of what regulators are doing, and why, helps those who have to make, or live with, difficult decisions.

---

[20] *Maintaining Public Water Supplies,* 1999; Report on Tariff Structure, 1995, Report on Leakage, 1997; Office of Water Services, *Report on Cost of Water Delivered and Sewage Collected,* published annually, 1992–6.

THE SUCCESSES OF REGULATION

Regulation has, I believe, produced a good deal for customers and a good deal for the environment. It has done this for the following reasons.

- We regulate by outcomes, not by expenditure; by outputs, not inputs. State-owned regional water authorities did not have clear quality, environmental, and service objectives: privatized water companies do. Their performance is widely monitored and they are held to account for failure.

- We have adjusted price limits to allow companies to finance ambitious investment programmes to improve water quality and to protect the environment.

- Incentives work. We allow companies to make money by reducing costs (but not by cutting corners). At price reviews we transfer the benefit of a lower cost base to customers.

- We provide incentives for good outcomes. Companies performing well are rewarded at price reviews; companies performing badly are penalized. Companies who share benefits with customers between price reviews have this recognized in future price limits.

- We have maintained, and stimulated, comparative competition to the benefit of customers. We have published comparisons of levels of service[22] and pushed the laggards to catch up with the leaders. We have examined costs comparatively. While expecting everyone to do better, we have assumed that the less efficient would catch up with the more efficient. Companies do not like to be left behind, and shareholders do not like to have failures in their portfolios. Incentives work.

[21]Office of Water Services, *Water Company July Returns*, submitted annually since 1990.
[22]Office of Water Services, *Report on Levels of Services for the Water Industry in England and Wales*, published annually since 1990.

- As the original dual product companies have diversified, we have strengthened the ring-fencing of the core water business to avoid crosssubsidy or putting the appointed business at risk from other operations.
- We are creating a level playing field for market competition to develop.

We live in a global market; protection is not good for sound business. We benefit from the presence of French, Scottish, American, Spanish, and German companies in the water business in England and Wales. If our companies do well at home, they should be able to compete in world markets – and vice-versa.

Water companies are subject to takeover, thus keeping up pressure on management. To balance this with the maintenance of comparative competition, water-water mergers have to show a positive benefit to customers, while non-water-water mergers are allowed to proceed unless there is a detriment to customers.

WORKING WITH OTHER REGULATORS

Regulators do not work in isolation. We cooperate both with the quality regulators and with the other utility regulators. We work closely with the DWI and the EA on the details of the quality programme to be allowed for in price limits. We monitor the performance of the companies in tandem.

Work with the other utility regulators has involved debate on regulatory strategy, exchange of experience on particular issues, and day to day cooperation. We have a joint work programme[23] and report publicly on its progress.

---

[23]Office of Water Services, *Statement by Oftel, Ofgem, ORR and Ofreg on Joint Working*, Birmingham, October 1999.

LEARNING FROM EXPERIENCE

I have enjoyed the way my role, and that of OFWAT, has developed in the last ten years. We started with an Act of Parliament, the Water Act,[24] a licence for water companies,[25] and a clean sheet on process, methodology, information and publicity. We have built up an efficient and effective office, with excellent staff at all levels. We have developed a comprehensive system for reporting on company performance, including financial performance, their costs and efficiency, and the prices they charge.[26]

We keep a systematic, and sometimes beady, eye on outcomes and take action where things are going wrong. In 1996 the first €64 million 'fine' was levied on Yorkshire Water following an investigation of its performance during the drought of 1995.[27]

We tell the world what is going on, through:

- my annual report[28] and those of the Customer Service Committees (CSCs) and the OFWAT National Customer Council (ONCC),[29] and

---

[24]*Water Act 1989*, London: HMSO, 1989.

[25]*Instrument{s} of Appointment of the Water and Sewerage Companies*, 1989.

[26]*Report on Financial Performance, 1991; Report on Cost of Water Delivered, 1992–6*; Office of Water Services, *Report on Water and Sewetage Service Unit Costs and Relative Efficiency*; published annually since 1997; *Report on Tariff Structure, 1995.*

[27]Office of Water Services, *Report on Conclusions from Ofwat's Enquiry into the Performance of Yorkshire Water Services Ltd*, Birmingham, June 1996.

[28]Office of Water Services, *Director General's Annual Report*, published annually since 1990, London: HMSO/ Stationery Office.

[29]OFWAT National Customer Council, OFWAT Customer Service Committees, *Representing Water Customers: The Annual Report of the OFWAT National Customer Council and the Ten Regional Customer Service Committees*, published annually since 1997; individual OFWAT Customer Service Committee annual reports, published annually 1991–6.

- our regular publications on companies – on their financial performance, levels of service, on efficiency and tariffs.[30]

I like to think of this as a model for other services still in the public sector.

I am proud that we have been able to do this within a modest budget. Including regulation and customer representation, we spend €18 million a year, equivalent to £0.60 for every customer.

CUSTOMER REPRESENTATION

CSCs are making sure that services meet the needs of citizens. Each regional committee has built up its own network using practical skills and local knowledge. They deal with complaints that customers have not been able to resolve with their companies. They monitor the quality of companies' customer service, using independent audits. They have lobbied for the appointment of non-executive directors, with skills in customer service, to utility boards; in a number of cases such directors have come from their ranks. CSCs have been involved in the arrangements for the market research conducted by companies.

As the water industry has a strong regional dimension, the CSCs naturally have different views, often reflecting, quite rightly, the preoccupations of the area. A striking example is provided by the debate I encouraged on *Paying for Water*[31] in the early years of regulation. The differing views on metering were well expressed by the CSCs: half favoured metering and half opposed it.

The chairmen meet together about six times a year in the

[30]*Report on Tariff Structure*, 1995; *Report on Financial Performance*, 1991; *Report on Cost of Water Delivered*, 1992–6; *Report on Levels of Service*, 1990; *Report on Water and Sewerage Service Unit Cost*, 1997.
[31]Office of Water Services, *Paying for Water: A Time for Decisions. A Consultation Paper issued by the Director General of Water Services on Future Charging Policy for Water and Sewerage Services*, Birmingham, November 1990.

ONCC (originally the Chairmen's Group). This gives them an opportunity to exchange their different regional experiences and to talk to the regulator. I have always found it useful to listen to chairmen; we have done much useful work together. Where there has been consistency of view, the ONCC has formulated a national position.

PAYING FOR WATER

We in OFWAT have also been concerned with water services as a market.

The use of a tax basis (1971 rateable values) for charging restricts consumer choice and hampers the normal working of supply and demand. Hence we consulted at an early stage on *Paying for Water*. Following this consultation, we adopted policies for selective rather than universal metering.

Progress has varied, having been much more rapid in East Anglia than in Wales. Penetration of meters is now, however, rising steadily and may be stimulated by the recent Water Industry Act,[32] which gives all households a right to a meter free of charge for installation. Under that Act, OFWAT has to approve companies' charges schemes before they can lawfully collect money from most customers. We will use these powers to ensure that charges for particular services and for particular groups of customers properly reflect economic costs.

MARKET COMPETITION

The scope for competition in water is less than in telecoms, gas, or electricity. But the agenda is now opening up. The Competition Act 1998 is a milestone. Companies have already set out principles for access to their networks and we have asked them to translate these into access codes governing 'common carriage' of an entrant's

[32]*Water Industry Act* 1999, London: Stationery Office, July 1999.

water. Ministers have agreed to reduce the threshold for inset appointments,[33] and I hope they will legislate to liberalize trading in abstraction licences.[34]

At present competition is concentrated on large users, but the right to optional metering and the installation of meters in new properties and, indeed, when occupancy changes could open up competition for household customers, particularly in conjunction with the development of common carriage.

Our objective is to create a level playing field, i.e. to provide opportunities for competition to flourish,[35] by giving competitors access to the monopoly inherent in the water and sewerage networks. This access would be on fair terms and include access to abstraction rights not allocated through a market process. It would not be our intention to force competition or to stipulate dates for achieving specific goals. Rather, we aim to create a framework to allow competition to develop where customers can benefit.

CONCLUSION

Four years ago I said that RPI − X was alive and well and living in the water industry, but that it was an adolescent, vigorous, but sometimes gauche and with much to learn.[36] Since then it has matured − while retaining its vigour.

Good process has been established with wide consultation. There is an accepted methodology. Sound information is collected and widely disseminated. The RPI − X arrangements have developed,

[33]Department of the Environment, Transport and the Regions, National Assembly for Wales, *Competition in the Water Industry in England and Wales*, London: Department of the Environment, Transport and the Regions, April 2000.

[34]Department of the Environment, Transport and the Regions, *Economic Instruments in Relation to Water Abstraction: A Consultation Paper*, London: Department of the Environment, Transport and the Regions, April 2000.

[35]Office of Fair Trading, *Competition Act 1998: Application in the Water and Sewerage Sectors*, London: Office of Fair Trading, January 2000.

within a reasonable budget, into medium-term incentive regulation with a mechanism for transferring the benefits of a reduced cost base to customers at successive price reviews. These should continue along present lines to provide incentives for companies to improve performance.

CSCs are making sure that services meet the needs of citizens. Each regional committee has built up its own network, using local knowledge and expertise to represent customers and deal with unresolved complaints. The meetings of their chairmen in the ONCC enable them to exchange information, talk to the regulator, and formulate a collective national voice. Any changes in institutional arrangements should respect this good practice.

Arm's-length working of regulators and ministers has been effective in achieving results while reducing costs. Regulators work together within a statutory framework. They are well placed to take a medium-term view and to resist specific pressures from interest groups. Siren calls to nationalize regulation should be resisted. Where ministers wish to implement social or environmental measures they should use specific legal provisions, and the costs should be clear to those paying the bills.

Finally, the time is ripe for more competition in the water industry. The Competition Act 1998 has shifted the legal balance. The job of the regulator is to create a level playing field so that market competition can develop. To facilitate competition further, the scope for inset arrangements should be widened and abstraction licences opened up to trading. Market competition will inevitably take time to mature, however, and until then we should preserve the conditions where comparative competition can flourish. Any further reduction in the number and range of comparators should – and will – be examined by the Competition Commission and approved only if there are positive benefits to remedy the detriment to comparative competition.

[36]Ian Byatt, *Price Control Review: Letter to Clare Spottiswoode, Director General, Office of Gas Supply*, Birmingham, August 1995.

3.2   Water Regulation

Centre for the Study of Regulated Industries (CRI),
University of Bath, Regulatory Review 2000/2001,
Millennium edition, 2001

THE HIGHLIGHTS OF THE YEAR

1999–2000 was a significant year in the history of the privatised water industry. The main highlights were:

- The second Ofwat 'price review' transferred to customers – in the form of substantial reductions in bills – the gains made by the English and Welsh water companies in reducing their costs.
- The review also set forward price limits which would give the companies the ability to finance the continuation of a large investment programme to improve water and environmental quality.
- The Competition Act came into force on March 2000. It provides the legislative framework for competition to develop in the water industry – as in the other utilities.
- The Water Industry Act 1999 established an independent regulator linked closely to a customer council to regulate the Scottish Water Authorities. It will be interesting to compare the progress of a privatised water industry in England and Wales with a publicly owned one in Scotland.

This chapter sets out the main events of the year; links them to the past and then looks at their implications for the future. The final section points out the choices facing Ministers and regulators. In short, should they follow the post-1997 drift to greater involvement by Ministers and more detailed regulation, both of environmental obligations and of charges to individual customers, or should they work towards greater competition and re-emphasise the primacy of the customer?

THE EVENTS OF THE YEAR

The key milestones in the price review were:

- The submission – in April – of the companies' business plans to Ofwat. These plans set out the price *increases* which the companies believed they needed to be able to finance their existing functions and the new water quality and environmental obligations that were being placed upon them by Ministers. The key elements in these plans, including the proposed increases in prices, were published.
- The publication of draft price limits by Ofwat, in July 1999, proposing large reductions in prices in April 2000 and stable prices for the next five years.[1]
- The final round of representations by water companies and customers on the draft price limits and some fine-tuning of the timing of environmental obligations.
- The determination of price limits by Ofwat for all the water companies in November 1999, involving a 12% reduction of bills in 2000, but some increase thereafter, especially in the North West, to accommodate additional environmental obligations.[2]

[1]Draft Determinations: Future water and sewerage charges 2000–05, Ofwat, July 1999.
2Final Determinations: Future water and sewerage charges 2000–05, Ofwat, November 1999.
[3]1999–2000 Report on tariff structures and charges Ofwat, May 2000, published annually.

- The approval in February 2000 of companies' charges schemes incorporating the new price limits and the Regulations made by Parliament under the 1999 Water Industry Act for the protection of vulnerable customers taking measured supplies.[3]
- The Appeals to the Competition Commission by two out of the twenty five Water Companies against the price limits set by Ofwat.[4]

There was progress towards greater competition as follows:

- ministers published a long-awaited consultation paper on competition in the water industry;[5]
- a number of commentators argued the case for more competition in water services and some water companies became more active in pursuing it;
- all water companies published, in March 2000, principles for access to their networks. This was followed, later in the year, by full access codes;
- ministers laid Regulations before Parliament to reduce the threshold for inset appointments for large users from 250 to 100 Ml/year, thereby trebling the number of users able to profit from competition.

The regulator modestly rolled back the frontiers of regulation by removing large customers from price control (ie, those customers with consumption above the threshold for inset appointments) and significantly reducing the number of water companies subject to externally imposed leakage targets. Companies who had demonstrated robust systems for achieving economic levels of leakage were allowed to set their own targets.[6] Despite fears by Ministers and MPs the Millennium bug did not cause any problems

[4]Competition Commission: Sutton and East Surrey and Mid-Kent, August 2000.
[5]The current state of market competition, Ofwat, July 2000.
[6]1999–2000 Report on leakage and die efficient use of water, Ofwat, September 2000, published annually.

in the water industry. Companies worked well to avoid problems and Ofwat ensured that there was external validation of company systems.[7]

Ministers included in the Utilities Bill a large number of clauses relating to the regulation of the water industry. They were withdrawn a month later. They have subsequently been republished in a Water Bill, but without any timetable for legislation. Whether, in due course, this Water Bill will also include legislation to facilitate competition and better regulate abstractions remains unclear.

One water company, Hyder, became overextended and was obliged to sell to another operator. The transition was managed without damage to the interests of either the customers or the environment. Water companies began to consider what structural changes would help to reduce their costs, in order to maintain their profitability under the new price limits. They sought to reduce operating costs and the cost of capital. The regulator made it clear that such changes should not prejudice the position of customers, in particular by shifting risk from providers of capital to customers. Ofwat's costs were carefully controlled, enabling a £0.5m refund to be made to water companies.

THE LINK TO THE PAST

Prices

The price limits set by Ministers at privatisation in 1989 allowed for increases of 5% a year above the rate of inflation for the five years from 1990 to 1995, followed by increases of 4% above inflation in the five years from 1995 to 2000. The 1999 price review showed customers that water prices could fall because:

- the 1994 price review stopped this 'escalator' of 5% real increases and set price limits to rise modestly over the ten years from 1995 to 2005;[8]

---

[7]Millennium compliance studies, Ofwat, October 1998, June and October 1999.

- the 1999 review set price limits which involved a substantial fall in prices in 2000, followed by broad stability thereafter, ie, a significant reduction in prices over the five years from 2000 to 2005. This is set out in Table 1:

Investment

Since privatisation the water companies have invested heavily in refurbishing their plant and equipment and improving water and environmental quality. Gross capital expenditure has been running at some £3bn a year, double the level of the 1980s. The new price limits provide for a continuation of broadly this level of investment. This includes the continuation of a high level of expenditure on capital maintenance as well as on quality enhancement.

The 1999 price limits allow for capital expenditure of £15.6bn over the five years from 2000 to 2005. It amounts to £135 per property per year. The price limits will allow companies to spend:

- £7.4bn on improving water quality (£2.2bn on drinking water and £5.1 bn on wastewater);
- £6.4bn on maintaining their assets;
- £1.7bn to maintain supplies, mainly to new customers.

These amounts represent a broad continuation of the amounts allowed for – and spent – on capital account in the 1994 Review for the years 1995 to 2000.

Exactly how much money they will spend in the next five years will depend on how efficiently the many schemes for quality enhancement are carried out. There should be scope for significant savings if companies develop imaginative solutions. Examination of several projects during the Review showed that environmental benefits could be achieved at much lower costs by, for example, discharging into rivers with greater absorptive capacity and using supplies of water from other water companies. Environmental

[8]Future charges for water and sewerage services, Ofwat, July 1994.

Table 1: Comparison of Ofwat price limits
First and Second Price Reviews (See sources (2),(4) and (8))

Water and Sewerage Company	1995–2005 (1994 Review)	2000–2005 (1999 Review)	
		Business Plans	Final Determination
Anglian	1.5	7.8	-0.5
Dwr Cymru	0.5	5.3	-1.9
North West	1.2	5.8	-0.5
Northumbrian[b]	1.6[a]	0.0	-4.6
Severn Trent	0.2	0.2	-3.2
South West	0.5	2.7	-1.4
Southern	3.5	3.1	-2.3
Thames	0.5	4.5	-2.6
Wessex	1.0	6.8	-0.9
Yorkshire	1.2	2.5	-2.9
Bournemouth & W Hants	-0.5	4.9	-1.0
Bristol	-1.0	1.8	-2.1
Cambridge	-2.0	0.4	-3.5
Dee Valley[b]	-1.5	-0.4	-3.9
Essex & Suffolk	0.2	-0.5	-2.9
Folkestone & Dover	-0.8	8.6	2.0
Mid Kent	0.0	3.5	-2.5[c](-4.0)
North Surrey	0.2	0.9	-2.4
Portsmouth	-0.8[c](-1.5)	4.4	-1.4
South East	-1.0	2.0	-3.9
South Staffordshire	-0.8	4.5	-1.3
Sutton & E Surrey[b]	-1.4	12.3[d](1.5)	-2.3[c](-5.1)
Tendring Hundred	-0.5	5.6	0.0
Three Valleys	0.7	2.6	-3.2
York	0.0	2.9	-2.1
Industry Average	**0.9**	**3.8**	**-2.1**

[a]Weighted average of Northumbrian and North East Water

[b]2000–2001 figures include merger discount to customers.

[c]Final determinations by Competition Commission. Ofwat determinations in brackets.

[d]Sutton and East Surrey submitted a statement of case to the Competition Commission which differed from the business plan submitted to Ofwat.

regulators should allow companies to exploit such solutions rather than insisting on the details of the project as submitted to Ministers.

The financing of the capital programme has substantially increased companies' gearing. This will rise further over the next five years. The companies have, however, shown skills in raising money and should be able to exploit the demand for secure investments when governments need to borrow much less money than in the past. Immediately after the price review some concerns were expressed about the ability of the companies to finance their large investment programmes. Since then, markets have looked more favourably on water companies and share prices have risen.

Efficiency

In the five years from 1995 to 2000, water companies greatly increased their efficiency by improving delivery to customers and to the environment, while at the same time reducing their costs. They outperformed the regulator's assumptions made in 1989 and 1994.[9]

At the 1994 price review, companies were expected to improve operating efficiency, with the relatively inefficient companies facing more demanding expectations. This increased efficiency was expected to be offset by the additional costs of meeting new obligations, notably the implementation of the EU Wastewater Directive. In the event, all quality obligations were met and operating expenditure in 1998–99 was £420million less than had been expected.

As a result customers got a good deal in 2000. Prices fell by 12% on average. They saw that incentive regulation meant lower costs and that in time higher profits had led to lower prices. Over the decade, customers and the environment had enjoyed a substantial improvement in the quality of the product at a modest increase in prices above general inflation (nationally around 20%).

[9]1998–99 Report on water and sewerage service unit costs, Ofwat, March 2000, published annually.

The regulator has a statutory duty to 'secure that water companies can finance their functions'. It is now very clearly established that this does not mean the prices should be set on a cost-plus basis, nor that they should be at a level to allow an inefficient company to make a good return.

The 1999 price reviews for water and electricity left Hyder, the owner of Dwr Cymru, in an exposed position. The legacy of inefficient operations, poor acquisitions and over-extended management had made Hyder non-viable. The company had to be sold and new management put in charge. At the time of writing the new arrangements are not yet settled. There has been some pain to shareholders and to previous management but no loss in service either to the water customers or to the environment in Wales.

Supply and demand

A sensible approach to managing supply and demand depends on proper pricing, which depends in turn on the installation of meters and the proper setting of tariffs.

Ofwat's first consultation was on *Paying for Water*.[10,11] This showed that instant universal metering was not the way ahead. A more selective approach was better; installing meters where it was economic to do so and where savings could be expected in the use of water. In order to encourage metering in the right places, Ofwat devised and enforced policies to ensure that the price for measured customers was fair. Many water companies had overcharged customers taking measured supplies.

Meanwhile, Ministers of both political parties struggled with the politics of metering. The present administration compromised between the view that metering was good for the environment and the worries that some customers would be disadvantaged. The Water Industry Act 1999 gave all household customers the right

[10]Paying for Water: a time for decisions, Ofwat, November 1990.
[11]Paying for Water: the way ahead, Ofwat, December 1991.

to a meter without installation charges. But water companies lost their right to require current customers in their current residences to have a meter unless they had a garden sprinkler or a swimming pool.

Customers, especially those in high rateable value property, have come to appreciate the amount of money that they can save by having a meter. As a result, there is now a progressive switch to meters – at a rate which differs between company areas. As a result of the accidents of politics, however, metering is spreading where it can be expected to save money rather than water.

The net result is, nevertheless, much more sensible than might have been expected from the disputes of the early 1990s. It will be interesting to see whether, as provided for in existing legislation, Ministers are prepared to allow water companies to install meters compulsorily in area of water stress.

Meters facilitate economic pricing. Sensible tariffs also need to be devised and put into operation. While remaining simple, so that customers can understand them and therefore respond to them, tariffs should be based on the continuing cost of supply (known in the trade as long run marginal cost (LRMC)). This takes account of the cost of augmenting supplies of water and removing wastewater, including the capital costs of new reservoirs, where this is the most economic method of increasing supplies.

During 1999-2000, all companies provided estimates of LRMC, although there must be doubts about the quality of their work. The estimates were published by Ofwat and are, therefore, open to informed public challenge. Ofwat has, I believe wisely, told companies to do the job on the basis of a published methodology. But the range of answers does not suggest sufficient effort has been put into this important area.

Standards of service for customers

Standards of service, as measured by the regulators, have improved regularly over the years. This includes drinking water quality, the quality of wastewater discharged to rivers, beaches and coastal waters, as well as customer service. This has been well documented in Ofwat's annual publications.[12]

Customer protection

Customer Service Committees (CSCs), closely linked to the regulator's office, have represented customers. Individual committees and the regulator have worked closely together in an amicable and effective way. The CSCs provide a regional dimension, which is essential for the water industry. They come together in a non-statutory body, the Ofwat National Customer Council, which consists of the Regional Chairmen. The regulator always attends the Council.

The CSCs were closely involved in the 1999 price review. The Regulator consulted them at all major stages of the review. Customers had the advantage of being represented by well-informed CSCs whose role was complementary to that of the regulator.

The CSCs have also dealt with individual complaints. With some exceptions, they have mediated between customer and company to the satisfaction of customers. They have regularly met company executives to press the case for customers. Their audits of complaints have provided measures of the quality of service provided by the companies, which complements the quantitative information collected by the regulator.

Maintenance of capital

There have been disputes about what is needed in order to maintain the physical assets of the companies satisfactorily. This is a badly under-researched area. Companies have taken an engineering approach, arguing that what matters is the maintenance of the physical condition of the assets. Ofwat has approached the issue from the other end, beginning with the service provided

---

[12] 1999–2000 Report on levels of service for the water industry in England and Wales, Ofwat, July 2000, published annually.

to customers. So, for example, where bursts can be reduced by reducing unnecessarily high water pressures, it is sensible to improve service to customers in this way rather than involving them in the expense of replacing mains, or repairing them at high cost.

Both sides are agreed that this work should:

- involve a sufficient number of indicators to cover all the elements of serviceability to customers and to the environment;
- look at the long term trends and not concentrate too much on the past;
- be properly based on good information.

There is much patient work to be done in combining the economics of asset replacement with good information on the operation of company systems. Companies have done useful work on the condition of their assets. But it needs to be supplemented by work on the cost of operating these assets if capital is to be maintained in an economical way. Until this is done the debate risks being dominated by assertions and inappropriate statistics.

Competition Commission

The Competition Commission heard two appeals, as in 1994. Unlike 1994, the panel's conclusions were somewhat different from those of the regulator. The two companies, Sutton and East Surrey and Mid-Kent had, in their business plans, asked for annual average K factors of +12.3 and +3.5 respectively over the five years from 2000 to 2005. The regulator had concluded that the appropriate numbers were -5.1 and -4.0. The Competition Commission finally set the price limits for these companies at -2.3 and -2.5. The Commission's conclusions were much closer to those of the regulator than those of the companies.

The Competition Commission did not publish sufficient material to explain why they took a different position from the regulator. A significant part of the divergence seems to result from the decision of the Commission to allow these companies the legal and other costs of their appeals. These amounted to nearly £4m for both companies. Whether, from the point of view of the customers who will pay them, these costs were reasonable appears not to have been examined (taxed), as they would have been in a case before the Courts.

Another reason for divergence between the competition Commission and the regulator seems to be the treatment of depreciation. The regulator set price limits on the basis of broad equivalence between the allowance made for depreciation in price limits and company expenditure on the maintenance of assets. When revising price limits upwards the Commission appears to have accepted without question the company's own estimates of depreciation – although it did say that this area required more consideration in future.

The Commission used different econometric models for comparing efficiency, although the resulting differences do not seem to have been large. The Commission also took a different position on the allocation of responsibility between shareholders and customers for expenditure necessary to maintain standards, such as clean water. It also took a different view of the adjustment the regulator had made for poor service on the grounds that this could be considered retrospective

Transparency and communication

Ofwat achieved more consultation and more transparency for the 1999 price review than ever before. The consultations on methodology and information in 1997 were followed in 1998 with the presentation of options in *Prospect for Prices* and the publication of draft price limits in advance of decisions. Documents were fuller and contained more detail than in 1994. Considerable effort was put into wide dissemination of the essential issues.[13]

City analysts provided a stream of useful and often illuminating comment on the progress of the review, even though their predictions were sometimes wide of the mark. Not all the parties, however, were as open as they could have been. Companies were economical with the rationale behind their forward thinking. Did they really want level prices after allowing for inflation – as they often said – or the rising prices set out in most of their business plans?

The Environment Agency provided little relevant information on the benefits of environmental spending. This was a worrying gap. The Agency has a statutory duty to consider costs and benefits in its advice to Ministers. In practice little systematic information was provided for customers and for the public. The attempt to develop a 'multi-attribute' technique appears to have been abandoned.

Nearly all the figures were excised from the reports of the Competition Commission. Ministers said little, except in very general terms, about their involvement in the price review, particularly about the rationale for the scale of the environmental programme.

The utility regulators continued to work closely together, in particular, Ofwat and Ofgem co-operated closely over the water and electricity distribution reviews.[14]

THE IMPLICATIONS FOR THE FUTURE

There are four areas where the events of the recent past point to changes, not all in the same direction:

- the financial regime and the search for efficiency;
- customer representation;
- the increasing detail of ministerial involvement;
- the scope for competition.

[13]Prospects for Prices: a consultation paper on strategic issues affecting future water bills, Ofwat, October 1998.
[14]Statement by Oftel, Ofgem, Ofwat, ORR and Ofreg on Joint working, October 1999.

Finance and efficiency

During the last ten years the water companies have consistently outperformed the regulators' efficiency assumptions. In the short run, this has increased shareholders returns; in the long run it has reduced customers'prices.[15]

As companies are now mature, there can be more sticks and fewer carrots. Companies are now required to work hard to meet shareholder's existing dividend aspirations. They must continue to improve the efficiency of their operating expenditure and their capital expenditure. They must borrow on good terms to finance heavy investment. They know from the fate of Hyder that their survival depends on their ability to keep up with these assumptions.

Various proposals for restructuring were being discussed as the price review proceeded. It was suggested that the parts of the water businesses which could be subject to competition, ie, by contracting out, should be separated from the basic monopoly of the distribution system. It was also suggested that capital could be raised more cheaply if these two elements were unbundled. These discussions were accelerated when the new price limits were known, reaching the public domain in the summer of 2000. Yorkshire water proposed a sale of its assets to a mutual owned by its customers, linked to enhanced dividend payments to shareholders.[16]

These proposals did not get regulatory approval. Many of the ideas behind them, for example to reduce the cost of capital by substituting debt for equity and to reduce the cost of operations by more contracting out, make eminent sense. But customers will only benefit if they are operationally sound and not simply the results of financial engineering. The latter may involve an undesirable transfer of risk from shareholders to customers.

Following the price review companies seem to be more concerned to concentrate on what they can do best rather than to diversify

[15]1999–2000 Report on financial performance and expenditure of the water companies in England and Wales, Ofwat, July 2000, published annually.
[16]The proposed restructuring of the Kelda Group, Ofwat, July 2000.

further. This may be achieved by selling part of the business, as suggested by South West water, or contracting out elements that can be provided more satisfactorily by specialist firms.

Customer representation

The recently published Water Bill repeated the proposals in the Utilities Bill to separate regulation and customer representation, while, at the same time, giving the regulator a primary duty to protect customers. This would mean giving two separate bodies similar objectives, risking duplication or confusion, or both. The existing customer representatives prefer the existing arrangements, which provide for independence of thinking and consistency of action.

Detailed involvement by ministers

Throughout the ten years since privatisation, ministers have had ambitious environmental objectives. These objectives became more detailed after the election of 1997. In the 1999 price review, ministers examined thousands of projects. Because the Environment Agency would not accept the use of generic costs, ie, the costs of a type of solution, projects were individually costed. Monitoring of results will be in corresponding detail. This could lead to over-centralisation and undesirable rigidity.

There is also a danger that politicians will become involved in the details of capital maintenance projects. This would further derogate from the responsibility of management. The companies may become more concerned to get higher price limits by lobbying than by using their business skills to maintain and improve service to customers.

Ministers have decided to pursue social objectives at the expense of water customers. The 1999 Water Industry Act gave them extensive powers over companies's charges schemes. They now have a greater ability to influence the prices paid to individual customers then they did when water was in public ownership.

These powers have, so far, only been used to limit bills payable by low-income customers on welfare benefits, who either have three or more children or a disabling skin disease. Steps have been taken to ensure that this is carefully policed. The financial effects on other customers are likely to be small. Customer representatives have, however, shown some concern about these developments and have said that they would not want to see them extended.

In addition, ministers are, in the Water Bill, seeking legislative powers to set performance targets for water companies, without a request from the regulator. As they have ample powers under existing legislation to set health and environmental standards, these new powers seem designed to increase the scope for ministerial intervention in operational matters, such as leakage targets.

Greater scope for competition

During the last year, various blocks on competition have been removed. The threshold on inset appointments has been reduced substantially. Common carriage has become a possibility. Companies have now set out terms for access to their networks. I do nor believe that further legislation is required, although it would be helpful for the government to make sure that the controls exercised by the Drinking Water Inspectorate apply to all water carried through public supply networks. The water companies want all suppliers using their networks to be licensed to ensure water quality.

Existing suppliers are now in a better position to increase their profits by competing for new customers through common carriage. Water supplies are accessible from a variety of sources. Greater trading of abstraction licences would help to make them more readily available. Progress is possible without legislation but it requires a more positive and active approach from the Environment Agency.

The regulator has given a lead. Yet there is still uncertainty which is inhibiting action by companies. If Ministers were to give competition a favourable wind, they could release market forces to the benefit of customers.

CONCLUSIONS

The future offers exciting possibilities. There is little doubt but that companies will become more efficient. But there is a choice about how they will be regulated. Two scenarios are possible. One is *the heavily regulated, scenario,* with more detailed prescription by Ministers and regulators. This may achieve the results that the public authorities want, but at the cost of more prescription and higher costs for customers. The other scenario is *the competitive one,* where market structures and price signals give increasing power to customers. They want high quality water and a better environment, but in a cost-effective and affordable way.

At privatisation, ministers aimed for reasonably light-handed regulation. Experience has shown that a more hands-on approach is necessary in some areas. But this can go too far, to the point where regulation can operate like nationalisation. To do that would push up costs to the disadvantage of the customer.

Following the competitive scenario could avoid this. Government needs, however, to be committed to competition as a key objective. This is not immediately apparent. Progress in consultation has been slow. But the scope for action is still there. If the nettle is grasped, all regulators should then concentrate on making markets work well by being clear about objectives and avoiding detailed intervention.

3.3 Managing Water Resources Past and Present

in *The Linacre Lectures; Eds: Julie Trotter and Paul Slack*, Oxford, 2002

To understand how things have worked is the best preparation for looking ahead. So I will not gaze into a crystal ball but explain what is happening in England and Wales. I will, however, set out and discuss some scenarios for the future.

THE PROGRESS OF THINKING

In 1989 the water industry emerged from the nationalization era which it had entered only fifteen years earlier. It was a late entrant into the world of public corporations that had emerged between the wars, and particularly after 1945 – a world that was a product of Fabian thinking and wartime experience. The Fabians provided the intellectual base for 'gas and water socialism' in the late nineteenth and early twentieth centuries. Two world wars encouraged people to believe that the state could manage our basic industries efficiently, and the inter-war depression drew attention to deficiencies in the working of the market economy.

'Gas and water socialism' started in the last quarter of the nineteenth century, in the municipalities, with gas, water, electricity, and tramways. In the inter-war years there was a movement towards regional, then national operations, culminating in the post-war Nationalization Acts. Consolidation in water followed slowly.

The amalgamation of municipal undertakings into ten Regional Water Authorities did not take place until 1973. It brought a host of water and wastewater undertakings onto a river basin basis. A further step was taken in 1983 with the substitution of smaller, more executive boards for the much larger bodies that had included local authority representatives.

THE NATIONALIZED WORLD

The model for nationalization in the UK developed from the experience of Herbert Morrison, a key figure in the post-war Labour Government. It involved an arm's-length relationship with government. By the 1970s, the flaws in this model were evident.

The boards of the nationalized industries were required to act in the social interest, subject to breaking even financially. The definition of the social interest was the responsibility of the boards, without any clear mechanisms for ministers to influence their decisions. It was never clear what 'breaking-even', 'taking one year with the next', meant in practice. Moreover, having delegated social functions to such a public not-for-profit body, ministers found it difficult to stay clear. The power of general direction of the nationalization statutes was never used but there was regular and frequent non-statutory involvement in the affairs of the nationalized industries.

When I worked in the Treasury in the 1970s, there were constant disagreements between the boards of the industries and ministers and, within government, a gulf between those who were concerned with 'the efficient allocation of resources' (Treasury speak) and 'social and sectoral considerations' (Departmental speak). The Treasury was concerned with the scale, and poor quality, of their investment programmes and about their frequent loss-making activities. The Sponsor (*sic*) Departments were concerned with sectoral strategies, such as fuel policies, and social objectives, such as not raising prices for essentials of life. There was also a running concern with nationalized industry pay, because of its effect on

149

pay in the economy generally. Pay policy inevitably involved interference with commercial objectives and behind-the-scenes deals.

The nationalized industries represented the high point of producer domination of business decisions. They provided what *they* thought the nation required. Until 1978 there were no performance objectives or service standards. There was no ultimate sanction for failure to meet performance standards or efficiency (or cost-reduction) targets. Consumer committees were established but never given a significant role. Operational matters escalated to the top as unproductive arguments between senior managers and civil servants – or worse between chairmen and ministers. Investment was constrained and capital was wasted. Industries wanted to invest in grandiose schemes, while the Treasury was concerned to limit the macroeconomic consequences of capital expenditure. Industries complained of lack of investment. Yet financial returns consistently fell short of the cost of capital (Treasury 1961, 1967, 1978).

The institutional structure had produced the wrong incentives.

THE NEW APPROACH: 'GAS AND WATER CAPITALISM'

Conservative ministers elected in 1979 dramatically changed the levers of macro-and microeconomic policy. They resolved to control inflation by monetary policy and to increase labour market flexibility to generate full employment. They believed that competition would liberate consumer choice and put pressures on management to increase efficiency. Traditionally governments had sought to correct market failure. The new approach took account of public sector failure and the power of markets to deliver what customers wanted. This was a profound intellectual change, much approved of by those of us who had observed government failure in our daily work.

Ministers could not remedy investment deficits in the public corporations through the public finances. Privatization was as necessary for investment by BT as it was for investment in the water industry.

'Gas and water capitalism' is not the same as market capitalism generally. The utilities belong to the infrastructure sector of the economy, where there is considerable natural monopoly power through the provision of essential facilities. Independent specialist regulators were, therefore, given statutory powers to act as servants of government in its wider sense, not as servants of ministers. The primary duty of the water regulator was to 'secure that the companies properly carry out their functions and can finance them'. It is for the regulator, not ministers, to decide what constitutes the proper carryingout of functions. The regulator may consult ministers, but retains final responsibility. The regulator must determine the price limits need to finance the operations and investment of efficient companies, but not how much they should spend.

Subject to these primary duties, the regulator is charged to protect customers, promote efficiency, and facilitate competition. The government wisely provided for appeal by a company to the Competition Commission should it disagree with the regulator's pricing decisions. The regulator appoints ten Customer Service Committees (CSCs) to represent customers. He brought together the chairmen in the OFWAT National Customer Council (ONCC).

Because of the health and environmental importance of water supply and wastewater disposal, the government also appointed specialist quality regulators – a Drinking Water Inspectorate (DWI) and a National Rivers Authority (NRA), subsequently the Environment Agency (EA). Each organization had a specific set of statutory duties. The endemic confusions of the nationalized regime were avoided.

Initially it was not thought that competition was likely to develop rapidly, either in water supply or wastewater disposal. Nevertheless, the Privatization Act made a start by enabling the regulator to make 'inset' appointments of new suppliers to serve new customers on green field sites within the area of existing companies. In 1992 this was widened to include large customers already served by an existing company.

'GAS AND WATER CAPITALISM': THE RESULTS

Since the privatization of the water authorities in England and Wales in 1989 (OFWAT 2003), water quality has improved:

The percentage of river and canal water classified as good or fair has risen from 84 to 94 per cent.

Bathing water compliance has risen from 66 (1988) to 99 per cent.

Sewage treatment works compliance has risen from 90 to 99 per cent.

Sewer flooding incidents have fallen from 0.05 (1993) of connections to 0.02 per cent.

Compliance with drinking water standards rose from 99 to 99.9 per cent.

Customer service has also improved:

Properties at risk of low pressure have fallen from 1.3 (1993) to 0.06 per cent.

Unplanned interruptions over 12 hours have fallen from 0.42 per cent of properties to 0.05 per cent.

Written complaints from customers answered within ten working days has risen from 82 to 99.8 per cent.

Billing contacts dealt with within five working days has risen from 80 (1992-3) to 99 per cent.

This required a large increase in investment. Investment, running at about £1.5 billion a year (today's prices) in the 1980s, rose to average of £3.0 billion a year during the 1990s. By 2005, some £50 billion will have been invested in the privatized transmission and treatment of water and wastewater.

Customers' bills have had to rise by some 20 per cent about inflation to finance this. Within this increase, however, bills have *fallen* for customers (most business customers and, now, over 20 per cent of household customers) taking a measured supply. Prices would have risen much more but for the greater efficiency of the water companies. The annual average regulated household water bill (now around £230 a year) would have had to rise – between 1990 and 2005 – by £100 in order to finance the provision of better quality water and wastewater. In the event it will have risen by £38 (Byatt 2001). Most of the increases in price took place in the first half of the 1990s. Greater efficiency, delivered largely in the second half of the 1990s, enabled the regulator to reduce prices substantially in 2000.

THE FRAMEWORK FOR THE FUTURE

Good governance involves some unbundling of government. Ministers cannot, and should not, try to run everything. Conservative ministers recognized the advantages of distancing themselves from the operations of the utilities. New Labour is taking time fully to learn this lesson. The principles, set out in the Green Paper on Utility Regulation extol the advantages of an arm's-length relationship between ministers and regulators (DTI 1998). Those principles did not, however, prevent the Deputy Prime Minister from wanting to set leakage targets. Nor did they prevent DETR ministers from legislating to give themselves powers – which went beyond the ministerial powers under nationalization – to set water charges for individual groups of customers, and to deny companies the right to disconnect household customers for non-payment of bills.

Politicians are experienced and skilled in playing the zero-sum game of distribution. But they are pressured into action by the politics of the saloon bar. They mistrust the invisible hand of the market and want to pull their own levers – without fully considering all the consequences. And, because they are often fighting battles on several fronts, they baulk at tough economic action, even when they know they should be taking it.

Regulators are perhaps better able to engage in the positive-sum game of enrichment. They need to encourage as well as to complain if things are to be put right; and they need to be patient. They might need to act as a buffer, so that energetic ministers do not overreact to every adverse event. Regulators can also make markets work better: for example, in utility pricing, they can act as a proxy for the market.

EXPOSURE TO THE MARKETS

Before privatization, water was largely insulated from the market economy. Water companies are now part of global business. Expertise, in economics and customer service as well as in engineering, is now freely traded internationally. Water companies raise their own finance and account to their shareholders. They have incentives to increase their profitability by reducing their costs. They are no longer enmeshed in the culture of the public sector labour supply. Customers taking measured supplies now face tariffs that are increasingly related to costs and so have incentives to use water wisely. Businesses have stronger incentives to treat wastewater before discharging it to sewer.

Privatization of water has not simply substituted a private monopoly for a public monopoly. Water companies can use, and are now subject to, market forces in a number of overlapping ways.

1. *Markets for Water Resources.* The abstraction of water from rivers or aquifers is regulated in the interest of the environment. Abstraction licences can, however, be traded, albeit with some complexity. This could usefully be simplified. Water can be bought and sold between companies – with the regulator available to determine the price if the parties disagree. Companies can tap capital markets to finance investment in water abstraction, storage, and transfer schemes. The regulator can allow for this in setting price limits.

2. *Water Product Markets.* Water pricing is being released from the straitjacket of tariffs based on an extinct property tax (rateable

values) and from overreliance on standing charges when supplies are metered. Meters are now routinely installed in new properties and there is a steady switch of existing households to metered supplies. If tariffs reflect the continuing cost of supply – including the capital cost of augmenting facilities – customers can enjoy an economic choice of the volume of water bought. Regulators supplement existing market mechanisms.

If, as a result of regulatory and other pressures, the price of water is equal to the incremental cost of supply, including capital costs, water companies are able to finance additional supplies within existing price limits (OFWAT 1993). Where new households are connected to a company's network, it is able to levy an additional, regulated charge to cover the capital costs of new local infrastructure. Large users (water and wastewater) are able to choose their own supplier, and are increasingly doing so. The threshold of the definition of a large user has been reduced. The potential for competition has already reduced prices for large users.

Cross-border competition is possible for domestic supplies, but the scope is limited because borders do not generally pass through well-populated areas. If common carriage is developed commercially, as in telecom, gas, and electricity, customers will get choice and lower prices. Following the 1998 Competition Act, the market is poised for this. The Act requires companies not to abuse a dominant position. OFWAT requires companies to produce a code for access to their networks, including an access price (OFWAT 2002/7: 1). Potential entrants can take disputes to the regulator. The quality of drinking water in public networks is subject to the inspection of the DWI, or can be made so subject by the process of making inset appointments (see above) for new suppliers.

I believe the market is now contestable. So far there have been few contestants. Yet ministers legislated in 2004 to restrict competition.

3. *The Labour Market.* At privatization the water companies were able to free themselves from historical rigidities in both pay

and conditions. And unions are less powerful when ministers are removed from direct involvement. Companies have been able to change internal arrangements to achieve much more efficient working practices, without threats of strikes.

Companies are also able to unlock executive remuneration to pay salaries better related to other private sector companies and to recruit higher quality staff. Where senior managers have failed, shareholders have acted to replace them. Despite the temporary turbulence of the 'fat cat' accusations, a much better framework for executive pay is now in place.

4. *The Market for Procurement.* Privatization also increased the incentive to efficient buying of goods – both capital equipment and operating materials. Savings could be retained up to the next price review. In the case of capital expenditure, this probably affected specifications for projects more than techniques of tendering. One-well publicized example concerns sewerage on the Isle of Wight. Southern Water's original plan for a number of sewerage treatment works along the coast was changed into one that involved piping sewage to a central works and treating it more cheaply to the enhanced standard required by the EU.

As the 1990s progressed, ideas of contracting out substantial elements of operations began to develop into practical schemes. People were even beginning to talk of a 'virtual' utility with a small core staff, ensuring licence conditions were met and letting managing contracts for operations. Following the last price review this activity has intensified and is a major route for water companies to seek to reduce their costs to beat the regulator's projections. Contracting out, i.e. outsourcing – a feature of many private markets in recent years – allows companies to specialize in what they can do best. It enables individual managements to exploit their comparative advantages. Managing distribution networks requires rather different skills from those needed to compete for customers.

As outsourcing develops, it could provide increasing competition while allowing some concentration of the ownership of elements of transmission and distribution networks. Some merger of networks could be combined with increased contracting out of other activities.

5. *The Market for Finance.* Water companies have been, and still are, engaged in an intensive search for new – cheaper and better – sources of finance and to achieve an optimal balance (equity, bonds, loans, etc.) of existing instruments. In contrast to the complexity of estimating the opportunity cost of capital for nationalized industries, the cost of capital for private utilities has become a market phenomenon.

The initial estimates of the cost of capital at privatization were shown to be too high as companies tapped markets in a variety of ways – nominal bonds, indexed bonds, leasing, loans from the European Investment Bank, etc. In the last two years, water companies have shown that they can reduce their cost of capital further by increasing the gearing of a ring-fenced water and sewerage business. Some companies are now talking about gearing (measured by the debt: debt plus equity ratio) of around 85 per cent. This is significantly more than the 50 per cent assumed by the regulator at the 1999 price review.

This has involved new techniques, such as the formation of a private not-for-profit company (Glas Cymru) able to buy Welsh water at a discount to the regulatory capital value (OFWAT, 2001, and the 'thin equity' approaches of Scottish Power/Southern Water Services and Anglian Water (OFWAT, 2002c: 2-4 2002d and e). The emergence of monoline insurers (who combine insurance on capital value or interest payments with lending) may have reduced the cost of borrowing while imposing greater financial discipline on companies. Because water companies, unlike water authorities, pay the full cost of capital, they have an incentive to economize in its use – working existing assets harder and balancing the cost of replacement investment against its benefits.

In a capital-intensive industry such as water there can be additional constraints that are not fully reflected in conventional calculations of the cost of capital. In particular, companies have

157

needed to sustain a level of interest cover necessary to ensure investment grade rating on their bonds. These additional constraints on borrowing were important at all the three water price reviews. Their importance declined as it became progressively clear that levels of gearing could be raised. But they will not disappear while high investment is needed to meet new water quality and environmental obligations.

6. *The Market for Corporate Control.* Water companies are subject to takeover, although legislation restricts internal concentration to preserve a sufficient number of comparators. The threat of takeover is a continuing spur to better performance. The desire to maintain a good share price led companies to try to outperform the cost assumptions the regulator made at a price review. City carrots have proved to be more effective than Treasury sticks. The takeover mechanism made it possible to replace a poorly performing utility, Hyder, without detriment to customers or the environment.

The regulatory restrictions on internal mergers have ensured that a merger would be accompanied by a direct benefit to customers, usually in the form of lower prices. Under this regime there has been significant consolidation of smaller companies and two large mergers, both involving multinational corporations, which were accompanied by substantial reductions in prices. There are no restrictions on entry from outside the water businesses and from outside England and Wales. There have been takeovers by French, German, Spanish, Dutch, American, and Scottish companies.

Markets have shown themselves better able than political processes to cope with institutional change. Incremental changes can be made and tested. The political process struggles with institutional change – too often risking the preservation of obsolete structures or making dramatic changes with unintended effects.

THE REGULATORY COUNTERPART

Incentive regulation is the natural counterpart to the greater use of markets. It has translated greater efficiency into better service and lower prices to customers and into a better environment.

1. *Ringfencing.* The regulated business must be ring-fenced so that losses (or profits) made by other parts of the company are not attributed to the customers of the regulated business. This involves proper accounting separation, regular visits to understand what is happening, and policing of what companies are doing. It also involves ensuring that any losses incurred in a non-water activity could not impact adversely on the customers of the regulated water utility. This no-recourse rule meant that the collapse of the Enron Corporation, and the downgrading of its bonds to junk status, did not affect the status of the bonds of its subsidiary, Wessex Water, which retained investment-grade status.

The ring-fencing arrangements also involved ensuring that licensed water companies had good governance arrangements to ensure they made decisions in the interests of the water company rather than the diversified parent. There is growing evidence that this is reducing the cost of capital by insulating licensed companies from some of the risks faced by their parents.

2. *Incentives to Efficiency.* The setting of medium-term limits (price caps) on prices charged to customers is a key element in the provision of incentives. OFWAT ensured that companies were able to keep any savings they made on both capital expenditure and operating expenditure for a full five years. So, for example, when Scottish Power took over Southern Water well into the five-year period of the price cap, it was allowed to carry over savings at the next review.

3. *Expectations.* Incentives are not always sufficient. Price limits can – indeed should – be set which require management to work hard to achieve reasonable profits. OFWAT used comparative analysis to establish what expenditure should be allowed for in setting price limits. This involved judging how quickly, and to what extent, companies could be expected to improve their efficiency.

Comparative analysis builds on the costs revealed by the more efficient companies, i.e. those who responded best to incentives. Sticks and carrots are linked.

4. *Focus on Outcomes.* Regulation is about achieving outcomes effectively and efficiently, not saving costs by cutting corners. Measures of performance to customers, such as adequate water pressure and continuity of supply, and measures of performance for the environment, such as compliance of sewage treatment work with EU standards, were established and regularly monitored.

The incentives given to water companies to improve customer service standards were strengthened progressively as regulation matured. Initially, OFWAT recorded, published, commended, and encouraged. Rejecting a call from a Parliamentary Committee to set absolute standards from the regulator's office, we prescribed minimum standards and pushed laggards hard. In the 1999 Price Review, we used a composite indicator of performance. Companies at the top end of this indicator were allowed higher price caps, while those at the bottom were given tougher ones. This is now being developed further, better to incentivize the provision of good service (OFWAT *2002b*: 5).

5. *Interface with Ministers as Standard Setters.* The independence of the regulator from ministers does not preclude seeking guidance from ministers as setters of water quality and environmental standards. As part of the 1994 periodic review, a set of procedures was established that involved:

1. An open (i.e. public) letter to ministers, setting out the consequences for customers' bills of proposals for improvements in water quality and the environment.
2. Consideration of the issues by ministers collectively and guidance to the water regulator on legally enforceable water quality and environmental obligations.

At the 1994 Review, this included the establishment of an important quadripartite group involving government departments quality regulators (NRA and DWI), companies and OFWAT, under DoE chairmanship. This enabled ministers not to be concerned with the details. Unfortunately, by the 1999 review, ministers had become entangled in detail and the significance of the quadripartite group diminished.

6. *Dealing with Failure.* Monitoring does not always reveal success. Failure has to be dealt with effectively as well as firmly; penalties must be proportional and lead to better results. Failures might simply affect individual customers or could be on a much larger scale. A Guaranteed Standards Scheme (GSS) was set up at privatization so that individual customers would be compensated for specified service failures, such as an unplanned interruption of supply. The CSCs have – in addition – audited complaints and extracted compensation for failures in service. In cases of dispute, companies have ceded binding mediation to CSCs.

The biggest company failure to affect customers occurred in Yorkshire during the drought of 1995. To avoid running out of water, Yorkshire Water took it up the Dales by tanker at a cost of £45m. to the shareholders and loss of sleep to those living by the lorry routes. When the crisis was over, the company commissioned an 'independent' report, which concluded – in those well-worn words – that this was an 'accident waiting to happen' and recommended substantial investment. Ministers wisely kept out of this and left the governmental inquiry to be carried out by the regulator.

The inquiry team was given full access to the company's records. The facts were agreed by the company. The team concluded that there were serious failures in customer service and deficiencies in the governance of the utility business. Also, as then Director-General of Water Services, I concluded that the special dividend of £50m. that Yorkshire Water Services had just paid to its parent company was not appropriate in the circumstances (OFWAT 1996). Following discussions with the new management, the company agreed to lower price limits – costing some £40m. It also agreed formal undertakings to improve service to customers.

It agreed to amend its licence to ensure that the utility would conduct its business as though it were a separate plc and not pay dividends which could impair its ability to finance the regulated business.

The episode revealed a hole in the compensation arrangements The legislation apparently did not provide for compensation should the supply be interrupted when a drought order was in place. Despite promises by two administrations to remedy this, nothing has been done. As an 'interim' solution, I negotiated changes in the companies' licences to provide for compensation in all cases. There the matter rests. There is now an automatic financial penalty awaiting a company that fails its supply duty.

7. *Information and Consultation.* Privatization and regulation has led to much greater transparency. Regulators need information and publishing it provides a basis for informed public debate. One of the early jobs in OFWAT was to devise a regular (annual) flow of information from the companies to the regulator. It drew on the internal information systems used by the previous water authorities. It has been modified during the years, in consultation with the companies and other stakeholders.

OFWAT was careful to ensure that information is consistent and comparable. Much midnight oil was burnt in getting the definition right. Independent Reporters were appointed, with a duty of care to the regulator, to validate the data collected by the companies. Wide distribution of this material was ensured, in a series of published annual reports, through *ad hoc* publications, and by making the basic data available to research workers. Key points were set out in leaflets that were widely accessible to customers and to the general public. This information also protects the regulator against asymmetry of information – a very real problem for regulators.

8. *Capital Expenditure.* Much has gone well, but the position on capital expenditure remains imperfect. Investment is not an end result: it is a cost and not an outcome. Only where investment produces a sufficient return does it provide value for money for customers.

Forward estimates by companies are often biased. Investment appraisal is often poor; those promoting schemes can be resistant to the search for better alternatives. Frequently the right information has not been collected. There is a tendency to overspecify work. There is a temptation to press for capital expenditure which can push up price limits in order to reduce operating costs and pay higher dividends. Much regulatory effort has been needed to improve the capital cost estimates used for setting price limits.

By no means all the proposals for investment by water companies have been on worthwhile projects. At the 1999 Periodic Review there were a number of uneconomic projects, notably the expensive Wessex low-flow project, which were postponed for further investigation.

LOOKING AHEAD

The fixed point in looking ahead is the 1999 Periodic Review, which reduced prices in April 2000 by over 12 per cent – the famous (or infamous) – P_o adjustment. In the first year (2000/1) of the new price limits, prices were reduced so that profits would be no higher than the cost of capital. This contrasted sharply with the approach of the 1994 Price Review where price limits were designed to transfer efficiency to customers by reducing profits to the cost of capital over a ten-year period – although most of the reduction would take place over the first five years.

The logic behind the P_o (first year) reduction was twofold. First, it was felt that customers, who had endured substantial increases in prices since privatization, should have – and see – the benefit of the efficiency generated by privatization. Secondly, the goal was to ensure transparency in environmental decision-making. Any further environmental – or social – obligations imposed by ministers on water companies would be seen to raise prices. There would be no cushion provided by shareholders.

SCENARIOS FOR THE FUTURE

Attempts to forecast are so often doomed to failure that I have chosen to present my views in the form of three scenarios for the future. In putting them together, I have combined possibilities in a number of variables. The key ones relate to capital expenditure, its financing (i.e. the cost of capital), the structure of the companies, and the nature of the regulatory regime. The broad nature of the pressures on these fronts is clear. The demands for environmental improvements, involving continued capital expenditure on water quality and environmental improvement, are likely to remain strong.

The companies will be much more geared up at the next Periodic Review and the scope for further gearing may be relatively small. The government, meanwhile, is getting increasingly involved in the detailed working of the regulatory arrangements. At the last review, it looked at thousands of environmental improvement projects.

The vertically integrated structure has persisted to a greater extent than in gas and electricity, but is now being challenged as companies increasingly come to concentrate on what they can do best and outsource other activities.

Progress on competition has been slow compared with what has happened in energy. Partly this reflects the underlying situation, partly it reflects the different attitude to competition within government. Environment ministers, particularly under Labour, seem more worried about any downside than excited about the potential benefits. Increased competition is not compatible with detailed control; ministers prefer the control and fear the competition.

Out of this I can image three scenarios: (A) high capex: high prices; (B) competition: high efficiency; (C) muddling through.

Scenario A: High Capex: High Prices. The pressure for a continuation of high capital expenditure could arise from new, poorly targeted water quality and environmental Directives from the EU and poorly appraised national schemes.

By the next price review in 2004 companies may have *projected* interest covers that are barely sufficient to maintain investment grade status on their bonds. If so, there will be pressure on the regulator to advance revenue when setting price limits. Alternatively, appointed water companies may need to raise equity, either through an injection from their parent companies or directly.

It may become increasingly difficult for water companies to raise their efficiency more rapidly than that of the economy as a whole. Many of the gains from the initial transfer from the public to the private sector may already be achieved.

If both capital and operating expenditure stay high, and the cost of capital rises, the price escalator will start again. This will not be popular, whatever the underlying desire for quality. It will exacerbate disputes between those who are content to see bills rising to improve quality and the majority who may not – particularly if other taxes are rising.

Scenario B: Competition: High Efficiency. The effect of competition on energy prices, where large reductions have taken place, shows the scope for increases in efficiency in the water sector once it is driven by competition. Some of this is taking place as companies compete with each other for outsourcing contracts, but the advent of market competition would further stimulate the search for better performance and lower costs.

It is possible substantially to improve investment appraisal, particularly where enhancement projects are concerned. The Environment Agency could, and should, move away from using its political muscle to support any project, however expensive, to developing a system for improving the effectiveness and efficiency of projects, and concentrating on the better ones. The Agency has neglected its statutory duty to consider costs and benefits. It would also improve performance and efficiency if ministers were to concentrate on strategy and not look at a myriad of small schemes – where they and their civil servants have limited expertise.

There is work to be done better to understand capital maintenance, by improving information on service to customers and its relationship to asset conditions and operating costs. When information is available, economic techniques can.be used to improve effectiveness and efficiency.

If investment becomes more efficient, costs, including the cost of capital, can stay down. In such a world, we could look forward to steadily improving water and environmental quality, where customers' bills remained broadly stable in real terms.

Scenario C: Muddling Through: Neo-nationalization. In politics, where there are conflicting objectives and no easy answers, muddling through can often be a good strategy. In business life, it is more often the way to oblivion. If water is dominated by politics, we could drift towards neo-nationalization. Ministers would set generalized objectives and intervene in particular events. They would use their extensive powers on water charges to promote social agendas. They would be driven by the sound-bite and the ballot box rather than by business logic.

Nor do ministers have a good track record when it comes to an open assessment of strategic possibilities. The cost of better water and environmental quality was never openly estimated and appraised under nationalization. Immediately after privatization, things even took a turn for the worse. Relieved of having to go to the Treasury for finance for investment, ministers believed the financial markets could be milked. But, as could have been predicted, only at the cost of rapidly rising water prices. It was left to the water regulator to protect customers from environmental taxation, by constantly reminding them about the cost of improving quality.

Muddling through can create tensions while it tries to negotiate through them. Unresolved conflict is the last thing that business leaders want. It leads to paralysis, high costs, and constraints on investment. The end result is poor performance and inefficiency.

WHERE DO WE GO FROM HERE?

It is easier to see who gains from each of the scenarios than to say which will prevail. The companies would welcome Scenario A, the customers, Scenario B. Environmentalists would gain from

166

both, but their instincts probably point them to A. Ministers would instinctively welcome the high investment of Scenario A but recoil from rising prices. Unaided, they may not be able to exercise the self-restraint needed to avoid Scenario C.

My own preference is for Scenario B. It involves recognizing that there are differences in objectives and that centrally imposed solutions do not work. It involves continuing to use markets to allocate resources. It involves unbundling government and involving all stakeholders in making decisions on water and environmental quality. It involves taking risks in encouraging competition, by reducing substantially the threshold for inset appointments, by opening up the market for abstraction of water from rivers and aquifers (subject, of course, to environmental constraints) and by facilitating common carriage, in particular by extending the functions of the DWI to all water supplied through public networks. It involves accepting that capital markets will manage new suppliers. It also involves an evolution of tariffs based increasingly on cost and the extension of metering.

I would scarcely be human if I did not finish this chapter by arguing for maintaining the position of independent regulators, able to act in the public interest at arm's-length from the political concerns of ministers. They are needed to ensure that water companies have sufficient finance for well-appraised investment, to facilitate competition, to achieve an efficient structure of prices.

Independent regulators have been able – under their statutory powers – to act both transparently and dispassionately. They do this within a framework of good process – a process able to involve all stakeholders in a situation where there are no simple answers.

Let us use the available tools to achieve a sensible balance by keeping water in the market economy.

REFERENCES

Byatt, Ian, The Water Regulation Regime in England and Wales', in C. Henry, Michel Matheu, and Alain Jeunemaitre, *Regulation of Network Utilities: The European Experience* (Oxford: Oxford University Press, 2001).

DTI, *A Fair Deal for Consumers: Modernising the Framework for Utility Regulation* (London: Department of Trade and Industry, 1998).

OFWAT, *Paying for Growth* (Birmingham: Office of Water Services, 1993).

—*Report on Conclusions from OFWATs Enquiry into the Performance of Yorkshire Water Services Ltd.* (Birmingham: Office of Water Services, 1996).

—*The Proposed Acquisition of Dwr Cymru Cyfyngedig* by Gias Cymru Cyfyngedig (Birmingham: Office of Water Services, 2001).

—*Access Codes for Common Carriage* (Birmingham: Office of Water Services, 2002*a*).

—*Linking Service Levels to Prices* (Birmingham: Office of Water Services, 2002*b*).

—*Proposals for the Modification of the Conditions of Appointment of Anglian Water Services* (Birmingham: Office of Water Services, 2002*c*).

—*Proposals for the Modification of the Conditions of Appointment of Southern Water Services Limited* (Birmingham: Office of Water Services, 2002*d*).

OFWAT, *The Proposed Takeover of Southern Water Services Ltd. by First Aqua Holdings Ltd.* (Birmingham: Office of Water Services, 2002*e*).

—*Water Regulation: Facts and Figures* (Birmingham: Office of Water Services, 2003).

Treasury, Cmnd. 1337, *The Financial and Economic Obligations of the Nationalised Industries*, (London: HMSO, 1961).

—Cmnd. 3437, *Nationalised Industries: A Review of Economic and Financial Objectives* (London: HMSO, 1967).

—Cmnd. 7131, *The Nationalised Industries* (London: HMSO, 1978).

3.4 Economic regulation of water and sewerage services

With Tony Ballance and Scott Reid

International Handbook on Economic Regulation.
Eds: Michael Crew and David Parker, 2006

INTRODUCTION

Effective regulatory oversight of utilities begins by making appropriate decisions on industry structure, competition and regulation. Where it is feasible competition provides a spur to good service and efficient provision and there are therefore strong arguments for developing structures that facilitate it wherever possible. But should water services be treated like other utilities (i.e. energy and telecoms) in terms of how the sector should be organized, how competition should work and how it should be regulated (see for example Robinson, 1998)? Or are they a natural monopoly, in which the potential for competition between multiple suppliers for the same group of customers (i.e. competition in the market) is limited and hence some form of regulation is required to protect the customer interest?

In this chapter we examine these important questions by looking at two key themes in the regulation of water services: the regulation of *structure* and the regulation of *conduct*.

Consideration of the regulation of *structure* provides the necessary context for understanding the scope for competition *in* the market for water services and approaches to the regulation of industry structure. It also provides a framework for understanding the structure of costs in water services. We review the evidence on economies of scale and scope in water services, focusing on the situation in England and Wales. We then address the public oversight of the conduct of the water sector where competition is limited, in particular the need for and the role of a regulatory agency where there is private ownership of the assets, as is the case in England and Wales. We then consider the need for public oversight where there are other forms of private sector participation (PSP) (i.e. through contracts). We focus on the French model of water PSP and then broaden the discussion out to consider the likely requirements for regulation in other countries. We complete the picture by examining these issues in the context of public owned water services, as is the case in Scotland, where there is an independent regulatory body.

REGULATION OF INDUSTRY STRUCTURE

The importance of 'getting industry structure right' for water services lies in two related factors. First, the experience of history suggests that a laissez-faire approach to water services has not resulted in industry structures that are economically or socially efficient. Second, policymakers have a public interest in an efficient structure for what are essential services and where, because of that essentiality, cross-subsidization is often a requirement to make service provision affordable.

The structure of costs in water services – economies of scale and scope

There are significant differences in the organization of water services worldwide, despite the production technology for those services being relatively well established and homogeneous.

At one extreme is the UK, where large vertically and horizontally integrated water and sewerage providers dominate the sector. At the other, and more common, extreme are the more fragmented municipal-based industry structures observed, for example, in Germany, France, Italy, the USA and Japan.

The evolution of these different industry structures reflects in part historical and geographical differences, but also competing views about the most appropriate model of organization for the production of water services. In England and Wales the reorganization of the sector in 1973 into ten regional water authorities was largely driven by a desire to see integrated river-basin management whereby a single entity where possible, should plan and control the uses of water in each river catchment. As such the reorganization was driven by factors broader than purely economic ones, although the assumption was that the industry was characterized by substantial economies of scale. With the implementation of the Water Framework Directive across the European Union, which will focus attention on issues of catchment management, these influences on sector structure may become more important more widely in Europe.

In this section, we examine in more detail the available evidence on the cost structure of water services to shed light on these debates and their implications for public oversight.

Some definitions

Water supply and sanitation services comprise the production of distinct multiple outputs, which could potentially be supplied by distinct markets. For example, the water supply process comprises: abstraction from underground sources and surface sources such as aquifers and rivers; storage (natural or artificial) in order to be able to maintain supplies during times of shortage (i.e. drought situations); treatment to remove natural and other pollutants; bulk transport before and/or after treatment; local storage (to cover diurnal variation in demand); and distribution via a network of mains to consumers.

There is also the customer interface retailing, which deals with connections, billing and payment systems. A simplified three-stage categorization of the production process might be bulk water supply, water transport and distribution, and retailing, as summarized in Table 17.1. A similar categorization of the

Table 17.1. The water supply chain

Supply chain		Components of supply system
Stage	Element	
1	Bulk water production/supply	• Raw water sources
		• Raw water trunk main
		• Water treatment plant
2	Trunk distribution	• Trunk main
		• Pumping station
		• Service reservoir
	Local distribution	• Local distribution system
		• Communication pipe
3	Retailing	• Meter and billing
		• Customer services

production process for the wastewater sector also applies.

With multiple outputs, the key issues for efficient industry structure are the scale of operation and to what extent operations should be vertically and horizontally integrated. In simpler terms, how many independent suppliers should there be (within a defined market) and what services should they provide?

Baumol (1977) and Panzar and Willig (1977) provide important elements of the necessary conceptual framework for addressing these issues. A first concept, but by no means the most important, is that of *economies of scale,* which characterizes the relationship between unit costs and the scale of output. In the multi-product case this can be further refined in terms of *ray economies of scale,* which indicates how total costs vary when each output is varied in fixed proportions, and *product-specific economies of scale,* which measures how costs vary with changes in a specific output, holding the quantities of other outputs constant. Second, *economies of scope* exist where the joint production of outputs involves costs

172

of production that are less than the sum of the production costs by separate specialized firms. Positive economies of scope can have two sources: the sharing across outputs of indivisible fixed costs (such as head office costs) that are not specific to each output or service, and cost complementarities in production activities, where the production of one output reduces the cost of producing the other output because of the ability to share inputs across production activities.

The presence of economies of scale in a multi-product firm need not imply lower total costs of production if diseconomies of scope are also present. Equally, it can be efficient to operate under diseconomies of scale, if the economies of scope from the production of multiple outputs are sufficiently large. Baumol (1977) shows that the appropriate test is whether costs are *sub-additive*; that is, joint production by a single firm results in lower costs than independent production of the same outputs. Scale economies are neither necessary nor sufficient in determining the most efficient industry structure for water services. In practice, moreover, as discussed below and in Chapter 6, yardstick or comparative competition can be a valuable element in the regulation of conduct in water sectors and because of this there are benefits to preserving a sufficient number of comparators.

Measuring scale and scope economies in water services

The textbook model of the production process assumes that firms are free to adjust in the long run the level of all factor inputs to ensure that costs are minimized. For water services this formulation may be less than helpful for two reasons (see, for example, the discussion in Saal and Parker, 2000). First, the technology used in water services can be indivisible and associated with very long service lives. Second, managers do not have total influence over fixed factors, such as capital investment, as this is often determined or influenced by regulatory requirements. Legal obligations to meet quality standards or to connect customers to the network mean that capital, in particular, is a quasi-fixed input and this needs to be recognized when measuring scale and scope economies (see Stone and Webster Consultants, 2004a).

Evidence from England and Wales

The consolidation of the water sector in England and Wales on the basis of better management of water services over a river basin provides important evidence on the extent of economies of scale and scope in water services. Recent work commissioned by the industry regulator for England and Wales, the Office of Water Services (OFWAT) provides the first systematic attempt in the post-privatization period to estimate scale and scope economies in this sector using a multiple output methodology (Stone and Webster Consultants, 2004a).

The 1945 Water Act encouraged the amalgamation of small municipal-based undertakings through self-organization in Britain (see Richardson, 2003).[1] By 1970, however, the industry was still relatively fragmented comprising 198 separate water supply undertakings (including 33 privately owned statutory water companies) and over 1300 publicly owned sewerage and sewage disposal authorities. The 1963 Water Resources Act had increased the centralization of planning with the creation of 29 river authorities with a range of water and waste disposal planning and licensing functions. The catalyst for consolidation of the operational undertakings was the work of the Central Water Advisory Committee, which was tasked in 1969 with examining the organization of water services in England and Wales. It was considered that water needed to be transferred between river basins, and that the planning of water resources should no longer be carried out by 29 separate authorities.

The Central Advisory Water Committee report (1971) laid the foundations for Integrated River Basin Management (IRBM) and provides the genesis for the ten Regional Water Authorities (RWAs) organized around major river catchments created in 1973. It also recommended an operational industry structure of about 50 water supply and sewerage undertakings to exploit available scale economies. However, the 1973 Act established the ten RWAs as multi-purpose bodies with responsibilities for water supply, sewage disposal, river management and planning and coordination functions.

The privatization legislation of 1989 transformed the RWAs into the privately owned water and sewerage companies (WaSCs), with the important exception that regulation of abstraction and the setting of quality standards were retained in the public sector (under the auspices of the Drinking Water Inspectorate and the National Rivers Authority, later absorbed into the Environment Agency). Thus the functions that had motivated the highly concentrated industry structure were not transferred to the privatized WaSCs, whose responsibilities were now solely operational. OFWAT was established at privatization as the economic regulator.

The privatization legislation also limited consolidation of the bigger companies (the ten WaSCs).[2] This reflects regulatory resistance to a reduction in the number of comparators, despite claims that significant cost savings could still be achieved through mergers (see for example Indepen and Accenture 2002).[3] The Competition Commission's report into the proposed take-over of Southern Water by Vivendi Water (now Veolia) in 2002 motivated OFWAT's commissioning of an investigation into scale economies in the England and Wales water industry.[4] The subsequent work – reported in Stone and Webster Consultants (2004a) – was extended to consider economies of scope and employed econometric methodologies to estimate models of industry costs over the period 1992–93 to 2002–03.

The main findings of the recent OFWAT study were as follows. First, there is clear evidence of scale economies for the smaller companies (interpreted here as companies serving populations below 400,000) with the average size water- only company characterized by constant returns to scale. Based on this study, the cost-minimizing scale for water supply undertakings is estimated to be around a population served of 650,000.[5] In contrast, the larger water and sewerage undertakings tend to be characterized by diseconomies of scale, which concurs with earlier evidence presented in Saal and Parker (2000). Similar findings have also been repeated in further work reported in Stone and Webster Consultants (2004b) using a similar methodology and Saal et al. (2004).[6]

On economies of scope the study provides mixed evidence about the horizontal integration of water and sewerage services. There is evidence of positive economies of scope from the integration of water and sewerage *production* activities, where there is the ability to share inputs across such similar activities, for example through the purchase of power for water and sewage treatment works. There may also be economies of scope through shared network management and common billing. However, the study provides no evidence that combining vertically integrated water and sewerage businesses yields economies overall. The diseconomies of scope seem to arise across the activities where the sharing of inputs is more limited, for example water production and sewerage connections, and sewage treatment and disposal and water connections.

The study also provides some support for the vertical integration of water supply. The cost savings are most evident for the smaller WoCs, with the management of network losses through leakage control appearing to have an important influence on these overall savings.

International evidence

International studies on water industry structure have tended to find similar results to the recent OFWAT studies on economies of scale.

Studies from the United States find evidence of 'u-shaped' cost functions for water supply. Kim (1985), Kim and Lee (1998) and Hayes (1987) present a range of evidence for different jurisdictions and time periods. A consistent finding is that economies of scale characterize the smaller firms that comprise the main part of the industry. Diseconomies of scale appear to characterize the largest firms. Average size firms tend to exhibit constant returns (though the average firms in these samples are significantly smaller than enterprises in the water industry in England and Wales), while most of these US studies find evidence of economies of scale for smaller-sized suppliers.

These findings are reiterated in the case of Italy by Fabbri and Fraquelli (2000), Garcia and Thomas (2001) for the Bordeaux region of France and Kim and Lee (1998) for Korea. Tynan and Kingdom (2005) review a range of international evidence and report that utilities, particularly those serving a population of 125,000 or less, could reduce operating costs per customer by increasing the scale of operation. Finally, Mizutani and Urakami (2001) present evidence for Japan, where the characteristics of the sample (in terms of the size distribution) are probably most similar to water supply in England and Wales. They also find evidence of diseconomies of scale and calculate the minimum efficient scale to be a population served of about 760,000. As highlighted above, this is comparable to the cost-minimizing scale for water-only undertakings in England and Wales, as calculated in the recent analysis for OFWAT.

Summary

The empirical evidence on water industry cost structures confirms that it is overly simplistic to regard water (and probably sanitation) as standard natural monopolies. Rather, the available evidence points to important trade-offs in the organization of water services. The most important trade-off – confirmed by engineering analyses at works level – is between the production (abstraction, treatment) and network functions. Economies of scale are most likely to lie in production activities (lower unit costs from larger sources and treatment works, for example), while diseconomies are fundamentally a function of distance and network size (Kim and Clarke, 1988; Garcia and Thomas, 2001).

Two important policy issues flow from this evidence. The first is whether an efficient operational configuration for water services needs to be matched by a similar pattern of independently owned and managed water service providers. In this respect the evidence is less clear-cut and the French concession system provides an example where operations are organized around municipal areas, while ownership and management are much more highly concentrated.[7]

The second relates to developing 'in market' competition. The available evidence reinforces the conclusion that the benefits of competition between competing producers (as opposed to competing retailers) are likely to be limited. An important consideration will be whether these benefits are able to offset the costs of forgoing the advantages of vertical integration of production and delivery.

Developing competition in water service markets

The scope for promoting competition in water services may be rather less than in other utility sectors, such as electricity and gas, where in many jurisdictions market reforms have now taken place. In part, this reflects the conditions necessary for sustaining competition in this particular network industry.

With water distribution and sewerage systems, barriers to entry due to the high level of sunk costs are generally considered to be substantial because of the frequent existence of spare capacity and the impracticality of multiple connections to individual premises.[8]

In utilities such as electricity and gas, competition has been facilitated through the separation of transmission and distribution systems from other components of the industry (either in terms of management, legal entity or ownership) and the introduction of competition in the upstream activities. This analogy begins, however, to break down when consideration is given to the ability to ring-fence the distribution network from upstream production processes. The clear-cut separation between resources (production) and distribution, which is the key to introducing competition in gas and electricity, does not exist to the same degree in the water sector. Small-scale localized supplies, as compared to supply by a large impounding reservoir and long-distance pipes, may make ring-fencing bulk supply from distribution difficult (and goes some way towards explaining the empirical findings on the benefits of vertical integration noted earlier).

While the scope for competition in the market may be limited, there is scope for facilitating competition in some areas, such as supplies to large industrial customers. Suppliers can be encouraged to consider outsourcing work where there are competitive markets for inputs. Where there is competition *for* the market, it is important to ensure that the industry is structured in such a way as to promote a high degree of competition for concessions of various kinds.

Is competition in bulk water supply possible?

Competition between multiple suppliers of bulk water on a large scale is constrained by a number of factors (see Ballance and Taylor, 2002). Bulk water supply is, like water distribution, highly capital intensive with many fixed assets having relatively long lives and few, if any, alternative uses. These large sunk costs create substantial barriers to entry for new suppliers. It is easier to provide for competition between smaller, localized sources.

Furthermore, high transportation costs for water relative to the cost of production, when compared to gas and electricity, mean that there are substantial locational monopolies for large-scale suppliers of bulk water. Even if a new entrant is able to construct a new reservoir and operate it more cheaply than an incumbent's existing facilities, it must be located sufficiently close to the final distribution point to ensure that these production cost advantages are not overwhelmed by additional transport costs.[9] Long-distance transport and distribution costs in the water sector are likely to account for the large proportion of total (average) costs, while, in comparison, in the electricity and gas sectors these costs are more likely to be a relatively small proportion of total (average) costs.

A third factor that is likely to constrain competition in bulk water supply is the rising cost nature of large increments to water resources. The least expensive water resources are developed first and as capacity is increased more expensive resources are commissioned.

Arrangements for introducing competition in bulk water supply must allow for a supplier of last resort, which is potentially far more complex for water than for other utilities. A significant element of the cost of supplying bulk water arises from the provision of water resources for exceptional droughts, which may occur once every 10-20 years, even in countries in Northern Europe, and maybe more frequently with climate change. If a new entrant is not required to provide standby supply for exceptional drought situations, this may place a substantial cost burden on an incumbent operator that is obliged to be the supplier of last resort.

There may be other problems restricting the scope for competition. First, the threat to water quality must be safeguarded if competition is to develop in the water sector. The entry of poorly treated water into a common main could cause contamination. Alternatively, there may be deterioration in perceived water quality even when water of the appropriate quality is input into a common main. Examples of this might be changes in water quality for industrial customers or changes in taste or water hardness for domestic customers. Finally, the unwinding of historic cross-subsidies in charging may cause consumer resistance to change.

Competition in retailing

It should, however, be possible to introduce competition in water services retailing, that is, the customer billing and payment function. Competition in this area is certainly the norm in a number of other utility industries, such as electricity and gas, in many countries where energy sector reforms have been adopted.

In terms of the practical separation of retailing from other functions in the water sector, there are examples of this type of separation taking place in locations as diverse as Serbia and Indonesia, although not linked to competition in retailing services. Often it has been linked to the establishment of municipal billing companies, which act as monopoly providers of billing services to a range of municipal service providers.

The scope for the development of competition in retailing will depend critically on the allocation of costs between those for providing wholesale water and the costs of providing retail services.

Summary

It is difficult to argue that the supply of water services in their entirety is a natural monopoly. There are clearly areas, such as retailing and supply to larger customers, where competition is possible, though the scale of the gains is not yet fully established. There is an argument for pursuing water sector reform to increase the scope for competitive forces both *in* the market and/or the market.

There are doubts, however, about how far a model of competition in the market for water would be the widespread success that it has been for other utility sectors. Yet there are interesting developments in a number of jurisdictions. These include, perhaps most notably, the United Kingdom. The 1989 Water Act made provision for 'inset' appointments where a new supplier could be licensed within the area of an existing undertaker. This has been taken up in relation to large customers and has resulted in significant reductions in the charges they pay for bulk water. The recent Water Act of 2003 allows for common carriage to customers using in excess of 50 Ml/d per day, and the Water Services (Scotland) Act 2005 provides for competition in retailing for all business customers from 2008.

In Southern California, water 'wheeling' through bulk networks has been the subject of policy and legal debate since severe droughts in the late 1980s.[10] The scope for competition and water market liberalization in the European Union has also been the subject of recent investigation and policy debate (see for example WRc and Ecologic, 2002). The publication by the Commission of the European Communities (2003) is widely seen as an attempt within the EU to encourage greater harmonization (and hence reduce legal uncertainty and market distortions) within European water sectors, and to promote greater competition through the unbundling of vertically integrated water utilities. At the global level, the European Commission has advocated the incorporation of water services into the GATS regime for international trade in services, though liberalization is expected to take the form of competition *for* the market rather than *in* the market (see Stone and Webster Consultants, 2002, for an assessment). In Australia national competition policy arrangements provide for competitive entry.

As a result of the limited scope for competition *in* water and sanitation markets there is usually a need for a comprehensive framework for the regulation of the conduct of the sector, to which we now turn.

REGULATION OF CONDUCT

The regulation of the conduct of a sector associated with considerable natural monopoly requires either regulation or competition *for* the market in the form of franchising – though franchises may not remove the need for regulation. Conduct regulation constrains a natural monopoly by rules covering areas such as quality, pricing and access. This requires an effective regulatory system.

The nature of the regulatory system, however, will very much depend on the type of private sector participation (PSP) in operation. We begin by discussing the case of England and Wales where the type of PSP resembles more closely that found in other sectors and hence the regulatory arrangements are more similar.

The regulation of water in the market economy – the case of England and Wales

In England and Wales where the ten publicly owned water authorities were privatized in 1989 and the independent water regulator OFWAT was established, the regulation of the conduct of the water companies is a major aspect of the industry's organizational framework.[11]

Responsibility for setting water quality and environmental standards has been distinguished from responsibility for setting price limits that allow companies to achieve these standards. In this way, ministers and their quality regulators are responsible for collective objectives, while the economic regulator is responsible for the individual objectives of customers.

Conduct is regulated by the economic regulator, OFWAT, and two quality regulators, the Drinking Water Inspectorate (DWI) and the Environment Agency (EA). Standards for water and wastewater quality are set by Ministers, following both national policies and European Union (EU) Directives. There are also regional and national customer service committees (WaterVoice). Some changes are planned for 2006, when OFWAT becomes the Water Services Regulation Authority (WSRA) governed by an executive board rather than an individual Director General, and a Water Consumer Council for Water (CCWater) takes over from Water Voice, but these changes are unlikely to have a significant effect on economic regulation.

The prime purpose of OFWAT is to ensure that companies properly carry out and can finance their functions, while protecting customers, promoting efficiency and facilitating competition.[12] Prices, but not profits, are controlled by a price-cap formula. The RPI − X regime applied to the other UK utilities has been modified into RPI +/− K, where K is a combination of the cost of higher water and environmental quality (Q) and the cost (allowing for increases in efficiency) of providing existing quality and better services to customers (X). K may be positive or negative, depending on the balance between the cost of higher water and environmental quality, and the ability of the companies to deliver water and dispose of wastewater more effectively and more efficiently.

Price limits are set for a period of five years, subject to annual adjustment in specific circumstances, such as a new legal objective. They cannot be altered in response to changes in circumstances within the control of the companies. With the exception of the

Welsh company, Gias Cymru,[13] which now is a private-not-for-dividend company, they are all owned by private, often institutional, shareholders in the UK and abroad.

Although the price control regime was designed to regulate the outputs of the companies and the prices they can charge, there has, over the years, been a growing emphasis on the detailed measurement of costs, especially where new water quality and environmental obligations are concerned. This focus on input measurement with detailed costing imposes regulatory burdens, and can damage incentives to efficient behaviour. In a survey of water companies commissioned by OFWAT, SWC Consulting (2003) highlights these concerns in the context of capital investment.

Under this regime, there has been a substantial increase in investment to meet higher water and environmental quality and to improve service to customers. Very substantial improvements have been made to water services. Efficiency rose sharply following privatization as clear accountability was established for the governmental and regulatory bodies and effective use was made of comparative competition (though see Saal and Parker, 2000). As incremental quality improvements are becoming progressively more expensive, however, prices are now set to rise significantly (confirmed by an average 23 per cent real increase in prices determined by OFWAT for the 2005–10 period).

Linking the responsibilities of the different regulators has involved a structured dialogue. OFWAT devised a process involving the publication of open letters between Ministers, and an open and transparent dialogue with customers and other interested parties. This dialogue depends in turn on the collection, analysis and presentation of high quality information, most of which did not exist under nationalization.

Comparative competition has played a major role in achieving better performance for customers and greater efficiency. The importance of comparative competition in water was recognized in the privatization legislation that provided for a compulsory reference to the Monopolies and Mergers (now the Competition)

Commission for all mergers of larger water companies: in judging a case, the Commission had to take account of its effect on the ability of OFWAT to make effective efficiency comparisons. A number of mergers of smaller companies have taken place, and in the case of some bigger ones, remedies had been agreed in the form of price reductions for customers. Some proposed mergers have been blocked.

Comparative competition has also involved good measurement, good analysis and good process. Guidelines for Regulatory Accounts are published and enforced to ensure that the operations of the water utility are properly separated from any other activities. Key performance indicators have been specified, covering water quality, compliance with discharge standards and customer service. Comparable information, verified by independent reporters appointed by OFWAT, is collected from each company. The results are published, and the supporting information made publicly available. The measures have been used in price reviews to ensure that the regulated tariffs are set at levels which ensure that an efficient company could finance its operations, while putting pressure on less efficient ones to reduce their costs without, of course, reducing service to customers or companies failing their environmental obligations.

In setting price limits, comparative analysis has been used separately for (1) operating costs, (2) the costs of maintaining serviceability of the system to customers, (3) the costs of enhancing quality; and (4) relative customer performance. Operating costs have been analysed econometrically. For enhancement costs a unit cost base has been used, where specified projects are costed by different companies revealing their relative efficiency. Both methods have been used for capital maintenance. Good performance in customer service is rewarded in higher price limits and vice versa.

Privatization has provided powerful incentives for efficient capital markets, in equity and, increasingly, in bond markets. As a result of innovations, the cost of borrowing has fallen and companies have responded to the incentive to reduce the cost of capital by exploring optimal gearing, which has turned out to be much higher than expected. When, however, companies have large capital programmes and are highly geared the need to maintain investment status for the bonds can add to the effective cost of capital. Privatization and regulation have driven substantial changes in how households and businesses pay for water services. Traditionally households and small businesses paid in relation to a property tax (rateable values) base. After privatization most, and now all new, households pay by meter. Existing customers have the right to opt for a meter and are doing so progressively. By the end of the decade, about one third of households will pay a volumetric charge. Metering has been extended to all businesses except where meter installation is difficult or expensive.

Extension of volumetric charging has been associated with significant reforms of tariffs. Cross-subsidies have been reduced. OFWAT has ensured a proper balance between the bills paid by households for measured and unmeasured consumption, resulting in significant savings by those paying volumetrically. Greater choice has resulted in wiser use of water as well as saving money. OFWAT has also acted to ensure that standing charges – for both household and business users – are kept down so that all users can exercise a proper economic choice.

Wastewater tariffs cover the costs of surface and highway drainage as well as the costs of collecting, treating and disposing of foul sewage. Customers who do not connect to the public network for surface drainage do not pay this element of charges. In principle, surface water charges should be related to the area drained, but this has been difficult fully to implement in practice. It has not proved practicable to charge highway users with the costs of draining roads.

Apart from England and Wales, private ownership of assets only occurs in very few places (e.g. Chile and parts of the USA) and as such the type of regulatory arrangements found here are not widely replicated. France has a highly developed system of franchising for water services, which is the most common form of PSP to be found around the world, and we will now discuss this.

Competition for the market and regulation – the case of PSP in France and lessons for elsewhere

The form of PSP most commonly found occurs through some form of contract with assets remaining in public (e.g. municipal) ownership and has its origins in France,[14] at that time driven by the need for financially starved municipalities to finance ambitious urbanization plans.

The large French companies (Veolia – previously Vivendi – and Suez) have been the world market leaders in the market for PSP in water. There are a variety of contract forms in France that are commonly used elsewhere in the world, the main ones being as follows.

Management contracts

There are two major forms of management contract in France. These are the *gérance* and *régie intéressée*. For both types, the contract's duration is typically around five years.

A *gérance* contract is a comprehensive operations and maintenance contract, where the private contractor provides all of the staff and expertise required to run a system, for a fixed fee. Under a *régie intéressée*, part or all of a contractor's payment is based on measurable results, which may relate to productivity or profits. The operator has responsibility only for operating the network, and no role in planning or undertaking capital investments or renewals.

Affermage contracts

The *affermage* contract (more commonly known as a lease) is the most common form of water sector delegation contract in France. The municipality or syndicate remains the owner of the assets and is responsible for financing capital expenditure and making investment decisions. The private operator is responsible for the operation of the system as well as asset maintenance, renewals and rehabilitation. The private operator is also likely to provide advice to the municipality on the need for new investment. The municipality may separately contract the private operator to implement capital investment decisions.

The private operator is remunerated directly by the consumer with a proportion paid to the municipality to cover its investment costs. The life of the *affemage* is usually of 10-15 years duration.

Concessions

Under a concession arrangement, the private operator is also responsible for financing new investment in the network and treatment facilities over the life of the contract, as well as operations and maintenance. The assets are, however, owned by the municipality. At the end of the contract, control over the utility's assets reverts to the municipality.

The concessionaire is remunerated directly by consumers and pays a portion of the amount collected back to the municipality to cover its expenses or any services provided by it. In practice, some investment may be undertaken directly by the municipality in order to benefit from government subsidies or cheaper finance. The life of a concession contract in France is now limited, by law, to a maximum of 20 years. Concession contracts signed before this limitation was introduced may run for longer periods, for example, as long as 30 or 50 years.

Contract-based approaches can be attractive to private operators because they reduce the risk associated with investment and the regulatory rules are embedded in an agreement between the two parties, which should make it more difficult for the public authority to change these rules in its own favour. There are, however, two issues of particular concern in relation to the contracting out of water services in relation to effective regulation and oversight, which we now discuss, using the French case as the reference point to make more general observations later.

Contract incompleteness and contract monitoring

A major problem associated with franchising is the presence of contract incompleteness. In the face of uncertainty about the future, a long-term contract of any description is likely to be incomplete. In network industries like utilities, where there are inevitable uncertainties about such critical elements as future investment needs and maintenance levels, the problem is significant.

In France, the regulatory regime is well adapted to dealing with this problem. Water sector PSP contracts (and other contracts with the private sector for the delivery of public services) are not treated in the same way as ordinary commercial contracts, but are governed by French public service law. Two core principles of French public service law are 'continuity of service' and 'continuing adaptation to circumstances' (see Shugart, 1998). If a company is in financial difficulty, for reasons which could not have been predicted, an extra payment can be claimed from the contracting municipality and this claim will be supported by the legal system. Unforeseen circumstances include legislation or policy decisions that impose additional costs on a private operator. Modifications can be made in the contractual terms as long as the private operator is appropriately remunerated. This provides the public authority with significant freedom in its decision-making authority, and significant protection for a private operator from bearing the financial burden of these decisions.

In France, however, the monitoring of the performance of private operators has been a weakness of its regulatory arrangements. Since 1995, private operators have been required under national legislation to produce annual performance reports to the contracting municipality regarding their performance. Dissatisfaction with both the level of compliance with this requirement and the quality of these reports has, however, recently led to a proposal to establish a national agency that would collect, publish and disseminate information on the comparative performance of water utilities in France, including both publicly and privately operated utilities.

Handling contract incompleteness and contract monitoring in other countries

The 'French regulatory model' is not easily transferable to other countries. Promises by public authorities of compensation in the event of loosely defined 'unforeseen circumstances' may lack credibility in some countries due to political reluctance to increase tariffs. Furthermore, legal systems in other countries may lack the impartiality and expertise necessary to adjudicate where disputes arise regarding this kind of commitment. Alternative mechanisms are often therefore required.

It may be difficult to deal with this problem of contractual incompleteness by simply trying to specify as much as possible in the contract (see Frontier Economics, 2003). Complete specification is simply not possible; some issue will eventually arise, most likely concerning tariffs, which will require either negotiation between the parties or some form of external decision-making. Formalized international arbitration, through bodies such as the International Chamber of Commerce, while impartial, is likely to suffer from a lack of expertise and it is also expensive.

An important role and rationale therefore emerges for a water sector supervisory agency of some kind (see Ballance and Taylor, 2003). It can support the ongoing effectiveness of a water sector PSP contract through adjudicating on those issues that cannot be fully addressed or specified in the contract, particularly tariffs, which simply cannot be pre-set for a 15 or 20 year period. It can have both the necessary expertise and the independence from government to make the requisite decisions and avoid this function being done through a process of obscure negotiation. Guasch (2004) points out that where there is weak public governance there has been a high incidence of contract renegotiation for water (and other utility) PSP contracts. A regulatory agency in such circumstances, however, would have a limited set of functions compared to say OFWAT in England and Wales, because of the very different nature of the arrangements.

A body can be established by legislation, which may have certain powers in relation to the formulation of regulatory rules and the approval of concession contracts, while other public authorities can have primary responsibility for negotiating and agreeing those contracts with private operators for the provision of water and sanitation services.

Under this approach, responsibility for monitoring the concession contract may be undertaken by the public authority, the regulatory body or both. The regulatory body may have some role in terms of acting as an appeals body when disputes between the public authority and the private operator arise.

This approach has been used where national (or regional) governments wish to exercise influence over municipal provision of water and sanitation services and related PSP contracts. Variations on this approach have been adopted in Portugal and are in the process of being adopted in Bulgaria and Indonesia.

There is, however, potential for conflict between the supervisory body and the public authority entering the PSP contract (e.g. a municipality) as well as a greater likelihood of conflicting or inconsistent rules being formulated. Foster (2002) points out that where this has been tried in Latin America (an 'Anglo-French hybrid') tensions have been created that can undermine the functioning of the model.

An interesting development in the context of regulation in the UK has been the establishment of the PPP Arbiter, whose main role is to advise on the fair price for the services provided by the three private sector infrastructure companies (Infracos). These companies will maintain, renew and upgrade London Underground's infrastructure under 30-year service contracts, under the new Tube Public Private Partnership (PPP). Previously the London Underground was publicly owned and operated. The levels of prices can be re-set at periodic reviews of the PPP contracts every 7½ years, when the Mayor of London and London Underground are able to re-specify what they require from the private sector, allowing flexibility in the changing needs of passengers. Extraordinary reviews can also be called in certain circumstances when the Arbiter will advise on possible adjustments to the payments made by London Underground to the Infracos. The Arbiter is also able to provide direction and guidance on any PPP contractual issues that London Underground and the infrastructure companies choose to refer to him.

Similar arrangements could be put in place for water PSP contracts, where the functions of the regulator are limited in scope, even if the functions that are exercised remain some of the more important ones (i.e. the resetting of prices).

For a supervisory agency to be effective, the contract must adequately acknowledge the agency's future role and specify the procedural mechanisms or triggers whereby it will be required to make decisions (e.g. resetting or re-basing tariffs). Otherwise, the actual responsibility of the supervisory authority for a particular issue is likely to be a further source of dispute.

An alternative means of resolving tariff disputes is the use of expert panels (see Shugart and Ballance, 2005) or external consultants to undertake periodic price reviews. This may be advantageous in situations where it is difficult to ensure that a regulatory agency is able to take crucial decisions in an independent way. An external source of expertise may save costs and achieve a sense of legitimacy that a regulatory agency cannot and also obtain the necessary expertise. A number of issues, however, need careful consideration, not least whether such decisions are advisory or binding in nature. If they are not binding, this can open up a further area for dispute.

Contract monitoring

Responsibility for the monitoring of a PSP contract can also be delegated to an agency, such as a specialist contract-monitoring unit established under the contract. This has been adopted in a number of PSP contracts internationally in recent years, including in Sofia, Bucharest, Manila and Jakarta. This agency can ensure that the private operator is meeting its obligations where additional mechanisms or institutions may be required. In particular, there may be a desire to make the monitoring process more impartial, particularly where its results have important implications for issues of contract compliance or performance-related payments.

Where performance-related incentives involving bonus payments to private operators are featured, so-called 'technical' auditors are often retained to provide impartial reports on the parameters impacting on these payments. Examples of management contracts where technical auditors have been retained include Amman (Jordan), Tripoli (Libya) and Dushanbe (Tajikistan).

REGULATION OF PUBLIC UTILITIES – THE CASE OF SCOTLAND

The supervision of publicly owned utilities by a regulator offers an alternative to concession contracts when governments want to retain public operation as well as public ownership of water services. In such circumstances, it is worth considering the use of an independent regulatory body, which can analyse and supervise, as an intermediary between Ministers and suppliers. Scotland offers an example of how these arrangements can be, and are being, developed. They have already led to a considerable increase in the efficiency of the operations of the water services in Scotland. Similar arrangements are being developed in Northern Ireland.

Scottish Water is a public corporation, formed in 2002 from the three Scottish Water Authorities, owned by the Scottish Executive, the devolved government of Scotland. Under the Water Services (Scotland) Act 2005, Scottish Water is regulated by a Water Commission that is independent of ministers. (The Commission has taken over the work of the Water Commissioner, who had previously advised the Scottish Executive.) In November 2005, the Commission set price limits for Scottish Water, subject to appeal as is the case in England and Wales to the UK Competition Commission.

The Commission (and previously the Commissioner) is using all the comparative information collected by OFWAT to set price limits for Scotland that cover 'lowest reasonable overall costs'. Similar procedures have been devised to ensure that quality obligations are properly costed before being imposed by the Scottish Executive on Scottish Water. There is a transparent process, exposing the methodology used and involving consultation with all stakeholders before decisions are made. The performance of Scottish Water against these obligations and against standards of service for customers will be monitored by the Commission, jointly with the Scottish Drinking Water Quality Regulator and the Scottish Environmental Protection Agency (Water Industry Commissioner for Scotland, 2004 and 2005).

There are two major differences compared with the situation in England and Wales. First, because Scottish Water is financed from the Exchequer, its cost of capital is related to the cost of public borrowing and such borrowing is constrained by the UK public expenditure limits agreed for Scotland.

Second, the incentives facing management are rather different from those in England and Wales, because there are no capital market pressures for improvements in efficiency. To achieve the necessary hard budget constraints and comparable incentives for management, ministers, as owners, have said that they are ready to deny additional finance to Scottish Water where, owing to factors within management control, objectives have not been met and where greater efficiency has not been achieved. Customers cannot be expected to pay twice for the same outputs. The Scottish Executive may need to ensure that the pay – and bonuses – earned by managers are related to the achievement of customer and environmental standards and of greater efficiency in delivering them.

Notwithstanding the different incentives facing managers, the private sector has been used to good effect in Scotland. Scottish Water contracts out significant elements of its capital expenditure programme. Some of this was done (in the past) under UK Public Private Partnership (PPP) arrangements for a number of build-operate-transfer (BOT) type schemes for waste water treatment. There are nine PPP contracts presently in place.

194

In addition, Scottish Water Solutions was established in April 2002 for the purpose of delivering a large proportion (around 70 per cent) of Scottish Water's £1.8 billion capital investment programme. It was established as a joint venture limited company within a publicly owned organization, 51 per cent owned by Scottish Water and 49 per cent split equally between two private consortia, the rationale being that a joint venture would eliminate incentives to companies to act in their own self-interests. Scottish Water Solutions is managing a number of major projects throughout Scotland. This illustrates that other types of competitive pressures can be used to help deliver a good deal for customers.

The Water Commission is engaged in working with the Scottish Executive to achieve the objectives outlined above, including the creation of a financial cushion that would be available to deal with adverse shocks outside management control without involving additional public expenditure. It will also advise the Scottish Executive on the incentives needed to ensure that minimum standards for customer and environmental services are met.

CONCLUSIONS

In this chapter we have examined two particular themes in the effective regulatory oversight of water, which involves making appropriate decisions on industry structure, competition and regulation.

First, we examined the regulation of *structure*; that is, the appropriate organization of the sector including the scope for the competitive provision of services *in* the market. Second, we examined the regulation of *conduct*; that is, where there is considerable natural monopoly power, what form should regulation take or alternatively what is the scope for competition *for* the market and in such circumstances is there a need for further regulatory mechanisms? Implicit in our analysis is that where it is feasible competition provides a spur to good service and efficient provision and there are therefore strong arguments for developing structures that facilitate it.

In terms of structure, the available evidence indicates that there are economies of scale in the operation of water services, but also that there may be diseconomies of scale beyond some point. The international evidence provides support for a 'u-shaped' cost function.

The empirical evidence on water industry cost structures also confirms that it is overly simplistic to regard water (and sanitation) as standard natural monopolies. There are important trade-offs in the organization of water services – that is, between the production (abstraction, treatment) and network functions. Economies of scale are most likely to lie in production activities (lower unit costs from larger sources and treatment works, for example), while diseconomies of scale are fundamentally a function of distance and network size.

Considerations other than economic ones might at times also influence industry structure. In the case of England and Wales, the reorganization of the sector in 1973 into ten regional water authorities was largely driven by a desire to see integrated river-basin management, whereby a single entity where possible should plan and control the uses of water in each river catchment. Similar pressures may be seen in Europe in the future with the implementation of the Water Framework Directive, which will focus attention on issues of catchment management.

It is difficult to argue that water services in their entirety are natural monopolies. There are clearly areas, such as retailing and supply to larger customers, where competition is possible, though the scale of the gains is not yet fully established. Water sector reform could increase the scope for competitive forces both *in* the market and *for* the market. While there may be doubts whether competition in the market for water would be the widespread success that it has been for other utility sectors, there are interesting developments in a number of jurisdictions.

Turning to the examination of the regulation of conduct for the water sector, we focused our attention on the cases of England and Wales where there is an independent regulatory body (OFWAT) regulating privatized water utilities, of France where private sector participation (PSP) takes the form of contract and regulation is done primarily through contract (so-called 'regulation by contract'), and of Scotland where there is an independent body regulating a single publicly owned water utility.

Different approaches may be suitable for different circumstances. The regulatory models in England and Wales and France appear to have served their sectors well, despite being very different in many ways (see Ballance and Taylor, 2005; and Ballance, 2003). Regulatory models need to be tailored to the social and cultural circumstances of a country. Wholesale application of any one model to other jurisdictions is unlikely to succeed.

For the most part, where there is PSP it is usually in the form of contracts. As such, the England and Wales model is likely to have limited application. However, there are, as we have set out, features of the application of the French model that also make its application to other countries limited. These are associated with the legal system, the ability to deal with issues of contract incompleteness and the level of expertise required. The oft-cited public debate about whether, therefore, one should choose the 'English' or the 'French' model for regulation is misleading (see Ballance and Taylor, 2003). Where effective PSP contracts are desired (particularly deeper forms of PSP, such as concession and *affermage* contracts) there will be a need for the establishment of an effective institutional framework, particularly with respect to periodic tariff setting and contract monitoring. Consideration will need to be given to having a regulatory body but with far more limited powers than a traditional independent regulatory agency (such as OFWAT), like the PPP Arbiter for the London Underground in the UK, or indeed the use of expert panels for periodic tariff reviews.

The Scotland case is interesting in that in many jurisdictions the water sector is likely to remain under public ownership with a limited role for PSP. In such cases the Scottish model offers an example of the establishment of an independent regulatory body to ensure that the supplier delivers quality and customers standards in an efficient and acceptable way.

NOTES

1. An additional pretext was the amalgamation of undertakings serving urban and rural areas, thereby providing greater opportunities for cross-subsidization.
2. The most significant changes are for Northumbrian Water, which merged in 1995 with the contiguous North East Water and the non-contiguous Essex and Suffolk Water in 2000.
3. OFWAT's resistance is well illustrated by the response to the Department of Trade and Industry's White Paper setting out proposals for inclusion in an Enterprise Bill:
    OFWAT considers that the existing special provisions for dealing with mergers between water companies as set out in sections 32 to 36 of the 1991 Water Industry Act (WIA) should be preserved in the new merger regime. The 'public interest' test in these provisions expressly refers to the Director's need to be able to make comparisons in order to carry out his duties under the WIA. Due to the monopoly nature of the industry there is a need to retain comparative competition until such time as there is effective market competition even if ultimately it means that certain mergers have to be blocked. The current powers have been effective. (OFWAT, 2001)
4. The planned take-over of Southern Water by Vivendi Water received qualified approval from the Competition Commission (see Competition Commission, 2002), but was blocked by the Secretary of State for Trade and Industry, largely on the grounds of the detriment to comparative competition. The case was also noteworthy for OFWAT's consideration of the proposed remedy of Southern Water divesting their water supply operations in Hampshire to create a new comparator. Hampshire is a non-contiguous area within Southern Water's water supply area. This would have been the first instance of a reversal in the post-war trend towards consolidation, but the Competition Commission panel decided that the remedy

of Vivendi divesting their stake in another water supply company (South Staffordshire Water) was preferable to the creation of a new company in Hampshire. One reason was that the divestiture of the Hampshire area would have exposed significant cross-subsidies within Southern's regionally averaged charges.

5. Strictly, this is the scale at which operating expenditure is minimized for the sample average undertaking.

6. These latter studies extend the previous analysis by examining the impact of scale on productivity growth in the post-privatization period. Saal et al. (2004), in particular, find that increasing scale has a negative impact on productivity growth.

7. There are also parallels with the debate in England and Wales about further consolidation in the sector on two fronts. First, the regulatory requirements for the maintenance of comparative data have meant that even with increased consolidation in ownership and management, subcompany comparisons of operational efficiency (based on operational area) provide an alternative that OFWAT itself has expressed a willingness to develop further, as part of its benchmarking exercise, when setting regulatory price caps. Second, the threat of take-over remains an important market discipline on management in England and Wales and for this reason there are benefits to regulation from retaining a certain fluidity in the structure of ownership (in effect a form of 'for market' competition).

8. Competition in telecommunications has ultimately also been constrained by the impracticality of multiple connections to a single residence. While multiple networks have been possible for trunk networks, the connection into individual premises (the so-called 'last mile') has remained a stubborn monopoly, though unbundling of local loops is now occurring.

9. OFWAT has calculated that in gas and electricity the indicative additional costs of transportation can be approximately 2.5-5 per cent per 100 km, while in water they are approximately 50 per cent.

10. For example, the Californian State Water Code was enacted in 1986. The so-called Wheeling Statutes are formally codified in Part 2, Chapter 11, Article 4 Joint Use of Capacity in Water Conveyance Facilities (sections 1810-14). Section 1810 stipulates the mandatory requirement to allow access in return for fair compensation. In November 1998 San Diego County Water Authority (a retailer)

started a legal challenge to the wheeling rates established by Metropolitan Water District (the network owner) to comply with statutory requirements. The case, after appeal, concluded in 2000 in favour of the network operator.

11. This section draws upon Byatt (2004).

12. The Water Act 2003 changes the primary duties to protecting the interests of the consumer through promoting effective competition where appropriate.

13. Glas Cymru is a limited company by guarantee with no equity shareholders that now wholly owns and controls Welsh Water (Dwr Cymru), one of the ten water and sewerage undertakers. It was formed in 2001 to buy out Welsh Water from Western Power Distribution. The purchase was financed through bond issues. The majority of the operations conducted by Welsh Water have been contracted out. United Utilities and Kelda have been contracted to provide the bulk of the day-to-day water and sewage treatment operations and most site operations staff have transferred to the new contractors. Thames Water provides customer services.

14. In France private sector participation has been present since 1853 with the founding of Compagnie Générale des Eaux, which gained a water distribution concession in Lyon. Générale des Eaux gained further contracts in Nantes (1854), Paris (1860) and Nice (1864). Following the establishment of Générale des Eaux, Eaux de Banlieue was established in 1867 and Lyonnaise des Eaux in 1880.

REFERENCES

Ballance, A. (2003) *The Privatisation of the Water Industry in England & Wales – Success or Failure and Future Direction*, London: Stone and Webster Consultants.

Ballance, A. and Taylor, A. (2002) 'Competition in the Water Market: A Review of the Issues', *Water*, **21**.

Ballance, A. and Taylor, A. (2003) 'Regulation of Private Sector Participation in Water: The Myth of Clear Cut Choices', *Water*, **21**.

Ballance, A. and Taylor, A. (2005) *Competition and Economic Regulation in Water: The Future of the European Water Industry*, London: International Water Association.

Baumol, W. (1977) 'On the Proper Tests for Natural Monopoly in a Multiproduct Industry', *The American Economic Review*, **67**, 809-22.

Byatt, I. (2004) 'Managing Water for the Future: The Case of England and Wales', in J. Trottier and P. Slack (eds), *Managing Water Resources, Past and Present: The Linacre Lectures 2002*, Oxford: Oxford University Press.

Central Advisory Water Committee (1971) *The Future Management of Water in England and Wales: A Report by the Central Advisory Water Committee*, London: Central Advisory Water Committee.

Commission of the European Communities (2003) *Green Paper on Services of General Interest*, COM (2003) 270 Final, Brussels: European Commission.

Competition Commission (2002) *Vivendi Water UK PLC and First Aqua (JVCo) Limited: A Report on the Proposed Merger*, London: Competition Commission.

Fabbri, P. and Fraquelli, G. (2000) 'Cost and Structure of Technology in Italian Water Industry', *Empirica*, **27**, 65-82.

Foster, V. (2002) 'Ten Years of Water Service Reform in Latin America: Towards an Anglo-French Model', in P. Seidenstat, D. Haarmeyer and S. Hakim (eds), *Reinventing Water and Wastewater Systems – Global Lessons for Improving Water Management*, New Jersey: John Wiley & Son Inc.

Frontier Economics (2003) 'Water Under the Bridge', *Frontier Economics Bulletin*, April 2003.

Garcia, S. and Thomas, A. (2001) 'The Structure of Municipal Water Supply Costs: Application to a Panel of French Local Communities', *Journal of Productivity Analysis*, **16**, 5-29.

Guasch, J.L. (2004) 'Granting and Renegotiating Infrastructure Concessions: Doing It Right, Vol. 1 of 1', *WBI Development Studies (Report No. 28816)*, Washington, DC: World Bank.

Hayes, K. (1987) 'Cost Structure of the Water Industry', *Applied Economics*, **19**, 417-25.

Indepen and Accenture (2002) *Water Merger Policy: Time for Review*, London: Indepen and Accenture.

Kim, E. and Lee, H. (1998) 'Spatial Integration of Urban Water Services and Economies of Scale', *Review of Urban and Regional Development Studies*, **10**, 3-18.

Kim, H.Y. (1985) 'Economies of Scale in Multiproduct Firms: An Empirical Analysis', *Economica*, **54**, 185-206.

Kim, H.Y. and Clarke, R. (1988) 'Economies of Scale and Scope in Water Supply', *Regional Science and Urban Economics*, **18**, 479-502.

Mizutani, F. and Urakami, T. (2001) 'Identifying Network Density and Scale Economies for Japanese Water Supply Organisations', *Papers in Regional Science*, **80**, 211-30.

OFWAT (2001) 'Productivity and Enterprise – a World Class Competition Regime', *Response to the DTI White Paper*, October 2001, Birmingham: Office of Water Services.

Panzar, J.C. and Willig, R.D. (1977) 'Economies of Scale in Multi-output Production', *Quarterly Journal of Economics*, **91**, 481-93.

Richardson, H.J. (2003) 'The Water Industry in England and Wales: Constantly Changing Development over the Past Half Century', *Water Intelligence Online*, 1-11.

Robinson, C. (1998) 'A "crisis" in Water: The Wrong Sort of Privatisation', in J. Morris (ed.), *The Crisis in Water*, London, Institute of Economic Affairs.

Saal, D. and Parker, D. (2000) 'The Impact of Privatisation and Regulation on the Water Industry in England and Wales: A Translog Cost Function Approach', *Managerial and Decision Economics*, **21**, 253-68.

Saal, D., Parker, D. and Weyman-Jones, T. (2004) 'Determining the Contribution of Technical, Efficiency, and Scale Change to Productivity Growth in the Privatised English and Welsh Water and Sewerage Industry: 1985-2000', *Aston Business School Working Paper RP0433*, Birmingham: Aston University.

Shugart, C. (1998) 'Regulation by Contract and Municipal Services: The Problem of Contractual Incompleteness', PhD, Harvard University (Graduate School of Arts and Sciences).

Shugart, C. and Ballance, A. (2005) *Expert Panels: The Future for Public Utility Regulation?*, Washington, DC: World Bank 2005 (http://rru. worldbank.org/Discussions/ topics/topic66. aspx).

Stone and Webster Consultants (2002) 'GATS and the Liberalisation of Water Supply Services', in *Final Report to Gesellschaft fuer Technische Zusammenarbeit (GTZ)*, August 2002, Bonn: GTZ.

Stone and Webster Consultants (2004a) 'Investigation into Evidence for Economies of Scale in the Water and Sewerage Industry in England

and Wales', in *Final Report to Office of Water Services*, January 2004, Birmingham: OFWAT.

Stone and Webster Consultants (2004b) 'An Investigation into OPEX Productivity Trends and Causes in the Water Industry in England & Wales – 1992–93 to 2002–03', in *Final Report to Office of Water Services*, May 2004, Birmingham: OFWAT.

SWC Consulting (2003) 'Ofwat Study into the Effects of Regulatory Policy on Company Investment Decision-making', in *Final Report to OFWAT*, March 2003, Birmingham, OFWAT.

Tynan, N. and Kingdom, W. (2005) 'Optimal Size for Utilities? Returns to Scale in Water: Evidence from Benchmarking', *Public Policy for the Private Sector*, January, Note Number 283.

Water Industry Commissioner for Scotland (2004) *Our Work in Regulating the Scottish Water Industry – Volume 3: The Calculation of Prices*, Stirling: Water Industry Commissioner.

Water Industry Commissioner for Scotland (WICS) (2005) *The Strategic Review of Charges: Draft Determinations Volumes 1 to 7*, Glasgow: Water Industry Commissioner, June.

WRc and Ecologic (2002) *Study on the Application of the Competition Rules to the Water Sector in the European Community*, Prepared by WRc and Ecologic for the European Commission – Competition Directorate General, December 2002, Swindon: WRc Plc.

CHAPTER 4

The Scottish Papers

These lectures focussed on the regulation of the public water services in Scotland, when I was chairing the WICS. They were both given in Edinburgh and had benefitted from comments by my fellow Commissioners and by the staff of the Office.

4.1 *Changing the Taps:*
Regulating Water in Scotland

The 2006 Comiston Lecture, Edinburgh

Available from Water Industry Commission for Scotland.
Tel: 01786 430 217   www. watercommission. co. uk.
First Floor, Moray House, Forthside Way, Stirling FJ8 1QZ

A SPEECH BY SIR IAN BYATT

LADIES AND GENTLEMEN

It is a great honour to deliver the 4th Comiston lecture, in a series which is already becoming a significant event in the intellectual life of this "Athens of the north", the home of the Enlightenment. Scotland has been a model for the world, and can continue to be so in the CXXI. And we can note with satisfaction that your Water Commission is the only purely Scottish utility regulator.

It is a particular pleasure for me to talk to you about regulating the water industry in Scotland as I have been concerned with economic and political issues in the utilities throughout my working life.

THE OLD MODEL

My love affair with the utilities began 50 years ago as a research student at Nuffield College, where Herbert Morrison was a visiting fellow. I was studying the contribution that electricity made to the British economy before the First World War.

That took me into electricity supply, at a time when the current orthodoxy believed in central planning and statutory monopoly – owned by the state, but operating at arm's length from ministers. My interest in utilities continued when I entered government service. I became deeply involved in the difficult debates leading up to the last of the great nationalised industry white papers, published in 1978.

The 1970s were a gloomy period for the British economy, and for the state industries. The flaws in the Morrisonian model were becoming painful. Boards pursued their own agendas without democratic accountability; ministers damaged financial viability with industrial policies designed to correct the inflationary consequences of their economic policies.

It was clear by the end of the 1970s that things had to change. But not everyone thought that privatisation was the answer, and they still don't. Water in Scotland, and the Royal Mail, remain in the public sector.

The experience of the last two decades has shown that competition is best for customers where it is possible, and that in cases of natural monopoly, customers can be well protected where regulation provides incentives for efficiency.

These lessons can help us to develop a public sector model that can transform the provision of water services in Scotland – and provide an exportable template.

THE NEW MODEL

What seem to have been the keys to success in the new, post-Morrisonian model?

First, separation of powers between ministers and regulators, by giving regulators specific legal functions and making ministerial objectives explicit.

Secondly, the focussed use of business skills, through incentive regulation, with rewards for out-performance, to deliver public policy objectives.

Thirdly, the clarity provided by capital markets, where before there had been smoke-filled rooms. Budget constraints and requirements to perform became real, and those who sought to evade them found themselves on the streets.

Fourthly, the emergence of active customers rather than passive consumers. Competition returned to the scene – for example customers can now choose their electricity and gas suppliers – something that would have been science fiction a generation ago.

Fifthly, the separation of functions into ministerial government – a political function: the supply of services – a business function: and regulation – a supervisory function.

This required good information, much better information than existed in the former regime. Paper, not water – the jibe is familiar, but the provision of proper information provides the essentials for regulation, and a crucial platform for public understanding and consultation.

INSTITUTIONAL CHANGES IN SCOTLAND

In recent years, there have been rapid changes in the provision of water services in Scotland, and they are not yet over.

In 1996 water services in Scotland were still in the hands of local authorities, nearly a generation after they migrated to water authorities in England and Wales.

In 1996 three water authorities were formed, and in 2002 they were consolidated into Scottish Water.

The 2005 Act requires separation of retailing (billing, customer service and value-added services) from the core wholesale businesses of supplying water and removing waste water. Scottish Water retail is being split off from Scottish Water wholesale.

From April 2008, only two years away, other companies will be able to supply retail services to business customers.

Economic regulation has also developed rapidly in Scotland.

Initially, it was thought that the Customers' Council would help to manage prices. Then in late 1999, Alan Sutherland was appointed the Water Industry Commissioner for Scotland – the beginning of the modern age. He was to advise ministers rather than to make decisions, but his advice would be published.

Alan began with a quick review to get Scotland to the starting gate. He then undertook the first four-year review of prices; from 2002 to 2006. This review introduced, for the first time, a systematic set of comparisons between operating costs in Scotland and in England and Wales.

As a result, he concluded that substantial improvements in operating efficiency were possible. To its credit, and to the benefit of its customers, Scottish Water has over-achieved these efficiencies.

The second review of charges covers the four years from 2006 to 2010. It includes capital costs and capital efficiency as well as operating costs. Building on the work of the Commissioner, the new Commission concluded its final determination of prices on St Andrew's Day of last year.

This determination has now been accepted by Scottish Water. This involves acceptance of all the outcomes for which the financing is provided – a crucial element in regulation.

On average, customers will get price increases somewhat below inflation for the next four years. They will also get better customer service and Scotland will see better water and environmental quality.

The scene has also changed significantly on quality regulation.

The Scottish Environment Protection Agency regulates the quality of the water environment. The regulation of the quality of drinking water is in the hands of a statutory Drinking Water Quality Regulator.

Government has also changed. Water is devolved to Scotland although competition remains a Westminster competence.

The Scottish Executive owns Scottish Water – a matter of political consequence north of the border. The Scottish Parliament is actively concerned. MSPs handle a large amount of watery issues for their constituents.

Scottish ministers also set, as in England and Wales, objectives for water and environmental quality – that are then translated by the quality regulators into specific outputs.

Up to 2005, Scottish ministers decided the prices that Scottish Water could charge its customers. They have now passed that power to the Commission.

The Scottish Executive lends money to Scottish Water to finance investment, using funds that are available under the UK public finance arrangements. One £ more or less for water means one £ less or more for other Scottish public services, such as health and education.

The development of PFI has loosened this constraint and there is a growing debate in Scotland about the prospect of borrowing from other sources for Scottish Water. As the public finances are tightening, both in Scotland and in the UK generally, this debate is timely.

APPLYING THE NEW MODEL TO THE PUBLIC SECTOR

How we can we apply the lessons of regulation of water services in England and Wales to the public sector model in Scotland? What is the nature of the constraints facing Scottish Water and the resulting incentives?

The strategic review of charges for 2006 to 2010 involves five key elements.

First, the use of a comparative model to determine the costs of an efficient supplier. These are the costs that Scottish Water could be incurring if it was performing as well as other companies in England and Wales, allowing for the special circumstances of Scotland. In this way, public supply in Scotland is benchmarked by the results of pressures and incentives south of the border, giving Scottish Water a challenge to meet, or better, to beat.

Secondly, price limits allow Scottish Water to make a return on its capital that will cover interest charges and risks that are within the control of management. The price limits allow Scottish Water to meet the financial ratios required by lenders and credit agencies for English and Welsh companies and to manage the levels of debt incurred.

Where events, such as a new quality obligation, are outside the control of management, the Commission will be ready to change price limits within the four-year period or formally to recognise that such events will be fully dealt with at the next strategic review.

The Commission will shortly be issuing its guidance on how this will work in Scotland.

Fourthly, as an innovation in the 2005 strategic review, the Commission and the Scottish Executive have agreed a £50 million buffer to allow for events outside management control that may not be large enough to qualify either for an adjustment of prices or for logging up for the next review.

A further innovation was to create the potential for a fund, to be invested in index linked gilt-edged securities, in which out-performance on capital or operating costs can be held. In the Scottish public sector model out-performance will not leave the industry in the form of dividends.

Fifthly, should Scottish Water spend the financial resources available without achieving the required ministerial objectives and improving customer service, the Scottish Executive will meet the costs of remedying this. Customers will not be expected to pay twice.

INCENTIVES

These arrangements readily create a set of incentives.

Setting ministerial objectives and objectives for customer service establish minimum acceptable outcomes that must be met.

Out-performance remains in the system to be used – at the next strategic review – for lower prices, better water and environmental quality and better customer service – or some combination of all three.

At a wider level, greater efficiency in the water industry can release funds to deliver other public services to the Scottish people

– and vice versa where efficiency falls short of expectations.

The Scottish Executive has recognised that this creates a framework for bonuses that links rewards for managers and workers with the benefits to customers and the environment. Those who create the wealth and improve customer service can share in the benefits. Such bonuses would only be paid if minimum acceptable standards are exceeded.

COMPETITION FOR RETAIL SERVICES

Looking ahead for this year, and the next two, looms retail access and competition.

The Competition Act 1998 strengthened the legal presumption favouring competition.

Ministers have subsequently legislated in England and Wales (2003) and in Scotland (2005) to manage competition.

Household customers are excluded, both north and south of the border. In England and Wales only water supply is covered, and customers taking less than 50Ml/year are excluded. In Scotland, common carriage is banned but there is no restriction on the size of business customer and access applies to waste water services as well as the supply of water.

This permits retail access to more than 100, 000 business customers ranging from corner shops to paper mills.

By April 2008, the retail business market will be open to all who obtain licences from the Commission, that is all those who can show competence and sound finances.

The job of the regulator is to ensure that there is a level playing field, and one that is seen to be level, between Scottish Water's retail entity and any entrants.

Separation between Scottish Water wholesale and Scottish Water retail is crucial to success. This separation must involve separate management, and separate governance.

It is also necessary to separate the activities and assets of the two businesses. Further study is needed on this issue.

The Commission will continue to ensure that the wholesale business remains financially viable, provided that it is efficiently run. It has a legal duty to ensure that the opening up of the retail market does not prejudice the core functions of Scottish Water.

In due course, the Commission will shift to determining the wholesale charges that Scottish Water can charge to all retail suppliers.

The Commission is preparing for this through a study – to be undertaken jointly with Scottish Water – of the structure of costs of providing water and removing waste water at the wholesale level.

The financial viability of the retail business will be tested in the market. To avoid state aid, capital should be remunerated at commercial rates. There would be merit in borrowing directly from the market. That would both ensure that Scottish Water's retail entity was borrowing at proper commercial rates, and would release public finance to improve other public services in Scotland.

While competition for retail is developing, the Commission has to consider what protection may be needed for the customers of retail suppliers, either Scottish Water's retail entity or other suppliers.

Subject to this, the Commission believes that all retail suppliers should be able to offer whatever tariffs they think most suitable for any of their customers. Tariffs would be established by the market.

RECENT ACHIEVEMENTS

May I summarise what has been achieved in recent years and look at the main challenges for the future?

There is now a free-standing water service with clear objectives, better knowledge of its assets and defined costs set out in regulatory accounts.

Secondly, the supplier, now Scottish Water, is no longer monitoring its own performance. That is being done by independent regulators. It is not always comfortable, but it is always well meant. And external assessment of comparative performance provides a mirror for management.

Thirdly, customers of water services are benefiting from stable prices and are getting better service.

Prices increased sharply in Scotland around the turn of the century to overtake those in England and Wales, but they are now set to rise by less than in England and Wales.[1]

My second chart shows that while investment lagged behind England and Wales in the early part of the 1990s, it has now caught up and is surging ahead.[2]

Scottish Water seems on the road to be one of the better water companies, providing services at reasonable prices.

There is now clarity on the financial resources needed, and being provided, to enhance the quality of water and the environment.

The information is being put in place for productive consultation with all stakeholders, comprising all the Scottish people.

STEPS INTO THE FUTURE

Looking at the future, the Commission identifies four big challenges.

First, full delivery of all objectives, including the improvement in customer service set out in the price determination made last November. The Commission is delighted at the establishment of a high level monitoring group which will include the quality regulators. It will take the lead in servicing this group. It will also publish annually reports showing the progress of Scottish Water on customer service, on costs and performance and on relieving development constraints.

Secondly, continued progress on efficiency by Scottish Water. We have seen a substantial increase in operating efficiency, and expect

---

[1]See Chart A: Average household bills in Scotland and in England and Wales 1999–00 to 2009–10 (projected) (2005–06 prices).
[2]See Chart B: Average annual investment per property in Scotland and in England and Wales 1984–85 to 2009–10 (projected) (2005–06 prices).

more. We now need to see better delivery and better efficiency in the capital programme. We will report on progress.

Looking further ahead, preparation for the implementation of the EU Water Framework Directive. This requires cost reflective charging and good quality water, but does not specify what the latter might mean. Any solutions must be cost effective to ensure that tariffs remain affordable to customers. They must also ensure that Scotland will be able to invest efficiently in better water and waste water quality.

Finally, making retail competition work for the benefit of business customers. They must get proper choice and be protected against market power.

So, ladies and gentlemen, the taps are being changed in Scotland. What is emerging is a big step forward in providing the water services that the Scottish people deserve.

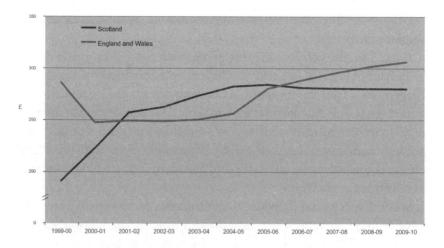

Chart A: Average household bills in Scotland and in England and Wales 1999–00 to 2009–10 (projected) (2005–06 prices)

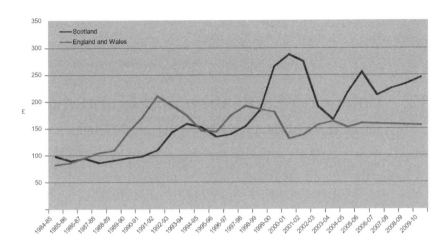

Chart B: Average annual investment per property in Scotland and in England and Wales 1984–85 to 2009–10 (projected) (2005–06 prices)

4.2 Balancing Regulation and Competition in the Water Business in Scotland

Hume Paper No. 67: *David Hume Institute*, April 2006

A speech given by Sir Ian Byatt at the
Royal Society of Edinburgh 19 April 2006

Ladies and Gentlemen,

It is a privilege to give this lecture tonight, and an honour to do so under the Chairmanship of my former colleague and long-term mentor, Alan Peacock. It is a pleasure to speak to the Institute early in the Directorship of my Treasury colleague, Jeremy Peat. It is a delight to address this distinguished audience in the city where David Hume lived and worked.

> *"Money ... is none of the wheels of trade: it is the oil which renders the motion of the wheels more smooth and easy"*
> David Hume *Essays:*
> *1741–2 Of Money*

Regulation may have been unknown to Hume – although there was a supply of piped water to Edinburgh in his days – but I believe that he would have regarded regulation, like money, as the oil, not the engine and, like money, believed there can be too much of it.

> *"Avarice, the spur of industry ... works its way through so many real dangers and difficulties ..."*
> David Hume *Essays:*
> *1741–2 Of Civil Liberty*

Avarice, or incentives as we would now say, permeates regulation as well as industry, providing its motor force.

"Does it contain any experimental reasoning, concerning matter of fact and existence? No. Commit it then to the flames: for it can contain nothing but sophistry and illusion"
David Hume *An Enquiry Concerning Human Understanding* 1748

Belief and action should be based on facts not received opinion.

How can we apply these concepts to regulating publicly owned utilities – and, perhaps, other public sector bodies? This is my task tonight, using water services in Scotland and the work of the Water Commission as an example, and perhaps a model, of what can be done.

First, let us put water in Scotland in the wider context of European utilities.

THE OLD MODEL IN EUROPE

The old model, the traditional European way of dealing with utilities – classified as services of general economic interest – has been to designate a body, typically state-owned, with a statutory monopoly, to deliver collective objectives such as universal service provision, or, to use European terminology again, to discharge its "mission".

In the UK these bodies, all with statutory monopolies, comprised the nationalised industries. They were part of a post-war world of national planning. Many of them have now been transformed into regulated privately owned businesses. Some, notably the Royal Mail and Scottish Water remain as public enterprises but with their own regulators.

Water services in Europe are generally fragmented and are often still at the municipal level. They have been consolidated in the UK into water authorities, and now water companies – in England

and Wales in 1974 and more recently in Scotland and Northern Ireland.

There has been much less change in Continental Europe than here in the UK. But the distinction between natural and statutory monopoly is recognised in the Treaty of Rome, where exemption is granted from the competition rules for services of general economic interest – only in so far as this is necessary to discharge their "missions".

The old model generated its own economics with a distinguished pedigree. It developed in France from the tradition of engineering economics. In the Anglo-American tradition it derived from the work of Lerner and Lange in applying classical micro-economics to state industry. It was used with great distinction by Boiteaux in developing pricing rules for electricity. It found its way into the Treasury White Papers on Nationalised Industries, particularly the one published in 1967.

This economics is, however, about how to run state industries, not how to regulate them. The economics that has proved useful in regulating utilities has derived from a different tradition, one concerned with the power of structures, institutions and incentives, not of internal pricing rules or how best to appraise investment projects.

THE NEW MODEL

To understand the new model let us go back to basics.

Utilities provide collective services as well as responding to individual or household demand. Decisions on the nature and scale of the implementation of collective objectives must be collective.

But it does not mean that they must be provided by a government owned supplier. Nor should we assume that a supplier should have a statutory monopoly.

Provided there are ways of ensuring that collective demands are met – through finance or regulation or by some combination of both – competitive suppliers can deliver them, while responding to the individual requirements of their customers. But where there is natural monopoly, that is where there are substantial economies of scale over the whole range of output, competitive supply is effectively prevented.

Where competition is possible we should facilitate or promote it; regulation will only be necessary to ensure matters such as product safety. Where natural monopoly is inevitable, it is necessary to turn to some form of regulation of outcomes and prices. But this does not imply regulation – as opposed to analysis – of costs or ways of producing these outcomes. Regulation should focus on outcomes and incentives, not inputs and micro-management.

Proper separation of responsibilities and accountabilities is a key to establishing helpful behaviour and proper incentives. Responsibilities divide between suppliers, a business function: ministers, a political function: and regulators, a supervisory function. Ministers should provide clarity on objectives and should refrain from intervening in the delivery process. Regulators advise on objectives, establish prices, facilitate or promote competition and monitor performance. Suppliers focus on business, competing for customers or achieving collective objectives.

Incentives may be positive or negative; either incentives to outperform expectations, or incentives to avoid failing to deliver what is required. They are sticks as well as carrots.

Good information is essential. It should be both comprehensive and comprehendible, not just data. It must be trustworthy and trusted, avoiding asymmetry in quality and understanding, and regulatory gaming. It must be designed to promote consultation with all the stakeholders in politically visible industries.

Paper, not water – that is always the jibe. But information, if consistent, and repeated, does change behaviour.

A CULTURAL GAP

There is a cultural gap between the old and the new models – a gap that is wider than matters of ownership. It is the gap between rule

221

by the Platonic guardians, who know what is best for us, and the contestable world of David Hume.

At a more mundane level, a switch towards outputs and outcomes, to the virtues of out-performance, and away from expenditure control and managing allocated moneys, can transform the culture of an organisation – to one that strives for achievement rather than doing no more than is strictly necessary.

Proper structuring of incentives is a major element in closing this gap. In a public sector model, regulators need to replicate the shareholder pressures that drive action in privately owned companies.

APPLYING THE NEW MODEL IN AN INSTITUTIONAL CONTEXT

How could this new model work in a publicly owned organisation? What is the role of the regulator? Specifically, how could this model work in the case of water services in Scotland?

Regulators need to be party to developments in institutional structures, and the way they operate. They need to search for opportunities to structure good incentives for all, i.e. for suppliers, customers, developers, ministers and regulators.

This involves supporting institutions and practices that create good information and incentives, generate cost-effective decisions, ensure openness to customers, and facilitate entry by new providers.

It means avoiding inferior institutional structures and bad incentives – to inflate costs, to use the political process to short-circuit analytic processes, and generally to do deals in smoke- filled rooms.

Regulators have limited opportunity to create institutional structures and may need to concentrate on developing incentives within existing structures. But there are areas, e.g. in developing competition, where they should exercise a benign influence on institutional structures.

WATER SERVICES AND INCENTIVES IN SCOTLAND

So what is the situation in Scotland concerning incentives, and what are we, the Commission doing to influence and develop it?

I will run through the incentives that are, and could be, facing the various actors on the scene – existing and new suppliers, customers, developers, ministers, and regulators. Inevitably there are overlaps.

INCENTIVES FOR EXISTING SUPPLIERS

Let us begin with existing suppliers.

As a result of recent reforms, there is now a single, externally regulated, Scottish Water, financed to deliver ministerial objectives efficiently, and to provide good service to customers. The Chairman now comes from a business background. These are major steps forward from a position where water was simply a department in a local authority with many other objectives.

Scottish Water does not monitor its own output. There are quality regulators, the Drinking Water Quality Regulator (DWQR) and the Scottish Environment Protection Agency (SEPA), together with the Commission and the customer representatives, Waterwatch, to provide an objective assessment of delivery.

Better information – flowing from the returns made by Scottish Water to the Commission, from the regulatory accounts and from a major effort by Scottish Water to improve its knowledge of its assets – provides the clarity required for proper accountability.

There are pressures for greater efficiency and for better customer service deriving from comparative competition. Price limits are set on the basis of comparisons with England and Wales, where the pressures from financial markets are driving increases in efficiency and customer service.

DEVELOPMENTS IN THE 2006–10 STRATEGIC REVIEW

New incentives were developed in the 2006–10 strategic review of charges to yield:

A hard budget constraint linked to a set of regulatory accounts that will be used to monitor financial performance

A cost of capital, linked to that used by Ofwat that allows for such risks as are within the control or influence of management

A process whereby material changes in legal obligations and ministerial objectives will trigger changes in price limits, either between reviews or at the next strategic review

A £50m buffer to act as a quasi-equity cushion that insulates customers from shocks that are outside the control of management. It can only be utilised with the consent of the owner, the Scottish Executive, acting on advice from the Commission.

The establishment of a fund, to be held in gilt-edged securities, for any out-performance of the financial expectations in the price determination. This fund would be available at the next strategic review to be used by ministers and regulators, to reduce prices, improve customer service, or improve water and environmental quality.

A requirement by the owner, the Scottish Executive, that bonus payments to management must be fully self-financing and only be made when regulatory expectations have been outperformed. This ensures a clear relationship between personal reward and delivery.

INCENTIVES TO NEW ENTRANTS

There is a statutory requirement for the separation of the retail services of Scottish Water to business customers and provision for the licensing of new retailers who can improve these retail services or supply them more economically.

To open up this market on a level playing field – and one that is seen to be level – will require the new retail arm of Scottish Water, Scottish Water Business Stream (SWBS), to be demonstrably separate from the wholesale supplier, Scottish Water – separate governance, separate management and separation of activities and assets.

From 2008, entrants will be able to provide retail services (billing, customer service and value-added services) to over 100,000 business users, both large and small, for the supply of water and the disposal of wastewater.

SWBS will require its own working capital. To avoid state aid, and to keep the playing field level, implies borrowing at commercial rates. The best way to achieve this would be for SWBS to borrow directly from the market. This would give it market incentives to invest wisely and efficiently.

Borrowing from the market would also have the advantage of involving bankers directly, as has happened in England and Wales, to improve discipline in the use of funds. It could be achieved by SWBS taking a minority share in a Joint Venture.

It would also release funds that the Scottish Executive could use for other public services.

INCENTIVES FOR CUSTOMERS

The price limits determined on St. Andrew's Day will finance rapid progress towards the full metering of business customers. When meters are installed, business users will have proper incentives to use water and wastewater services wisely. Retailers would be free to design tariffs that are attractive to customers.

The development of a competitive retail market would lead the Commission to limit wholesale rather than retail prices. It is studying, jointly with Scottish Water, the structure of costs in the wholesale business.

As the retail market develops, the Commission will protect customers by outlawing undue preference and requiring all suppliers to offer a "default" tariff that would be properly related to the regulated wholesale tariff.

The price limits set for 2006–10 allow for some unwinding of the cross subsidy from business to household customers. This will be further examined at the next price review, when the results of the study of the structure of wholesale cost will be available.

The Commission intends to examine the relationship between charges to customers, including household customers, taking a measured supply and those paying on a taxation basis. In England and Wales, metered bills – for a standard consumption – must not exceed unmeasured bills by more than the additional cost of metering. This led to a substantial reduction in measured tariffs, promoting a steady switch towards metering and greater care in using water and discharging wastewater.

INCENTIVES FOR DEVELOPERS

Finance has been provided, through the price limits set in November, for Scottish Water to deal with the peculiarly Scottish problem of development constraints. New regulations now ensure that incentives are in place to use the property market to prioritise aspirations.

The Planning Authorities have a crucial role in preparing Structure Plans and granting planning consents. They will facilitate, but do not control, construction activity by Scottish Water.

Builders are responsible for local development costs, subject to receiving a reasonable contribution from Scottish Water when the new properties are connected. Price limits allow Scottish Water sufficient funds both to make these contributions and to enhance the capability of the strategic network.

Scottish Water customers are making their contribution to development in Scotland where it is permitted, and where it is economic. They should not pay for extensions to the strategic network where local Planning Authorities do not want to see development or where developers do not want to build.

INCENTIVES FOR MINISTERS

The Scottish Executive accepts that any failure of Scottish Water to deliver the outputs financed by the price determination would fall on taxpayers, not customers. Customers are not expected to pay twice.

This provides a powerful incentive to Scottish Ministers. Under the UK public finance arrangements, every £ more for water will mean a £ less for other public services, such as health and education.

The public finances are tightening, in the UK in general, and in Scotland in particular I fear, lest economies in public expenditure lead to cuts in the amounts that the Scottish Executive lends to Scottish Water – as happened south of the border in 1976, when the investment programmes of the water authorities were reined back to meet the required IMF cuts in public expenditure.

This would imply a substantial increase in customers' bills. It could, however, be avoided by borrowing directly from the market. To do this would involve forming a trust or a cooperative within the public sector model, with powers to borrow directly to finance its investment.

Rates may be somewhat higher than those available from the Treasury. But greater efficiency could be expected, especially in relation to investment. Such a body would need to convince the capital markets that, although publicly owned, its financial strength and efficiency was comparable to privately owned companies elsewhere in the UK.

INCENTIVES FOR REGULATORS

Where there is good information and regulatory trust, regulators can concentrate on the achievement of outputs and leave the management of inputs to the supplier. Otherwise, there is constant temptation for all the regulators to micro-manage Scottish Water's activities.

The process (the Quality and Standards process) for planning projects for the enhancement of water and environmental quality, needs to be closely linked to monitoring the delivery of such projects.

A joined-up process for regular monitoring of the delivery of the outputs, required to meet ministerial objectives has been established. This should generate a strategic process for developing future objectives for the implementation of the EU Water Framework Directive (WFD) – a Directive that requires "good" water quality but does not specify what "good" might mean.

We need to recognise the constraints on the scale of an investment programme that can be efficiently delivered. There is already an overhang in a programme that is equivalent to half the output of the construction industry in Scotland. Investment per head of population is higher than in England and Wales.

Continuation of a scale of investment that is consistent with achieving proper efficiency in delivery, say an annual programme of some £400 – 500 million, would be compatible with a continuation of price limits that mirrored inflation.

For the early phases of the implementation of the WFD, it would seem sensible to develop a system of prioritising projects for the improvement of water and environmental quality within this level. The quality regulators would choose the most environmentally cost effective projects for early implementation, while avoiding a workload that would generate wasteful increases in prices.

WIDER APPLICATION OF THE NEW MODEL

In many parts of the world, countries want more effective and efficient water systems to cope with demands for rising standards – and in many cases for decent basic supplies. They want to maintain a public sector model and improve its performance.

Other utilities particularly intertwined in the public sector, such as railways and postal services, are striving for improved and more efficient services, using competition and the incentives deriving from private sector participation to the extent possible.

Other public services, such as health and education, are seeking to be more responsive to users, while avoiding the strings of central planning.

Perhaps they have things to learn from what we are doing in our Scottish public sector model. The key to success is the ability to develop incentives without opening these services fully to the capital markets.

CONCLUSIONS

To conclude, Ladies and Gentlemen.

I have attempted to set out the new model for regulating utilities that has developed, as a practical tool, in the UK in the last twenty years. It has stood the test of time and brought great benefits to customers.

Many elements of this model are now in place in Scotland, as a result of changes made in the last decade. They have taken place within the context of a public sector model.

Current developments include establishing tighter disciplines on managers and strengthening personal and institutional incentives for producers, customers, developers, ministers and regulators alike.

They also include the separation of a retail segment of Scottish Water and the licensing of new entrants to provide retail services to all business customers.

Looking further ahead, it would be wise to explore innovative ways of using private finance within a public sector model.

In doing this we must keep our eye focussed on the ball and be practical about what matters to customers and to the Scottish people. I believe that they want public control of objectives and public supervision of the delivery of these objectives. They also want stability in their bills.

Within this public sector framework, let us use the tools that David Hume might have recommended to deliver collective and customer objectives in the most cost-effective way.

CHAPTER 5

Regulating Publicly Owned Utilities

5.1 Regulating Publicly Owned Utilities – Outputs, Owners and Incentives

Occasional Lecture University of Bath, 2007

INTRODUCTION

It is a pleasure to talk to this distinguished audience and I thank the Centre for the study of Regulated Industries (CRI) for the opportunity to do so. May I preface what I have to say by quoting John Stuart Mill?

> "It is essential that the practical supremacy should reside in the representatives of the people [but] there is a radical distinction between controlling the business of government and actually doing it".

How can we achieve Mill's objective for publicly owned utilities, such as the Royal Mail/Post Office, Scottish Water, and Guernsey Electricity; for utilities that are classified to the private sector, but heavily dependent on public money, such as Network Rail; and for part publicly-owned utilities, such as National Air Traffic Services (NATS) and the London Underground?

I aim to assess why the nationalised model went wrong, to

Acknowledgement: Lecture given to the CRI on 18th April 2007 and revised in the light of the discussion. I am grateful for help from John Banyard, Chris Bolt, Mike Brooker, Harry Bush, Charles Coulthard, Ed Humpherson and David Simpson, and from questions and points made after the lecture. All responsibility for drafting rests with me.

identify the lessons of the regulatory regime set up to regulate privatised utilities, and then to apply them to publicly owned utilities.[1] I believe that there are common themes; although applications must be context specific. There may also be lessons for other public services.

My objective tonight is to provoke a discussion leading to further work by regulatory bodies and independent bodies such as CRI. I will concentrate on examples from water, because that is where I have a comparative advantage. Colleagues have helped me with other areas and I hope that your comments and questions will further fill out the space.

The balance between politics and business

The public believes, particularly in the utilities, that politics and economics are closely entwined. It makes no sense to ignore – or make assumptions about – the one and then to develop a string of propositions about the other, without bearing both in mind.

The drivers of politics and economics often conflict. Politics is a world of multiple objectives and short-term pressures. It is concerned with the protection of vulnerable groups from the winds of economic change. Economics is much more focused on more measurable bottom-lines. The balance between the two is one of the great strengths of an open society – but not easy to achieve.

HOW DID GOVERNMENTS TRY AND FAIL? – THE NATIONALISED/PUBLIC CORPORATION MODEL

The arms-length arrangements envisaged by Herbert Morrison did not work. Ministers appointed the 'right' people to operate statutory monopolies in the 'public interest', subject to general directions that were never given, and to financial controls that were rarely respected. Ministers spent little time on strategy, being

---

[1] It has been put to me that the nationalised regime started well. But it was not durable and by the 1970s it was performing badly.

234

more concerned to respond to events and to intervene to achieve particular ends, such as compliance with pay policies. Sponsor departments, not, note, regulatory departments, were concerned to defend their industries against the Treasury. The Treasury sought to impose financial discipline by setting financial targets and improving investment appraisal.[2] But targets were missed and investment made inadequate returns.[3] To quote an influential paper by Stephen Littlechild, ministers failed the "Sed quis custodiet ipsos Custodes?" test.[4,5]

For their part, the industries had few doubts about their objectives. As Christopher Foster put it:

"The chairmen and boards of nationalised industries had a great practical independence [which] they used to pursue what they believed to be the interests of their public corporation. For them that, not the interests of the public as Herbert Morrison or changeable ministers conceived them, or the improvement of economic efficiency, was the public interest".

In commenting on the failure of the 1968 Transport Act, Stewart Joy argued that *"The British Transport Commission assumed that virtually all the existing railway services would be provided for an indefinite period, and that if users would not pay their full cost,*

[2]HM Treasury (1961), The Financial and Economic Obligations of the Nationalised Industries, Cmnd 1337; HM Treasury (1967), Nationalised Industries; A Review of Economic and Financial Objectives, Cmnd 3437; and HM Treasury (1978) The Nationalised Industries, Cmnd 7131.
[3]Much government documentation, notably the 1967 White Paper, was about how nationalised industries should operate, for example, how they should do investment appraisal, not about how they should be regulated. Perhaps it would have been better to have recognised the importance of different accountabilities.
[4]"But who is to guard those guards?"
[5]Littlechild S (1979), Controlling the Nationalised Industries: Quis custodiet ipsos custodes?, Series B Discussion Paper No 56, Faculty of Commerce and Social Science, University of Birmingham, August.

taxpayers would be forced to". The industries were the priests of supply, with few doubts about what was good for consumers. They saw government primarily as an (unreliable) source of finance for investment, and, where necessary, to support unprofitable operations. They were big on aspirations and poor on delivery,

Not everything went badly; for example, British Gas switched smoothly from town to natural gas. But nationalised industries were inefficient on a scale that we only fully appreciated after they had been privatised. Strong unions captured the statutory monopoly. Investment was misdirected into prestige projects and few attempts were made to exploit existing assets. Hard budget constraints were absent and there were few political incentives to create or enforce them. There was inadequate information, both for industry managers and for government officials, on costs, performance and financial accounting.

Was reform possible?

We in the Treasury tried to harden budget constraints by imposing external financing limits (EFLs) as part of the reforms in the control of public expenditure in the middle 1970s.[6] We also promulgated the required rate of return (RRR) on investment in the 1978 White Paper. Following this, we developed a financial framework that could be used to set targets for a return on existing as well as new assets. I chaired a group of independent economists and accountants, whose report was published by the Treasury, to show how this could be done.[7] We were engaged, however, on the notoriously perilous task of changing the culture. Happily, that culture changed at privatisation and the report became a useful manual in the new world.

The culture of the old regime involved conflict and confusion on objectives, low efficiency and poor delivery. Systematic

[6]HM Treasury (1976), Cash Limits on Public Expenditure, Cmnd 6440.
[7]HM Treasury (1986), Accounting for Economic Costs and Changing Prices; A Report to HM Treasury by an Advisory Group, HMSO.

measurement was absent.[8] Its key words were pay, employment, conflict and politics.

THE NEW MODEL OF THE PRIVATISED UTILITIES

Privatisation and regulation of telecom, gas electricity and water in the late 1980s created a new model. Ministers moved to a new arms-length relationship, where they were obliged to make their objectives explicit through legal instruments. Their ability to intervene in response to 'events' was constrained. Nationalised industries became private companies whose purpose was to use commercial skills to meet the objectives of their customers (not, this time, consumers), subject to external regulation by a new breed of public servants with specific statutory duties, acting independently from ministers.[9]

These regulators were to enable, promote or facilitate competition, and, in the meantime, to protect customers by limiting prices and establishing proper incentives under an RPI-X regime. They succeeded, particularly in energy, in disentangling the natural monopoly elements from those that are contestable.

The new model was also developed, particularly in water, and subsequently railways, to accommodate collective objectives. In 1994, I asked ministers, publicly, for guidance on water quality and environmental objectives, reminding them that these objectives were powerful upward drivers of bills.[10] They duly gave guidance, publicly – having investigated how these objectives could be met in economical ways.[11] Ministers now have a statutory duty to tell the

---

[8]For example, there were no performance measures before the 1978 White Paper.
[9]Vibert F (forthcoming 2007), The Rise of the Unelected: Democracy and the New Separation of Powers, Cambridge.
[10]Ofwat (1992), The Cost of Quality: A Strategic Assessment of the Prospects for Future Water Bills and Ofwat (1993), Paying for Quality: The Political Perspective.
[11]This guidance proved to be a lasting feature of water price reviews – although subsequent ministers have not always been so careful to avoid high cost options.

Office of Rail Regulation (ORR) what they want to buy and how much money they have available.[12]

Outcomes, outputs and inputs – individual and collective objectives

I find it useful to distinguish between outcomes, outputs and inputs. By outcomes I mean the high level objectives delivered to customers, such as clean beaches, effective removal and disposal of sewage, and the provision of safe drinking water. Outputs are the means of delivering these outcomes, involving the provision and operation of effective – and cost-effective – systems of pipes and treatment works. Inputs are the resources, financial and other, that go into the enhancement, maintenance and operation of these systems.

The distinction between the objectives of citizens as customers, and those of citizens as guardians of the wider public interest is crucial. In an open society, outcomes are the concern of customers as well as politicians. Competition enables dissatisfied customers to go elsewhere. Politicians will stand or fall by whether collective outcomes are well-specified and delivered effectively.

The specification, measurement and monitoring of the outputs that will achieve desired outcomes for individuals are best left to competitive forces. Where collective objectives are concerned, regulators need to equip themselves with the requisite skills. They must be responsible, and be seen to be responsible, for the specification of outputs, their use in setting price limits, and the subsequent monitoring of their delivery.[13]

The management of inputs is best left to the suppliers of the service. If they are to be fully effective, they must have incentives to do their job efficiently and economically. They need to be free to assemble the resources that they need to do the job, not to be

[12]This should be systematically monitored.
[13]These activities should involve quality regulators as well as economic regulators.

238

constrained by restrictions on what they can pay their work force or how, or how much, they can borrow for capital investment.

This new model involves a culture of devolution of accountability and decision-making. It also involves transparency and the use of objective information. Its key words are competition, information, outcomes and incentives.

THE LESSONS OF THE NEW MODEL FOR THE PUBLICLY-OWNED UTILITIES

First, competition is crucial. Natural monopoly must be disentangled from statutory monopoly – as it has been in energy and telecom. Regulators need to identify all potentially competitive areas. Postcomm has promoted competition in postal services. In preparation for opening the market next year, the Water Commission in Scotland (WICS) is ensuring the contestability of retail services (ie, billing, value added services and complaints handling) for some 130,000 nonhousehold customers of water and sewerage services, by insisting that the retail arm, Scottish Water business services (SWbs), is fully separate from Scottish Water (SW).[14] ORR has acted to promote competition on the East Coast main line, despite train franchising having been taken back into the Department for Transport.

Good accounting and proper cost allocation are essential to success in creating and maintaining contestability. It is never easy, but we have seen in the case of water in England and Wales that retail-minus arrangements, such as the efficient component pricing rule (ECPR), can become a charter for incumbents. Contrast the provision of internet services in France and the UK. In France the market is dominated by Wanadoo, a subsidiary of France Telecom; in the UK, BT is only one of several players.

---

[14]SWbs has a provisional licence. A full licence will not be granted until WICS is satisfied that there is proper separation between SW and SWbs.

Second, where competition is difficult or impossible to achieve, comparisons are vital. We in Scotland have the advantage that we can use the comparative material on costs and performance of water companies in England and Wales collected and analysed by Ofwat. This means that the efficiency expectations generated for Scottish Water result from market driven performance south of the border.

Third, the importance of clarity in formulating desired outcomes for collective objectives. Examples are the universal service obligation (USO) for posts, water and environmental quality, and the balance between journeys by rail and road. It is no easy task to address the real issues, but the instinctive defence of the status quo is not productive. Regulators can help, as has Postcomm, in exploring the nature of the USO and its relationship to market forces.

Fourth, the recognition of the importance of transparency and proper accountability. This involves clarity on responsibility and the creation of incentives to improve delivery to customers and to the collectivity – society if you like – in efficient ways. It is achieved by having clear and well understood processes and well-defined accounting and other rules. Regulators have a responsibility to collect information and establish protocols. They can go far in ensuring that decisions are not made in 'smoke filled' rooms.

Fifthly, the need for better information about the wishes and preferences of customers and the cost structures of the suppliers. This is needed to underpin better decision making, better operations and more effective investment.

ISSUES OF OWNERSHIP

How can this model be applied to publicly owned utilities, when the prospect of failure and take-over is absent, and when ministers feel able, and even obliged, to intervene? Does it stand a chance?

Privatisation left ministers as standard setters, maintaining public control over the collective objectives of the supplying companies. Finance for investment was provided through the capital markets and the new owners were subject to a variety of pressures, some from markets, and some from regulators, to improve both delivery and efficiency.

As public sector owners, ministers are obliged to act as bankers, and to control the finance available to the supplier. They have to juggle conflicting demands for cash, which means that money will not always be available. They are also inevitably drawn into the application of public sector pay policies. In carrying out these tasks, what scope is there for ensuring hard budget constraints and for creating the right incentives, without being pulled into micromanagement? I will draw on developments in Scotland, hoping to elicit ideas and experience from others.[15]

History has shown that the existence of a hard budget constraint is essential to proper delivery and to efficiency. We in Scotland have achieved ministerial acceptance of the policy that 'customers should not pay twice'. Making good any deficit in Scottish Water's delivery of the outputs allowed for in the price settlement will not be financed from customers, but from the taxpayer. This gives a powerful incentive to the owner, the Scottish Executive.

At the 2006 Strategic Review of Charges, we created a £50m quasiequity buffer against new legal obligations, such new quality obligations under the threshold for an interim adjustment of price limits. This would only be available, when agreed by the Commission and the owner. In this way customers would be protected and Scottish Water, and its owner, incentivised.

The Scottish Executive has further agreed that the gains from outperformance by Scottish Water of the regulator's expectations, made when setting prices, would go into a fund, to be held in

---

[15]For a fuller account, see Sutherland A (2006), Efficiency Incentives for Public Sector Monopolies – The Case of Scottish Water, Beesley Lecture 16, November.

index-linked gilts. This would be available to finance unexpected adverse shocks without recourse to customers and, at the next price review, could be available for lower prices or better services to customers and the environment.[16]

Payment of dividends may have an important role to play, provided that they are dependent on good performance and declared after profits or surpluses have been calculated, and not predetermined payments to the Treasury. They would enable governments to point to the public benefits of greater efficiency – and can be related to bonus payments to employees.

There is currently no expectation that Scottish Water would pay dividends to its owner and the Executive would not, accordingly, accrue funds to reward it for the risks that it is taking. Provision needs to be made for this as price limits should allow for the risks of the business. This would take into account the entry of SWbs into a competitive market; for the wholesale business, the measure of risk should recognise that there is a monopoly provider of funds. These arrangements should allow for some build up of 'risk' funds, as well as of out-performance funds, in the gilts buffer.

The Scottish Executive has also indicated that bonus payments to employees of Scottish Water should be related to performance – as measured by the Commission. Bonuses should be self-financing, ie, result from out-performance and be related to delivery to customers – as measured by the overall performance assessment (OPA) created by Ofwat. Scottish Water discussed their bonus scheme for 2006 to 2010 with us before submitting it to their owner. It is Scottish Water's scheme, not ours, but it meets our criteria.

There is a licence condition requiring Network Rail to have a management incentive plan (MIP). But more needs to be done if MIP targets and regulatory targets are to be fully aligned. In the Royal Mail/Post office, senior management has been incentivised

[16]In Scotland a Strategic Review of Charges.

to improve performance, but there is some concern that this has been more to the benefit of the owner than the customers.

The Shareholder Executive

The creation of the Shareholder Executive, a new body set up to improve the use of assets and extend the role of the owner in the public sector, is an interesting innovation.[17] Ministers as owners should learn from the way in which this responsibility is discharged by private sector owners in comparable areas.

There are two issues here. First there is the confusion of objectives discussed above. Secondly there is the lack of expertise and experience in Whitehall. The Executive offers a welcome source of advice and expertise, advising on transparency and accountability, and on the monitoring of results

Finance for investment

Is it necessary for ministers to finance the businesses that they own? Public finance is no longer inevitably cheaper than private finance. The development of bond finance for privatised utilities in the last fifteen years has left only a small difference between public and private interest rates. As public finance is inevitably constrained, the weighted average cost of capital can be lower for utilities financed directly through capital markets.

Borrowing directly from the private sector can strengthen investment appraisal and improve efficiency in the use of capital funds. Bankers lending to utilities typically require quantified information on how the money will be used and cash flow projections that show the expected impact on the key financial ratios specified in borrowing covenants. By contrast, when publicly-owned utilities require funds for investment there is less likely to be a professional check on the use of the money than on whether is has been properly voted.

[17]National Audit Office (2007), The Shareholder Executive and Public Sector Business, Stationary Office, London.

Responsibilities of owners to customers

We need a new model for the ownership of publicly-owned utilities. In developing this model, public sector owners should bear in mind the responsibilities that they have to customers, responsibilities for delivery of outputs that will achieve desired outcomes in cost-effective ways – without trying to micro-manage such delivery, especially by subjecting them to the myriad of public sector systems, including constraints on pay.

Much progress has been made in setting prices that reflect costs and not political priorities. But further progress is needed for the public sector model to work in a fully effective way. In rethinking their position as owners, ministers should, perhaps, be taking their lead from the behaviour of owners of private sector businesses.

In particular, this should include rethinking the way that publicly owned bodies are financed. Under public ownership, the provision of finance is subject to public expenditure controls. These controls have often distorted investment and, particularly in the case of railways, have interacted in an uncomfortable way with regulatory decisions. Are there ways of disentangling these interactions that are consistent with commercial operation and public expenditure control? It is interesting to see that Network Rail is increasing its reliance on capital markets for the financing of investment, and reducing its dependence on public finance. This may be a useful pointer for other areas.

It has been argued that it would not be sensible to allow publicly owned utilities to borrow directly from bond markets – because we cannot exclude an implicit Treasury guarantee. But this needs to be revisited where commercial operations provide a revenue stream. Professor Stephen Glaister has told us that borrowing for Transport for London has involved careful scrutiny by lenders of the purposes and use of the money – greater scrutiny than is traditional in public sector lending.

Where a body receives both subsidy for operations and finance for investment, it is important to separate these quite different purposes, in particular, to disentangle criteria for payment and the monitoring of results. The ideal method would be to pay defined *ex ante* subsidies directly to the users of the service. Where this is impractical, subsidy should be closely related to the use of the service – or to some specific social objective. The worst method, which both confuses objectives and damages incentives, is to pick up the bill after the event.

AN ALTERNATIVE – THE CLG MODEL

But as pressures on public expenditure are intensifying, now may be the time to consider other ways to raise this money directly from the markets. We in Scotland believe that capital finance of some £200m a year is required for Scottish Water for the foreseeable future. Yet the public finances are tightening, to a greater extent than even in England. For political reasons, privatisation is out of the question. There is now an alternative, the 'mutual' model, in the form of Glas Cymru, a company limited by guarantee (CLG), that has been successfully developed in Wales.[18,19]

The emergence of Glas Cymru has shown that the power of the licensed, independently regulated, incentive driven, equity model, can be extended to a non-equity model. By buying out the previous owner at a discount, it had the initial advantage of a small quasi-equity buffer. Glas has operated transparently under the scrutiny of investors, with a high calibre board and members appointed on Nolan principles with a commitment to delivery. Customers can still gain from out-performance; Glas has innovated by paying 'dividends' to customers, dividends that can be easily linked to the bonuses earned by workers.

Is this the way ahead within a public sector model? Does a

---

[18]In a mutual, all customers would be members and carry risk. It can, however, be convenient to group a CLG under the general label of a 'mutual' when distinguishing it from a shareholder of a publicly owned company. The Canadian term 'no share company' is an alternative formulation.
[19]Sparrow J (2006), Glas Cymru 5 Years On, Royal Bank of Scotland, 6th July.

mutual model offer sufficient incentives for management efficiency? It can be effective where, as in water, the company is part of a wider industry, allowing comparative competition or where, as in the case of Canadian Air Traffic Control, it is more a matter of network operation than asset management.

London Underground Railways (LUL) provides an alternative model where operations are public and maintenance and enhancement private. This involves complexity in governance. Given experience with long-term contracts, it was also necessary to appoint a standing arbiter. The arrangements are innovatory, and the arbiter is imposing financial discipline, but will they pass a full evolutionary test?

NEXT STEPS

There is a big agenda to be explored. We in Scotland are committed to it. Could it be extended to the whole area of publicly-owned utilities, and, as a separate exercise, to the wider public sector, and if so, how?

I started by quoting John Stuart Mill. My own coda, in much less elegant language, is that 'the representatives of the people should identify what their constituents want and are ready to pay for, encourage competition and effective business models, and leave the rest to markets, regulators and management'. I hope that the discussion will extend and enrich what I have been saying, and, of course, correct vulgar errors. Thank you.

REFERENCES

(bold numbers refer to the footnote in which first cited)

HM Treasury (1961), The Financial and Economic Obligations of the Nationalised Industries, Cmnd 1337, HMSO. (2)

HM Treasury (1967), Nationalised Industries; A Review of Economic and Financial Objectives, Cmnd 3437, HMSO. (2)

HM Treasury (1976), Cash Limits on Public Expenditure, Cmnd 6440, HMSO. **(6)**

HM Treasury (1978), The Nationalised Industries, Cmnd 7131, HMSO. **(2)**

HM Treasury (1986), Accounting for Economic Costs and Changing Prices; A Report to HM Treasury by an Advisory Group, HMSO. **(7)**

National Audit Office (2007), The Shareholder Executive and Public Sector Business, Stationary Office, London. **(17)**

Ofwat (1992), The Cost of Quality: A Strategic Assessment of the Prospects for Future Water Bills. **(11)**

Ofwat (1993), Paying for Quality: The Political Perspective. **(11)**

Sparrow J (2006), Gias Cymru 5 Years On, Royal Bank of Scotland, 6th July. **(19)**

Sutherland A (2006), Efficiency Incentives for Public Sector Monopolies – The Case of Scottish Water, Beesley Lecture 16, November. **(15)**

Littlechild S (1979), Controlling the Nationalised Industries: Quis custodiet ipsos custodes?, Series B Discussion Paper No 56, Faculty of Commerce and Social Science, University of Birmingham, August. **(5)**

Vibert F (forthcoming 2007), The Rise of the Unelected: Democracy and the New Separation of Powers, Cambridge. **(9)**

CHAPTER 6

The lost decade; unfocussed regulation, 2000–2012

6.1 Do the taps need changing; Or the washers renewed?

Getting a better deal for water customers[1]

European Policy Forum, April 2007

Hose-pipe bans and rising prices are not what customers want. Investment is high; the water environment is being transformed: but those who pay the bills are wondering whether they are getting value for money.

The basic plumbing of water regulation seems sound, but market forces need to be strengthened to serve the interests of customers. It is now time to make a real effort to strengthen market competition. This would introduce innovation, challenge, and the development of better process and improved products. It would reveal information that is neither collected nor understood by buyers and sellers in monopolistic markets. It is the best option to improve customer service and keep down prices.

A better functioning market would liberalise supplies, particularly in south-east England.

This will require leadership by regulators, active support from ministers and an entrepreneurial response by companies. While the energy and telecoms sectors have been transformed by harnessing the power of the market, water has lagged behind. It should learn from other areas.

The key element is to replace competition by negotiation with competition by regulation. Under the present "retail-minus" arrangements incumbents have been able to prevent entry by competitors by "offering" them very low margins. They should be replaced by arrangements designed to allocate costs more fairly, using costs based on analysis of activities, not on estimates of marginal cost.

The application of pricing principles should be policed by regulators. This is the approach that we are using in Scotland to allow for access of new suppliers of retail (billing, customer and value-added) services for non-household customers (business, schools, hospitals and local authorities). If this does not work, legal separation of the ownership of vertically integrated regional monopolies, on the lines of what happened in the energy markets, will be required.

To ensure public support, such changes must take place within a framework of prices that are relatively stable, in relation to inflation and to the growth of household incomes.

The last 15 years have seen some £50 billion spent on capital projects in the water industry. This has significantly improved our rivers and our beaches; they are now in a good state. It has improved tap water above the standards of much of the bottled water we buy in our supermarkets.

How much further and how much faster do we need to go? Customers need to be protected from hasty implementation of environmental legislation, specifically from overzealous implementation of EU Directives – particularly where this would involve increases in carbon emissions. While continued investment is crucial to improvement of the water environment, we must accommodate the speed of improvement to the depth of our pockets.

In planning this investment, we must keep our eyes on the cost of the finance required. We have been through a benign period, when gearing has risen from a very low level at privatisation to quite high levels, in some cases up to 85%. And interest rates have fallen. More gearing may be possible, but risks are growing and we may soon find ourselves facing a rising marginal cost of finance.

The basic model created in England and Wales is now being

applied to publicly owned water in Scotland and Northern Ireland Customers now have their own independent regulators, the Water Industry Commission for Scotland and the newly formed Northern Ireland Authority for Utility Regulation.

Bills in Scotland are rising by less than the rate of inflation while financing a large environmental improvement programme. Customers must insist that incentives are developed to drive efficient behaviour and that adequate public funds are available to finance investment. Unless both can be guaranteed, some change in ownership, while remaining under public control, seems inevitable.

TODAY'S CHALLENGES

Watery issues are coming to the fore in the utility world. Are there too many leveraged take-overs from abroad? Is leverage too high anyhow? Is it time for consolidation into a smaller number of companies? Are capital market pressures lessening as fewer companies are listed? Why is competition not working – as it is in energy and telecom? What should be done about regular water shortages in south-east England? Are the pressures for ever higher water and wastewater quality straining the framework initiated in 1989? Is there a growing affordability issue? Is the scope for comparative competition diminishing as company performance converges? Are there problems in the information provided? And how do regulated publicly owned water businesses in Scotland and Northern Ireland fit into the picture?

Do all the taps need changing? Or just some washers? Are we talking about matters of behaviour – or of structure? Are there the right incentives for change? This needs to be investigated in a questioning way, not rushing towards answers, remembering that there is a continuing political interest in the monopoly supply of water, especially when there are shortages and hose-pipe bans. I will argue that while the basic plumbing is sound, the competition and supply taps – or perhaps it is a mixer tap, because both are closely connected – do need radical re-engineering. And a few taps seem to have become leaky as a result of "events".

The provision of water services is structured similarly, but owned differently, in the countries of the United Kingdom. In England and Wales (E&W), suppliers are private companies (equity owned in England and a mutual – technically a company limited by guarantee – in Wales), while Scottish Water is a public corporation and Northern Ireland Water is a government company. The regulatory arrangements are broadly similar – economic regulators, the Water Services Authority (Ofwat), the Water Industry Commission for Scotland (WICS) and the Northern Ireland Authority for Utility Regulation (NIAUR) set price limits subject to appeal to the Competition Commission and have duties with respect to competition.[2] The quality regulators – water quality, abstraction and compliance with discharge consents – have broadly the same functions in all three jurisdictions. The E&W structure dates from 1989, the Scottish structure from 2005, although in 1999 a Water Industry Commissioner was appointed to advise Scottish ministers on price limits for Scottish Water. The regime in Northern Ireland comes into operation this year.

THE NEW MODEL OF THE 1990s

A successful new model for the utilities was created at and following privatisation. Gone was the old nationalised model, where ministers appointed the "right" people to operate statutory monopolies in the "public interest", subject to general directions by ministers that were never given, and to financial controls that were rarely met. Sponsor Departments, not seen as regulatory departments, struggled, usually unsuccessfully, with policy issues. The Treasury expended much effort on economic and financial arrangements, notably in the White Papers of 1961, 1967 & 1976[3]; but with few practical consequences.

The arms-length arrangements that were envisaged by Herbert Morrison did not work. Ministers spent little time on strategy, being more concerned to respond to events and to intervene to achieve particular ends, such as compliance with pay policies. To quote an influential paper by Stephen Littlechild, ministers failed the "Sed quis custodiet ipsos Custodes?"[4] test[5]. The industries became the priests of supply, with few doubts about what was good for their consumers. It is always worth reminding ourselves of the failures of the nationalised model – Industries were big on aspirations and poor on delivery – and the need to preserve the devolution of accountability and decision-making of the new model.

In this new model, ministers moved to a new arms-length relationship, where the purpose of the companies was to use commercial skills to meet the objectives of customers (not, please, consumers), subject to external regulation by a new breed of public servants with specific statutory duties, acting independently from ministers[6]. These regulators were to enable, promote or facilitate competition, and in the meantime, to protect customers by limiting prices and establishing proper incentives under an RPI-X regime.

Water was special among utilities because of the scale of collective objectives[7], in the form of environmental objectives, largely, but not exclusively, emanating from the European Union (EU). It was necessary to disentangle these collective objectives from the objectives of customers. This was done at successive price reviews, by a public exchange of letters between the regulator and the minister. (The X in RPI-X was decomposed into X & Q where Q related to the cost of statutorily imposed water and environmental standards.)

In specifying desired collective objectives, ministers would set out the outcomes that they want to see achieved, not the details of implementation, nor the exact way that they should be achieved. The specification of the outputs that would achieve those outcomes and the dedication of the inputs to deliver them would be left to regulators and suppliers respectively.

The distinction between the objectives of citizens as customers, and those of citizens as guardians of the environment, is crucial to the public supervision of the industry. Customers benefit from an amalgam of competition and price control; environmental guardians from quality regulation. There are trade-offs between the two sets of objectives, different weightings of citizens' objectives are involved and incentives are different in each of them.

Water was also special because the legislators of 1989 thought that competition would only develop slowly. They therefore inserted special provisions that would protect the scope for comparative competition. Mergers above a threshold were to be referred to the MMC (now the Competition Commission). After several hearings, it became accepted that while some mergers should be blocked, others should be subject to remedies to ensure benefits to customers that would not, in the situation of a vertically integrated monopoly, otherwise accrue. The legislation has not, contrary to oft-expressed views from the City, prevented sensible consolidation of water companies. There are now 22, compared with 39 at privatisation.

The key benefits of the new model are:

- clearer accountability and much greater transparency,
- greater efficiency by suppliers, and more investment, both to improve efficiency and to improve the environment.

An indication of its success is that it is now being applied in the publicly-owned water industries of Scotland and Northern Ireland.

So far, these benefits have been achieved by regulation, not, with the exception of lower prices for large users, by competition. The plumbing is a distinct improvement on what was there before, but it is timely to improve it further – by re-addressing the competition framework in the light of experience.

BETTER REGULATION

Before doing this, I will go quickly through a number of issues where the regime may need to adapt to changing circumstances – matters involving changing washers rather than taps.

First, I think that it is timely to revisit the price/quality trade-off

In the early days of regulation, I was insistent that there were economic limits to the speed at which environmental improvements should be introduced. When living through several years of RPI + 5 price increases, and run-away increases in the south-west, I argued that customers would be unhappy at price increases in excess of inflation or the rate of growth of household income. It was our aim – and we achieved it – to stop this escalator in the Price Review of 1994. In 1999, it was our strategy to transfer a large proportion of the efficiency gains made by the companies to customers, so that prices came down and stayed down; but we continued to finance a large programme of quality enhancement.

There may be a growing "affordability" problem. Water bills are becoming more onerous for vulnerable groups and there are limits to the amounts that the bulk of customers are willing to pay without complaint. Customers may need to be protected against paying for cost-ineffective or ill-judged environmental improvements; there should be no question of imposing "stealth taxes" though over-zealous interpretation of EU Directives.[8]

There is also a growing debt problem although in part this may be a result of the outlawing of budget payment devices. There is some help for customers on metered supplies who are receiving social security benefits. But the pleas from consumer groups for extension of social security payments in this area are likely to fall on deaf ears. In Northern Ireland there are special arrangements to cap bills for low income households, but the Treasury has made it clear that they will not be extended to Great Britain.

I suggest that the strategies – for both regulators and companies – for the 2009 Price Reviews should involve an objective for the prices charged to customers. We have one in Scotland, namely to avoid inflation-busting price increases for household customers. In England & Wales the numbers might be different. This approach need not involve stopping environmental improvements but rather tailoring the speed and the precise implementation of the EU Water Directives – taking appropriate account of emissions of CO2 and other greenhouse gases – to an investment programme that is consistent with broad relative price stability. The crucial matter is often not the EU Directive as such, but the interpretation that UK government officials put on it.

We in Scotland are also concerned with the achievability of the scale of the investment programme – the biggest per capita in the Kingdom. In particular, significant increases in the price of construction will benefit no-one save contractors and land-owners.

Secondly, financing and cost of capital are rising up the agenda

At privatisation, commentators expected a high cost of capital because of the then perceived need to rely on equity finance. This happily proved ill-founded; debt became increasingly available on a large scale and companies have become increasingly highly geared.

These developments have progressively reduced the average cost of capital, while the marginal cost of capital has been much lower, being related to the return on debt alone. But how much further can gearing go, before it hits the buffers, requiring expensive equity finance, or leads to undesirable increases in risk for customers? I was ridiculed when I suggested that gearing could be 50% or even 75%, but the laws of arithmetic may be more difficult to shift than City perceptions.

Risks are already high for holders of equity, but will they become excessive for other stakeholders? Unless leverage increases further, the continuation of a high capital improvement programme will involve a higher marginal cost of capital than the industry has been experiencing.

It may seem odd to attract finance by a tax shield resulting from a relatively high rate of Corporate Income Tax. But while reducing the tax shield would reduce incentives for high gearing and so reduce risk, it is not clear that a lower rate of Corporate Income Tax would reduce prices to customers.

It may now be necessary to recognise that investment in the water industry since 1980 has been particularly high in order to deal with a back-log and need not continue permanently at quite the same level. What seems important is to achieve a steady, and affordable, long term programme, not to push short-term expenditure up against a rising marginal cost of capital, in isolation from wider economic objectives.

At the technical level, estimates of the cost of capital need some attention. What has become a standard procedure, the adjustment of a longer-term weighted average cost of capital by the financial indicators current in the market at the time, can be a messy business. Perhaps we should take a cleaner look at current market data relevant to companies that wish, or are required, to retain investment grade status, and provide specifically for embedded debt.

Allowing for embedded debt, or using some other method of allowing for the necessary costs incurred to meet required outputs, may be necessary to provide a reasonable return for long term investment in fluctuating market conditions. While the efficient market hypothesis may not do all that is claimed for it, it is scarcely the job of the regulator to second-guess the market, – particularly if allowing for embedded debt can correct original expectations.

Where companies are listed, it is possible to check estimates of the cost of capital by comparing a company's stock market valuation with its Regulatory Capital Value (RCV). There are two developments here; fewer companies remain listed, but diversification seems to be giving place to concentration on the core business. Does this matter? I feel relatively relaxed. It was never easy to use Tobin's Q in this context; the stock market valuation of a diversified company required a complex adjustment, it was never clear how financial indicators fitted in, and stock market expectations have been volatile.

In the absence of measures of public sector risk, we in Scotland make use of Ofwat's estimates of the cost of capital to provide market-based measures of risk in the provision of water services. For the 2009 Strategic Review of Charges, we will discuss these matters with Ofwat, with a presumption for using E&W comparators to identify the then current situation and allowing for embedded debt in line with our long term approach to capital investment planning.

Thirdly, questions are being raised about merger policy and the associated issue of comparative competition

These issues are entwined. There is some clustering of companies close to the efficiency frontier. The various econometric models used never give quite the same answer. The scope for cost savings in England & Wales, but not in Scotland & Northern Ireland, may now be lower than in the early days of privatisation.

Neither of these arguments seems to me to point to a retreat from comparative analysis, nor to a change in the broad thrust of merger policy. There are still differences in the costs and performance of the companies. They are driving better performance and influencing executive pay. For regulators in Scotland & Northern Ireland these comparisons are crucial.

These comparisons provide challenges (sticks) as well as incentives (carrots). Both are important. Unpublished work by Martin Cave and Fabrizio Erbetta suggests that the shock of the 1999 price review was an important element in driving efficiency.[9]

Should market competition develop, the situation may change. Disaggregation of the present vertical monopoly could allow certain elements to be exposed to competition. In those areas, the special merger arrangements might give way to the merger rules used in other parts of the economy; although the existing approach would remain relevant for the natural monopoly elements to be found in distribution networks.

Fourthly, institutional and management incentives need wider application

Where there is private ownership, the regulatory regime is rich in incentives – provided that they are left to work and not overridden, or confused, by intervention and exhortation. The big incentive, that to customers to use water more wisely as a result of volumetric charging, is slowly being put in place, despite negative ministerial action and more progress may be expected.[10] Ministers have now consulted on proposals to make it easier for metering to spread, in areas of water shortage, thereby partially removing the restrictions that they imposed when coming into power in 1997. Judging by history, this issue will require continued attention by regulators.

Where there is public ownership, incentives need to be developed for both institutional and individual behaviour. In Scotland, the Commission has developed a quasi-equity buffer that can cushion the effect of new obligations and provide an outperformance fund to be available for risks falling on the owner, the Scottish Executive, and so avoid customers paying twice; that can provide resources for management bonuses; and in the future perhaps, that could be used to pay "dividends" to customers on the Glas Cymru model.

The formulation of a longer-term approach to capital investment and the prices paid by customers would provide a framework of incentives for the Quality Regulators, such that they would choose those projects that offered the bigger environmental returns, rather than campaigning to maximise the size of the environmental programme with limited concern for its cost-effectiveness or for its consequences for customers.

Fifthly, information needs to be more closely integrated into decision-making

Transparency has been the hallmark of the new model. Regulators rely on it. Ofwat put great effort into the specification and the analysis of comparable information on companies' costs and performance. This is a necessary defence against information asymmetry, and can prevent companies from outwitting regulators. While a company may know more than the regulator about its own costs and performance, a system of well-based comparisons means that it will know less than the regulator about other companies' costs and so can be effectively regulated through consideration of what has been achieved by those other companies.

This has, of course, been given much greater leverage because of the pressures that the capital market has put on all companies to improve their dividend paying ability. They have driven improvements in customer service and in operational and capital costs.

Recent suggestions of dubious information are disturbing. Regulators must take proportionate steps to ensure quality of information – recognising that some information, e.g. on leakage, is inherently uncertain, especially where companies do not have a well-based household consumption monitor. But the power of good information should go further and drive management decisions. The concerns about information appear to have led to strengthening of internal checks but I hope that this will extend to the involvement of non-executive Directors, who should play a valuable role in challenging executives.[11]

Information is not, of course, a free good. It takes time to compile and time to understand. There can be too many data as well as too few. If information is to be really useful, it must be both accessible and comprehensible to the Boards of Regulatory Agencies and to the Boards of Regulated Companies. If regulation is left to regulatory departments in both Regulatory Agencies and Regulated Companies it risks becoming a numbers game. Unless senior executives are fully engaged, information will not be properly used and both sides will suffer.

Information also needs to be communicated to the public, primarily through the media. Public Relations Departments are a necessary complement to Analytic Departments. Neither can be fully effective on their own.

Information should be dynamic, reflecting changing circumstances. This seems to me to be particularly important with respect to customer service, where I hope that companies will be innovative in finding out what their customers want and are ready to pay for.

COMPETITION AND MARKET FORCES

The operation of a market goes well beyond the confines of neo-classical economics; it involves innovation, challenge, the development of better process and improved products. It involves the uncovering of information neither collected nor understood by buyers and sellers in monopolistic markets. Competition is an essential element in a well functioning market; it is not just a way of sharing out existing customers or existing supplies, but makes a major contribution to the expansion of supply, both in quality and quantity.

Vertically integrated regional monopolies are scarcely likely to welcome entrants eroding their markets, nor do they have an incentive to buy water from other suppliers. Markets also require measuring devices, i.e. water meters. These are widely spread among non-household customers, but for a competitive market to function well in the household sector would require an increase in meter penetration.

There is much to work out to achieve a fully functioning model, and there will doubtless be some devil in the detail. But I believe that the broad thrust should be to follow the successful energy model. Meanwhile, there are some interesting comparisons to be made here between the situations in E&W and Scotland – comparative competition among regulators.

England & Wales

Ofwat has told ministers that competition is not working to its full potential. It is true that the legislation governing inset appointments – the creatures of the 1989 & 1992 Acts has not led to much entry – although prices for large customers fell substantially. E&W ministers legislated in 2003 to restrict competition and have been reluctant – for many years – to improve the threshold for choice. There is little apparent activity, even in the form of complaints about uncompetitive activity. A fundamental reason may be that under present arrangements, competition can only arise by negotiation – a negotiation where incumbents hold most of the cards.

Competition is not actively facilitated by regulatory action; in particular, incumbents have believed that they can set access prices that avoid any prospect that assets would be stranded. There is no incentive for vertically integrated companies to welcome entry by specialist suppliers, e.g. those with access to supplies of water. A "retail-minus" approach has enabled them to avoid the usual challenges and pressures of competition – pressures that, like the prospect of being hanged, concentrate the mind. – and if they don't, mean replacement by someone else. Comparative competition could never be so effective.

Scotland

The situation is different in Scotland. The 2005 Scottish Act is also restrictive, as in England & Wales excluding household customers, although there is no threshold and sewerage is included. But the Commission has opted for full separation of wholesale and retail operations, creating a level playing field that is open to any entrant that can demonstrate competence.

The Commission has recently published the codes it is minded to use for trading and for operational coordination between wholesale and retail. It is in the process of establishing a Central Market Authority, following the example of the electricity market, but keeping the mechanics as simple as possible.[12]

At the next price review, price control will shift to the wholesale operation of Scottish Water (SW), leaving retail activities that account for some 10% of costs open to competition. When SW's newly formed subsidiary, Scottish Water business stream (SWbs) can satisfy that it is properly at arm's length from its wholesale supplier, SW, it will be eligible for a permanent Licence. This Licence will include the need to declare any commercial agreement between SW and SWbs and to ensure that the pricing of those arrangements properly reflects the costs incurred.

Regulation, not negotiation

Setting limits to the wholesale price paid by all entrants is only one method of superseding negotiation by regulation. Incumbents have demonstrated their protectionist instincts. Regulators could take a more active part in establishing transfer prices. This might take the form of willingness to settle disputes on the basis of the application of known criteria. Bigger cases may be more complex involving wider application of the arrangements for determining bulk supplies.

The 1998 Competition Act has the potential radically to change our economic life – equivalent to the abolition of Resale Price Maintenance 40 years ago.[13] A legal requirement that utilities must provide access on fair terms to an essential facility gives great leverage to regulators seeking to promote competition.[14] The ECPRgfa terms that are believed to be implied by the 2003 Act are fair only to incumbents.[15] But, as became clear during the hearings at the Competition Appeals Tribunal, the Act refers to "avoidable", not to "avoided" costs.[16]

I have seen it said that the whole of the 2003 Act may fall foul of EU Competition Law. It sits uneasily beside the attempts of the Commission to strengthen competition in European energy markets. There is now an opportunity, and a need to start again – reverting to the 1998 Act. This should at least involve more active regulatory involvement in influencing the prices that apply to transfers between different parts of vertically integrated systems.

Those who doubt the efficacy of this approach may wish to seek legal separation of different functions following the example of British Gas. It was only when the approach to competition in the energy market switched from negotiated to regulated competition and British Gas was broken up that rapid progress took place, culminating in the extension of competition to household customers.

Expanding supply in areas of shortage

Strengthening the market also offers the best chance of solving the supply situation facing South East England. Metering may help the "management" of demand, but also gives signals for supply to be expanded. Customers should be able to use water provided that they cover the resource cost of providing it.[17] Where metered, they should be able to continue to be able to use hosepipes until a drought order is imposed. If proper transfer prices are set, there is no need for a national grid. Companies should not be able to avoid penalties if they fail to supply customers, even when a drought order is in operation.[18]

Leakage control may help, but we are in danger of putting too much weight on this fashionable instrument. In particular we are in danger of inventing a new catch-all approach by aiming for a "sustainable"[19] level of leakage that may simply have the effect of pushing problems under the carpet at considerable cost to customers. Ifas abstractions are thought to be environmentally damaging, this can be dealt with by tradable abstraction rights.

An independent retailer has many more incentives than an incumbent supplier to provide assistance to customers experiencing a shortage of supply, either by reducing demand without prejudicing essential activities, or otherwise helping to get incumbents to face up to their responsibilities, rather than hiding behind generalised excuses. Judging by history they are likely to be more effective than consumer councils.

OWNERSHIP AND INCENTIVES

Does ownership matter? Most definitely. The switch from political ownership in 1989 changed the incentive structure radically, and for the good.

Politics is, rightly, a world of multiple objectives and short-term pressures. It is rightly concerned with the protection of vulnerable groups from the winds of economic change. Business is much more focussed on more easily measured bottomlines. The balance between the two is one of the great strengths of an open society.

Incentives

Privatisation reduced the power of ministers to intervene and forced them to be clear about their objectives.

Experience has shown the power of the independently regulated equity model, but the successful emergence of Glas Cymru has shown that this success can be extended to a non-equity model. Glas has also developed the valuable innovation of paying "dividends" to customers.

As we have seen in Scotland, much can be done within a public sector model to improve efficiency.[20] Incentives have been strengthened by the creation of a quasiequity buffer, a gilts fund and an assurance that customers will not pay twice, i.e. that failure to perform will, as in E&W, be met by the owner, in this case the Scottish Executive, and not by the customer. The quasi-equity buffer will protect customers against relatively minor changes in environmental obligations. The gilts fund will allow the financial results of outperformance to accumulate to pay for underperformance and other adverse shocks without requiring contributions from customers.

Further progress is needed for the public sector model to work for customers in a fully effective way. Ministers may need to re-think their position as owners, perhaps taking their lead from the behaviour of owners of private sector businesses. And negative effects of public ownership should be avoided. For example, the pay policies that are now emerging in the public sector should not prevent recruitment and retention of staff. Nor should it have taken 18 months in Scotland to agree a bonus scheme that rewards outperfomance of the regulatory contract.

Governance

Ownership also matters because of the importance of good corporate governance. There is the potential, in the plc model sector, for the use of well-qualified and independent non-executives in a decision making capacity. Regulators should encourage their involvement in regulatory issues. I would also like to see owners, e.g. infrastructure funds, play a greater role in important regulatory issues.

Finance
Ownership is also important because of the provision of finance. Under public ownership, the provision of finance is subject to public expenditure controls, controls that inhibited environmental improvements for many years and could do so again. But once the money is voted, no further checks are made on how it fits into the business plan. By contrast, banks lending to private water companies are more flexible about the amount, but actively ensure that it will be well used.

The issue of financing investment from capital markets rather than from public finance is now back on the agenda. Much recent investment has been financed by PFI/PPP schemes.[21] These schemes may have served useful purposes but in future could prove expensive. Meanwhile Scottish Water's investment programme requires lending from the Scottish Executive of some £200million/ year as far ahead as the eye can see. As pressures on public expenditure are intensifying, now may be the time to consider ways to raise this money directly from the markets. This may involve adjustments in ownership, provided that it can be done within an essentially public sector framework

NEXT STEPS
This paper has covered a lot of ground and it is now time to pull the threads together into three directions for action, recognising that the priorities will be different in different areas.

The most urgent task is to make progress on enhancing the role of the market, primarily, but not exclusively, by promoting competition. This will require leadership by regulators to ensure that the costs of the various elements in the vertically integrated chain of supply are disentangled and made transparent, either by regulating transfer prices or enforcing legal separation. It will require ministers to facilitate, no longer to delay the spread of metering. It will require companies to take positive steps, as did Anglian and Cambridge, to increase meter penetration rather than to worry about the loss of revenue certainty. It will require a more positive approach all round to expansion of supply, not to rely exclusively on traditional reservoir building, negative "demand-management", or even "sustainable" leakage control.[22] It may involve initiating a system for trading of abstraction rights. If ministers want to preserve crosssubsidies in the household sector, they should be explicit about what they want and take actions that would be transparent.

Secondly the trade-off between price to customers and the speed of environmental improvement needs to go back on the agenda. At each price Review, there should be a strategy for the medium and longer term evolution of prices, with the interest of the customer at the forefront. These strategies should be linked to issues of affordability, the speed of environmental improvement, the rising marginal cost of capital, to long term investment programming and to sustainable delivery.

Thirdly, there are significant issues in Scotland, and, in due course, in Northern Ireland, about the need to introduce and strengthen incentives in the public sector model. This includes the role of the owner, the opportunity cost of public sector capital, the scope for borrowing from capital markets, and the use of the fruits of outperformance. Much progress has been made, but much still remains to be done.

Finally, it will be interesting to see how the three regulators, Ofwat, WICS and the Utility Regulator in Northern Ireland handle these issues. We now have the prospect not only of competition between suppliers, but between regulators. And that must be a good thing.[23]

NOTES

1. A regulator's perspective on the water industry, based on a talk, and subsequent discussion, at the meeting of the Regulatory Best Practice Group of the European Policy Forum on 22 February 2007.

2. Ofwat has a duty to promote competition where it is in the interest of consumers and has concurrent powers with the OFT. As competition remains a Westminster competence under devolution WICS has a duty to regulate retail access under Scottish legislation. NIAUR has a duty to facilitate effective competition whenever appropriate in water and sewerage.

3. Cmnd 1337 *The Financial and Economic Obligations of the Nationalised Industries*, April 1961; Cmnd 3437 *Nationalised Industries: A Review of Economic and Financial Objectives*, November 1967; Cmnd 7131 The Nationalised Industries, March 1978.

4. "But who is to guard those guards?"

5. *Controlling the Nationalised Industries: Quis custodiet ipsos custodies?* Series B Discussion Paper No. 56 Faculty of Commerce and Social Science, University of Birmingham August 1979.

6. See Frank Vibert *The Rise of the Unelected: Democracy and the New Separation of Powers*. Cambridge 2007 (forthcoming).

7. i.e objectives of the collectivity of people decided by a political process.

8. Ofwat lost in a Judicial Review case brought by three local authorities, Birmingham, Liverpool and Oldham and was obliged to order water companies to remove budget devices even where customers requested them. The High Court decision was not appealed, because ministers were thought to be ready to legislate on this issue.

9. *Regulatory and Efficiency Incentives: Evidence from the England and Wales Water and Sewerage Industry* 2006

10. During the 1990s, companies began to insist on the installation of meters for new properties and some, notably Anglian and Cambridge greatly extended household metering. Others dragged their feet and following their election victory in 1997, ministers acted to prevent companies imposing meters on customers save in restricted situations. Although the legislation provided for ministers to designate areas of water shortage, they appeared reluctant to use these powers, even where shortages were endemic. Attitudes seem to have changed, but how quickly will there be action?

11. When I was the regulator, I encouraged the appointment of good non-executive Directors and suggested a separate listing of the appointed business (the utility). I was generally disappointed in the quality of those appointed.

12. *The retail market for water and sewerage services: a policy statement* Water Industry Commission for Scotland, Market arrangements – a consultation paper (January 2007). Available at: http://www.watercommission.co.uk/WaterServicesBill/Licensing/Consultaion.asp

13. Following the passage of the Act, Ofwat used its powers to draw up, concurrently with the OFT, guidelines for its implementation in the water sector. I did not believe, given the attitudes of the ministers involved, and my experience with Departmental officials, that further legislation would do other than delay competition.

14. Efficient Component Pricing Rule.

15 An extreme form of retail-minus where access prices are related only to costs saved by the incumbent.

16. Christendom was split in the filioque clause; here we have the economics turning on 2 or 3 letters in the Act.

17. There is an air of paradox in the pleas from Consumer Councils for customers to economise on the use of water. It might seem more appropriate to emphasise the need to satisfy their legitimate demands.

18. Licences were amended after the 1995 drought to strengthen the ability of the regulator to impose penalties for failure to supply even when a Drought Order was in place.

19. One of my disagreements with ministers after the 1997 election concerned their desire to impose leakage targets on companies. In my view this would have drawn ministers into the details of water company management and have led them back to trying to regulate inputs rather than outputs.

20. *Efficiency incentives for public sector monopolies – the case of Scottish Water* Lecture by Alan D A Sutherland, London, 16 November 2006.

21. Private Finance Initiative / Public Private Partnerships.

22. It is quite unclear what might be involved in "sustainable" leakage control. In my view, anything going beyond the economic level of leakage should involve clear ministerial guidance that has been publicly costed before decisions are made.

23. *1066 and all that.*

CHAPTER 7

The story and the lessons

7.1   The regulation of water services in the UK

Utilities Policy 24, 2013

ABSTRACT

Water services in England & Wales were corporatized in 1974 and privatised in 1989. Quality regulators were appointed to ensure good quality of drinking water supplied and waste water discharged. An economic regulator, Ofwat was appointed to secure that water services were properly provided to customers and that they could be financed. The economic regulator was also charged to promote efficiency, enhance competition and protect customers. A similar body in Scotland was appointed in 2005, following corporatisation of water services in 1996 and the formation of Scottish Water as a Public Corporation in 2002.

Ian Byatt was appointed the first Director General of Ofwat in 1989 and the first Chairman of the Water Industry Commission for Scotland in 2005. In this article he gives his account of the regulation and draws some lessons from his experience. Regulatory strategy, he argues, not detail, is the key to success. Constant adaptation to changing circumstances is both inevitable and highly desirable. To be successful regulation requires careful explanation both to key decision-makers and to the public.

I was working in Government when water services were corporatized, and then privatised, becoming the first Director-General of Water Services (Ofwat) and then first Chairman of the Water Industry Commission for Scotland. While I have tried to write this article objectively I am scarcely a detached observer.[1] I hope that recollections from the coal face may be helpful in understanding why things happened and the lessons that might emerge. As is to be expected in human affairs, nothing is perfect; mistakes have been made and not all paths have run smoothly.[2]

First, some History. In the post war period, there were still small private water supply companies, regulated by dividend control, mainly in the south east England and on Tyneside. Water supply

[1]Readers may find it helpful to see the development of water regulation in the previous papers I have written:- "Ian Byatt looks at how ring-fencing worked in the privatised water industry and draws some parallels" in *Views on Vickers; Responses to the ICB Report Centre for the Study of Financial innovation* November 2011, "Regulation of Water Services: some recollections and some suggestions" in *Reflections on Regulation; Experience and the Future* Adam Smith Research Trust 2011, "Innovation, Incentives and Competition; a new deal for the water industry" Tony Ballance, Ian Byatt, Martin Cave & Alan Sutherland European Policy Forum February 2009. *Do the taps need changing? Or the washers renewed? Getting a better deal for Water Customers.* European Policy Forum April 2007. "Regulating Publicly Owned Utilities; Outputs, Owners & Incentives" Centre for the Study of Regulated Industries Occasional lecture # 20 April 2007. *Balancing Regulation and Competition in the Water Business in Scotland* Hume Occasional Paper # 67 David Hume Institute Edinburgh 2006. "Regulation of Water services." with Anthony Ballance and Scot Reid in *Handbook of Regulation*, (Eds.) David Parker and Michel Crew 2005. 'Managing Water for the Future: the Case of England and Wales' *Managing Water Resources, Past and Present: The 2002 Linacre Lectures*, Oxford 2004. "The role of UK competition agencies in the regulation and deregulation of utility service industries: reflections of a former regulator" *Utilities Policy, Volume 12, Issue 2, June 2004, Pages 57-59*. 'Water Regulation' in *Regulatory Review (2000)/2001: Millennium Edition* Centre for the Study of Regulated Industries. Bath 2001 Chapter 8. 'The Water Regime in England and Wales'. *Regulation of European Network Utilities.* Claude Henry Michel Matheu, Alain Jeunmaitre (Eds.). Oxford 2001. "Audition de M. Ian C.R. Byatt. Directeur général de l'Ofwat, Office britannique de régulation du secteur de l'eau". *Quelle Regulation pour L'eau et les Services Urbains?* Haut Conseil de Secteur Public. Paris 1999. Competition in the water and sewage industry. *Paper in Competition in regulated industries.* Helm, Deiter; Jenkinson, Tim (Eds.). Oxford University Press, 1998. Customer choice through competition in

the water industry. *Defence management journal* 2(1), December 1998, 90-91, 94 and *Public sector information*. Taking a view on price review; a perspective on economic regulation in the water industry. *National Institute review* 1/97 [159, January 1997], 77-81. Diversification, ring-fencing and transparency: How can corporate governance and incentives help? *Utility finance* Personal Viewpoint 1, February 1996, 15-17. *Financial Times* Personal View January 9 1996. The impact of EC directives on water customers in England and Wales. *Journal of European public policy* 3(4), December 1996, 665-674. Valuing improvements. *The utilities journal* January 1998, 35. 'Water; the PR process.' Paper in Utility regulation; challenge and responses. Beesley, Michael (Ed.). Institute of Economic Affairs, 1995. "La Regulacicón y el control de los servicios públicos en Gran Bretana" La experiencia de la Oficina de Aguas (Office of Water Services – OFWAT). *Revista Argentina del Regimen de la administracion Publica* 18(206), November 1995, 55-65. Economic regulation of the water industry in England and Wales. *Briefing notes in economics* March 1994, 1-4. Water regulation: the periodic review. A response. *Fiscal studies* 15(2), 1994, 95-97. 'Economic regulation in a political climate; the case of the water industry.' *Proceedings of the Manchester Statistical Society* 1992. UK Office of Water Services: structure and policy. *Utilities policy* 1 (2), January 1991, 164-171. 'The Office of Water Services: structure and policy.' Address given to the David Hume Institute. *Hume Occasional paper*, 16, 1990. *Accounting for Economic Costs and Changing Prices* (Chairman of Group), HMSO 1986. 'Market and Non-Market Alternatives in the Public Supply of Public Services: British Experience with Privatisation' in Francesco Forte and Alan Peacock (Eds.) *Public Expenditure and Government Growth*, 1985 (conference volume). 'The Framework of Government Control' in J. Grieve Smith (Ed.) *Strategic Planning in Nationalised Industries*, 1984 (conference volume). *The British Electrical Industry 1875–1914: the Economic Returns of a New Technology*, 1979. 'The Test Discount Rate and the Required Rate of Return on Investment' (with GP Smith and P Short). *Government Economic Working Paper No 22*, 1979 (Proceedings of seminar with experts from Government Departments and Nationalised Industries). 'Theoretical issues in expenditure decisions' in: M. Posner (Ed.) *Public Expenditure: Allocation Between Competing Ends*, 1977. For an outside view see Jose A Gomez-Ibanez *Regulating infrastructure* Chapter 9 "Price-Cap Regulation: the British Water Industry" Harvard University Press 2003 & Stephen Wilkes In the public interest; Competition policy and the Monopolies and Mergers Commission, Manchester 1999. Further light is cast in reports of the Monopolies & Mergers Commission, now the Competition Commission, both before and after privatisation, & reports by the National Audit Office.

[2]I am very grateful for comments by the reviewers of the article.

elsewhere was in the hands of the big municipalities, dating from the period of municipal enterprise in the second half of the 19th Century. Sewerage was a local authority function from the beginning, except in London, where specialised, non-local-authority public bodies were established. River management was developed by drainage boards and river authorities.

1. CORPORATISATION IN ENGLAND & WALES

Radical legislation led to the regionalisation in 1974, in England and Wales (E&W), but not in Scotland & Northern Ireland, of the municipal suppliers of drinking water and waste water collection, treatment and discharge. Ten Regional Water Authorities (RWAs) were created, each designed to cover a major river basin, charged with the integrated management of water, to cover environmental as well as supply issues.

They became subject to the regime that had been established in the post-war period for other utilities, such as electricity, gas, railways, airways & airports. A National Water Council was established, to co-ordinate the activities of the RWAs and to take responsibility for national policies. The remaining private water companies became agents of the RWAs.

Successive governments always found it difficult to stick to strategies for Nationalised Industries, either individually or collectively. There was a continuing clash between the Treasury, concerned with financial discipline and resource allocation, and the Government Departments concerned with social & sectoral policies. They were used to pursue counter-inflation policy, holding down pay and restraining prices. Mixture of motives and failure to resolve tensions led to inefficiency and poor financial discipline. The finance of investment was a recurrent challenge; lending to Nationalised Industries scored as public expenditure, competing with expenditure on education, health, defence & social security.

Pressures on public expenditure became acute in the 1970s. Poor management of the economy led to a request to the IMF for financial assistance.[3] The "price" was fiscal tightening, in particular the reduction of public expenditure. Capital expenditure by the newly formed water authorities was consequentially substantially reduced (see Fig. 1).

2. PRIVATISATION OF THE WATER AUTHORITIES

The reforms of 1989 involved the transfer of the environmental and river basin functions of the RWAs to a new public body, the National Rivers Authority (NRA), subsequently incorporated into a newly formed Environment Agency (EA). A Drinking Water Inspectorate (DWI) was established, soon becoming a free-standing regulator.

The 1989 reforms also involved the creation of the Office of Water Services (Ofwat), to regulate the supply of water services, i.e. the delivery of drinking water and the collection and disposal of waste water. The primary functions of Ofwat, to be discharged primarily by the setting of limits to the tariffs that companies could charge their customers, were to secure that the companies properly carried out their functions and could finance them. Subject to this, Ofwat was charged to promote efficiency, enhance competition and protect customers, assisted by regional Customer Service Committees (CSCs). The privatised companies operated under licences issued by the Secretaries of State for the Environment and for Wales (SSoS). These licences were to run for 25 years in the first instance and could be revoked on the advice of the regulator.[4] The companies were able to appeal to the Monopolies & Mergers Commission (MMC) against price limits set by Ofwat.

---

[3]The seventies began with the Conservative economic U-turn, continued with the Labour pay policy & industrial strategy, leading to an unmanageable run on the pound in 1976.

[4]Licences could be amended by agreement or, in the case of disputes after appeal to the MMC, now the Competition Commission.

279

Investment in England & Wales 1920 to 2010

Industry actual total gross capital expenditure from 1920 to 2010 with Ofwat's projections for 2006–07 to 2009–10

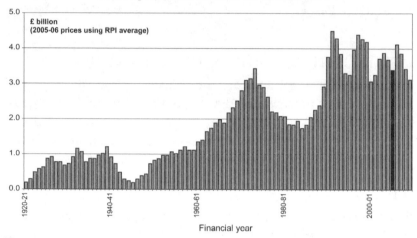

Notes

1. Original data for the period 1920 to 1980 was for water and sewerage companies only. These figures have been increased by 8% (based on a long term average of actual spend since 1980), to allow for expenditure by the water supply companies over this period.

2. Projected expenditure from 2006–07 to 2009–10 is Ofwat's projected gross capital investment included in the 2004 price limits assumptions.

Fig. 1. Investment in England & Wales 1920 to 2010.

3. THE CHALLENGES OF THE NEW REGIME

The changes made at privatisation involved considerable institutional change – involving fragmentation of governmental activities into separate regulators for abstraction and river quality (NRA), for drinking water quality (DWI) and price control and customer protection (Ofwat) and the emergence of international suppliers of finance in place of public finance – all with different objectives. Government, as architect of the system, set it in place, but left it to function without operational guidance.

The first challenge was to make the regime work, including making it politically acceptable. Water privatisation was unpopular especially when accompanied by significant increases in tariffs.[5]

It soon became clear that the privatisation price settlement was over-generous.[6] The prospective directors of the water companies had struck a good bargain with the SSoS, giving them, through rapidly rising price limits, the financial strength to diversify into other activities and into other parts of the world as well as to borrow from the markets to improve water and waste water quality and so meet European Directives.

The Government soon realised that the new arrangements could be exploited to finance water & environmental improvements. Under nationalisation, the Environment Secretary had to obtain Treasury agreement for borrowing; under privatisation, new obligations could be placed on water companies & Ofwat would sort out the financial consequences. Chris Patten's[7] advancement of the EC Waste water Directive, timed to coincide with a conference on the North Sea, had a major effect on South West Water, necessitating further increases in tariffs.

Government had legislated to abolish the use of the existing taxbased charging system for household customers after the year 2000.[8] Metering was the obvious alternative; it could create a proper relationship between suppliers and customers, introduce sensible incentives, and provide a charging structure for the introduction of competition. But because no "funding" had been allowed for in the privatisation price limits; most of the water companies, many of whom were opposed to volumetric charging, sat on their hands.

---

[5]The price limits set by the SSoS allowed prices to rise at a national average of 5% a year above the rate of in fl ation for the first 5 years, and 4% above inflation for the subsequent 5 years. General inflation was then running at uncomfortably high levels.

[6]The financial calculations that underlay the price settlement allowed for generous financial ratios, in particular wholesale debt write-off and a cap on gearing (debt/debt plus equity) of 35%.

[7]Now Lord Patten; then Secretary of State for the Environment.

[8]Bills were based on "rateable values", a form of property tax.

The CSCs provided more effective arrangements for customer representation than those put in place at corporatisation, which were primarily designed to maintain local representation when operating units were removed from local government.

To empower customers, the Government took two steps to encourage competition. First, it legislated to enable "inset" appointments, whereby a new supplier could take over a site away from the existing network and become a new supplier. Secondly, it stopped the creation of a national monopoly by encouraging comparative competition, and restricting the amalgamation of existing companies, by establishing a special merger regime,[9] – in a situation where economies of scale are limited.

4. OFWAT'S RESPONSE TO THE CHALLENGES

First, we needed to assemble the process for orderly discussion between Ofwat & the companies, Ofwat & the government & Ofwat & the quality regulators. Multipartite discussions proved dif ficult until the formation of the quadripartite (Government, Companies, Quality Regulators & Ofwat) group under the chairmanship of Neil Summerton,[10] for the specification of the quality obligations for the 1994 Periodic Review of Prices.

I initially visited all the companies to meet senior staff and arranged regional meetings which included the Chairmen of the local CSCs. I instituted a series of "Dear Managing Director" letters where we set out Ofwat's developing regulatory policies; I assembled informal working parties to discuss regulatory arrangements. My door was always open to Managing Directors; my relationship with the Board of the company was crucial. To the extent possible, we pressed the companies to act like private sector business in a competitive environment. A number of the Chairmen

[9]All mergers above a modest size had to be referred to the Monopolies & Mergers Commission.
[10]Head of the Water Directorate in the Department of the Environment (DoE).

282

of CSCs were chosen for their business experience.[11] They were supported by a powerful consumer affairs division headed by Michael Saunders.

Relations with the NRA were less harmonious. Lord Crickhowell,[12] the Chairman, did not favour a cost:benefit approach; he wanted to push ahead as fast as possible with quality enhancement. I wanted to keep bills acceptable to/affordable by customers, i.e. to increase no more than inflation, or the growth of household income.

Secondly, Ofwat used comparative competition to the full. We resisted amalgamations of large companies, such as Severn Trent's bid for South West. Where smaller mergers (the total number of companies fell from 39 to 22 in a decade) were involved Ofwat insisted on benefits for customers in the form of price reductions. The bigger cases had to be argued in front of the MMC under the terms of the special mergers regime.

Effective use of comparative competition required comparative information and proper analysis.[13] Ofwat built on the framework established in the nationalised period and in the special preprivatisation analysis; Chris Bolt[14] & Bill Emery[15] developed the system of Regulatory Accounts and July Returns that were

---

[11]I was hesitant about appointing traditional consumer representatives, not wanting to foster an anti-market atmosphere of protest and blame.

[12]Secretary of State for Wales in the Thatcher's Administration. Appointed as the first, and only, Chairman of the NRA.

[13]See Sanford V Berg *Water Utility Benchmarking: Measurement, Methodologies, and Performance Incentives*. London 2010. Benchmarking provided the regulator with powerful tools. But there is always a danger that it can grow into micromanagement, where regulatory analysts start to impose their views in how companies should deliver.

[14]Head of Charges Control Division in Ofwat, subsequently Rail Regulator, Chairman of the Office of Rail Regulation (ORR) & the PPP Arbiter for the London Underground. I had previously worked with Chris in the Government Economic Service.

[15]Head of Engineering Intelligence in Ofwat. Formerly with Yorkshire Water & subsequently Chief Engineer in Ofwat & Chief Executive of ORR.

the instruments both of monitoring and comparing performance. Econometric analysis was used to isolate special factors when making comparisons.[16] It was convenient to collect separate figures & conduct separate analyses of capital & current expenditure; this also fitted with the policy objective of increasing capital investment rapidly to meet new EC standards.[17]

This work enabled Ofwat to challenge the companies' bids, at successive price reviews, for ever-higher prices to finance their water quality and environmental obligations. The differences between companies that could be accounted for by explanatory factors were relatively small but there were huge differences between what the companies bid for and what they spent (see Fig. 2). Companies appealing to the MMC got little or no satisfaction.

Thirdly, Ofwat took the lead in arguing that water quality & environmental enhancements should be properly costed; the costs of EC obligations were rarely examined in other than a perfunctory way.[18] Ofwat published two consultative papers[19] showing the very large increases in bills that were at stake and arguing for proper consideration of costs by Ministers before decisions were taken.[20]

---

[16]Such analysis failed to find much in the way of systematic differences between companies, perhaps because they all contained a mixture of geographical characteristics and because individual companies quickly caught up on each other. Longer term assessment of productivity trends were vitiated by difficulty in constructing convincing water and environmental quality indices.

[17]The UK was alleged, by the environmental lobbies, to be the "dirty man of Europe".

[18]E.g. the costs of the adaptation of the EC Urban Waste Water Directive were initially estimated by the DoE at some £2 billion. As we moved into the preparations for the 1994 Price Review the numbers has increased to £10 billion. An exercise refining the requirements on the ground reduced this figure to £5 billion.

[19]The Cost of Quality 1992 & Paying for Quality: the Political Perspective 1993.

[20]It is often asserted that individual Member States have no control over the scale & costs of obligations set out in EC/EU Directives. But Government Departments are past masters of the process of winding-up costs which they could only justify with difficulty & then claiming that such costs were imposed by someone else.

Following the political fall-out from the substantial price increases in the South West, we ensured that the costs of new obligations were taken seriously at the 1994 Price Review.[21,22]

Fourthly, with the encouragement of Philip Chappell, formerly Morgan Grenfell and by then the first Chairman of the Thames CSC, Chris Bolt & I published two consultation papers,[23] arguing that the cost of capital was much lower than currently believed, in particular because gearing could be very much higher than assumed at privatisation,[24] and that the starting point for the Regulatory Capital Value (RCV), the base for the cost of capital, should be the price paid for the assets at privatisation, not the value in the Accounts. The Cost of Capital paper produced a furore, but the RCV proposals were more readily accepted, despite being considerably lower that the indicative capital values (IVs) calculated before privatisation.[25] We proposed to move away from reliance on financial indicators, whose "critical" values reflected

---

[21]Water prices became a major political issue in Devon & Cornwall, where several Conservative MPs were defending their seats against Liberal Democrat challenge. This political sensitivity has continued, resulting, recently, in special payments of public money to water customers.

[22]A later report (*The Independent Review of Charging for Household Water & Sewerage Services*), led by Anna Walker. Final Report (2009) debated the crucial issue of whether government or customers should be responsible for the financing of environmental improvements. It recommended that responsibility should stay with the customer − provided that new obligations should not be imposed on water companies without adequate costing.

[23]*The Cost of Capital* 1991 & *Assessing Capital Values* 1992.

[24]Rather than the 35% figure for gearing used for price setting at privatisation we suggested limits of 50%, or even 75%. This was regarded with horror/ incredulity in the City of London, but turned out to be a good predictor of what, in due course, happened.

[25]These IVs were calculated as the NPV of the future net income flow that would be available in the nationalised regime at the existing prices charges to customers and at the level of cost then incurred. The Water Authorities were sold for considerably less than the calculated IVs.

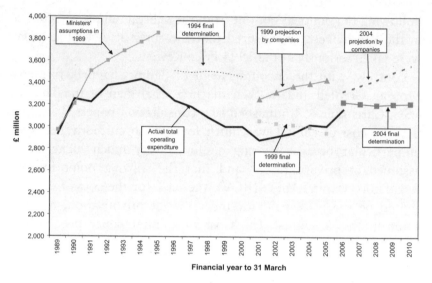

Fig. 2. Watch for information asymmetry.

fashions in financial markets, to a more analytic approach, the weighted cost of capital.[26]

Fifthly, Ofwat started a major consultation on systems of charging, primarily conducted through the CSC network.[27] Surveys showed differing views; metering scored better in the south than in the north, and was more popular among owner-occupiers than council tenants. We adopted a pragmatic approach: meters should be installed where simple and cheap, for example in new properties; customers should be able to opt for a meter on a fair tariff at a reasonable charge for installation; customers using large amounts

[26]The WACC had its own problems. It was a convenient way of expressing the information that was already in the financial markets but insufficient for the purpose of predicting the future cost of capital. Its use became tangled up with view about the "efficiency" of capital markets and the power of rational expectations. But it provided a useful grounding for the numbers to be used in price reviews.

[27]*Paying for Water; a Time for Decisions & the Director-General's Conclusions* March & December 1991.

286

of water, e.g. for swimming pools or garden watering, should pay by volume.

Tariffs were crucial, Those offered by the companies were unfavourable; in particular, standing charges were high. Troubles came to a head in Yorkshire where local authority & housing association tenants were metered as part of the renovation of their dwellings. Protest groups quickly formed; TV teams were invited into homes to film the babies in the bath. Ofwat then devised a "differential", the maximum extra charge that a company could make for a customer paying on a meter above the unmeasured charge.[28] As a result, metered bills dropped sharply; the Yorkshire problem was solved and an incentive created for customers to switch to a metered supply.

Customers began to switch, slowly but progressively, to paying volumetric charges.[29] Switching to metering reduced demand. Over a decade, charging households for their water services by meter became a widely accepted method of payment in England, but not in Wales, Scotland & Northern Ireland. It laid the foundation for a move towards compulsory metering after a decade of political foot-dragging, in areas of south-east England.[30]

Sixthly, Ofwat was determined to enhance the position & power of the customer. Customers need protection not only from monopoly water companies seeking high returns, but also from environmental groups, including Government Departments, pushing for water quality and environmental enhancement. Traditional political processes, involving the constraints of higher

[28]Installation of a meter cost money & meters needed to be replaced from time to time. Reading meters and sending out bills also cost money. These costs could be estimated objectively.

[29]The rate of transfer also depended on the policy of the company. Metering spread rapidly in the territory of Anglian & Cambridge Water resulting in welcome reductions in demand in dry area of the country.

[30]The incoming government in 1997 removed the right to impose metering on existing customers, except in water-stressed areas, subject to Ministerial agreement.

taxes were shifted from politics to regulation. CSCs took an active stance; the CSC Chairmen were closely involved in the first price review, reporting their views in the published documents. At the 1999 review, the Chairmen wanted to take a more distant stance, although I was able to get the views of a number of the CSCs from responses to Ofwat's pre-price review paper, *Prospects for Prices*.

Customers were the driving force behind my strategies for both the 1994 & 1999 Price Reviews, where I sought respectively to stop the escalator and to return the benefits of efficiency to customers. In 1994 price increases fell from 5% a year above inflation to 1.5% a year above inflation and in 1999, prices fell by 12%, with the prospect of stability in real, i.e. inflation adjusted terms thereafter.[31]

Seventhly, we made some progress, albeit hesitant, on the introduction of market competition. The original legislation involving a catch-22 situation; companies could only apply for bulk supplies if they were already licensed suppliers, but only become licensed suppliers if they had a bulk supply. This was remedied in the 1992 legislation, which also allowed for a wider use of "insets" for business and other non-household users. But I made the serious mistake of asking Ministers, for administrative reasons, to insert a threshold. Not only was the threshold, based on our imperfect knowledge, too high, but requests to reduce it as I had planned fell on deaf ears.[32]

---

[31]With the benefit of hindsight, I conclude that Ofwat was too generous in 1994, Prices probably should have been capped at inflation, completely stopping the escalator, and involving a correspondingly smaller price reduction in 1999. I would defend the record of the two price reviews taken together. I was criticised for being too tough in 1999, but subsequent events showed that the companies could cope adequately with 1999 situation. I note that the only companies to appeal to the Competition Commission in 1999 were Sutton & East Surrey and Mid-Kent. In both reviews the prices set provided sufficient scope for financing substantial investment in water & environmental enhancement.

5. DIVERSIFICATION & RING-FENCING

When privatised, many water companies planned to diversify, into other activities, such as waste management, and into water services in other parts of the world. They were concerned with the scope for making money; I was concerned with the risk of losing it to the detriment of the water customer. Ofwat's basic principle was to insist that the unregulated subsidiaries[33] should have no recourse to the licensed company; profits made in the unregulated activity would remain available for shareholders, who would absorb any losses. Each time a Water Company made an acquisition we took the opportunity to strengthen the licence conditions to avoid any unjustified transfers from regulated to unregulated business.

The big test came with the acquisition of Wessex Water by Enron, who wanted to enter the world water market; it believed that Wessex, a well-performing company of modest size, would provide credibility and expertise. I was nervous at Enron's ambition, but no knowledge of the wrong-doing that was later to emerge. We tightened the ring-fencing conditions in Wessex's license. This worked; when Enron collapsed, its bonds turned to junk while Wessex's bonds retained investment grade status, enabling it to continue to carry out its investment programme at no additional cost to customers.

This ring-fencing also enabled North-West Water and Welsh Water to acquire electricity companies, becoming respectively United Utilities & Hyder, and to separate back into water utilities. It enabled Macquarie Bank and other infrastructure funds to buy

---

[32]A threshold would enable us to learn how to handle applications for inset appointments and to make sensible decision about access prices when we had a number of other pressing problems on our hands. Thresholds had been set in gas & electricity and reduced when appropriate. I had underestimated the instinctive as well as the interested opposition to competition in water in any form.

[33]At privatisation, the Government had adopted a sensible corporate structure; floating a holding company, with the licensed water services company as one of its subsidiaries and scope for other activities to be put into other subsidiaries.

and sell water companies, thus bringing new skills into the water businesses and keeping down the cost of capital.[34] But experience revealed problems of corporate governance. Licensed water companies were subsidiaries; they had limited independence and limited ability to commit to actions vis a vis the regulator.

In the case ownership of companies owned by the French giants Generale des Eaux, now Veolia, Lyonnaise des Eaux, now Suez, and SAUR, power was in Paris, not in the English provinces. The regulator had to adapt to reality; sometimes the French companies came to Birmingham; I also went to Paris. It was crucial to be close to the decision-makers.

Similar issues arose with the British companies. Often the key decision makers were in the holding company: less often, in the licensed subsidiary. I encouraged the licensed companies to recruit powerful non-executives and to act as though they were free standing companies. But, ownership mattered.[35]

6. DIVIDENDS; AN UNDESIRABLE LOOP-HOLE?

The Licence charged the regulator to consider the borrowing position of a licensed company as though it was free-standing.[36] But, no expectations were set with respect to dividend policy. A free-standing company, when setting its dividend policy, might be expected to consider the financing of its future capital programme; but there were strong incentives on management to pay dividends

---

[34]Further study is required on the effect which the relative ease in buying water companies has on their management and hence on their delivery to customers.

[35]Further study of these relationships should yield some important conclusions on the differing patterns of contact between company & regulator and the lessons to be drawn from experience.

[36]This was an important issue when it came to assessing the cost of capital. Small companies, generally speaking, find it more expensive to raise capital than larger ones; in the early days, smaller companies were allowed a (somewhat) higher cast of capital. This produced some paradoxical results when small companies were owned by large ones.

to the holding company. This happened on a massive scale; some companies committed themselves to generous progressive dividend policies. At one point, I considered writing back, "excess" dividends into company balance sheets; but there are dangers in becoming involved with micro-management.[37]

7. YORKSHIRE WATER, SUPPLY PRESSURES AND LEAKAGE

1995, was a hot summer. Pressure on supply tightened and demand rose, largely for garden watering.[38] Companies such as Severn Trent changed their policy on metering, in particular insisting on the installation of a meter for households with swimming pools or using hosepipes and sprinklers.

Companies responded well, opening up old bore holes and using their grids to transfer water from one part of their area to another; there were hosepipe bans in some localities. Yorkshire Water, however, which had not completed its water grid and was experiencing a high level of leakage, got into real difficulties. As the rains declined to come, Yorkshire began to tanker water on a large scale up the Dales. The intensity of the traffic exacerbated customer's frustration and anger.

In the event, there were no cut-offs and no stand-pipes as there had been in 1976.[39] Ofwat set up an inquiry which found a number of deficiencies in Yorkshire's behaviour, including its corporate governance. Yorkshire had just paid a large £50 million dividend from the licensed company to the holding company. Following its inquiry, Ofwat reduced Yorkshire's price limits for the remaining years of the 5 year period, costing the company some £40 million. All of this was a direct benefit to customers. Yorkshire also agreed

---

[37]This issue deserves to be pursued further.

[38]Sales of hosepipes, etc. rose sharply in the summer.

[39]There was a major drought in 1976, just as post-corporatisation investment was rising. There were severe shortages in some area, necessitating shutting off normal supplies and the use of stand-pipes in the street.

to additional investment, to accelerate the completion of its grid, and to reduce its leakage to an economic level.

Leakage became a political issue in 1995. Frank Dobson MP, the Opposition spokesman, used Ofwat's estimates[40] of leakage to attack privatisation. He placed the issue firmly on the political agenda, committing a future Labour Government to action.[41] The companies responded sensibly by setting their own leakage targets and Ofwat suggested modest tightening. It also told the companies that they should follow Yorkshire by conducting value for money studies, seeking to identify where expenditure on reducing leakage was balanced by savings in running costs and investment in increasing supplies.[42]

The SSoS could set formal leakage targets, but only – as the law then stood – on the request of the regulator. That would have involved Ministers delving into the day to day operations of the companies at a local level and setting ambitious targets that could invite application for increases in price limits to finance yet another obligation.

When Labour returned to power in 1997, policy on utility regulation was reviewed. The outcome hung in the balance, but Ministers finally decided to keep the main elements of the existing system, maintaining the incentivising RPI-X arrangements, provided that the regulators thought this was in the public

[40]With a high margin of error, there were reasonable figures available for supply from water treatment works into transmission and distribution networks, but final consumption could not be directly measured for the majority of customers who paid on an RV (taxation) basis. Moreover, there was an incentive to overstate consumption to reduce the residual leakage figure calculated through estimates of residual figures in water-balance calculations.

[41]The Conservatives won the 1992 Parliamentary Election with a narrow majority. Since then the events of "Black Wednesday", when the UK was forced out of the European Exchange Mechanism (ERM) had increased the chances of a Labour victory in the 1997 Election.

[42]A template was available from work conducted by Yorkshire Water as recommended in the Ofwat inquiry.

interest. The main change proposed was to separate consumer representation from the regulator.

Labour's regret over privatisation evolved into a desire to reassert control through the regulator.[43] Incoming Ministers focussed on leakage. Ofwat had set its own leakage targets and all the companies had accepted them, but Ministers wanted to set their own. I declined to ask them to do this, but agreed to discuss (not consult on) proposals before making my final decisions.[44] The issue continues to regularly emerges whenever supplies are short; but Ministerial dictat has been avoided.

8. THE WINDFALL TAX & THE 1999 PRICE REVIEW

As the dust settled on the 1994 Price Review, it became clear that it had not fully dealt with the gains the companies had made at the privatisation settlement. Companies were also able to continue to make large efficiency gains. There was scope for a substantial transfer of greater efficiency to customers in the form of lower prices. We began to gear-up for a once-off price reduction (the infamous P_o, first year adjustment) – the scale depending on further analysis in the price review itself and on the scale of such new obligations that Minister might place on companies.

Meanwhile, incoming Ministers wanted to impose a Windfall Tax on all privatised utility companies to compensate for soft privatisations, on the understanding that it would not be repeated, and so risk raising the cost of capital. It also had the merit of healing political wounds.

---

[43]The Rail Regulator was eased out; his replacement had worked with Labour in opposition. The merger of Offer (electricity) & Ofgas (gas) into Ofgem (Energy) gave Ministers the opportunity to appoint a new regulator.

[44]The following year's discussions showed the wisdom of this; I was told by Michael Meacher (then the Water Minister) that the optimal level of leakage was 15% (the EA figure, presumably in all circumstances) & continued to make pragmatic decisions while requiring companies to improve their analytic work on optimal levels of leakage in different circumstances.

The price review involved an initial (P_o) price cut of 12% followed by broad price stability in real (inflation adjusted) terms over the five year period from 2000 to 2005. Initially, this was widely regarded as harsh, especially in the City, although none of the major companies appealed to the Competition Commission. Following it, companies made a renewed effort further to improve their efficiency – showing that avoiding the prospect of losses is a major driver of cost reductions.[45]

9. COMPETITION; LACK OF PROGRESS

The 1998 Competition Act,[46] changed the climate. Ofwat rapidly drafted guidelines for the implementation of the Act.[47] Unfortunately, progress was largely halted by the prospect of government legislation.[48] Ministers wanted to ensure that the scope for competition was restricted by the drafting of a section that came to be known as "the costs principle".[49] Ofwat also took a restrictive view in the Shotton case, taken by Albion Water against Welsh Water to the Competition Appeals Tribunal (CAT).[50]

The introduction of retail competition in Scotland seems to have led the Government to appoint Professor Martin Cave to investigate the scope for competition – and innovation – in the water industry.

---

[45]Erbetta & Cave Regulation & Efficiency Incentives; Evidence from the England & Wales Water Industry. Review of Network Economics December 2007, pp. 425-452.

[46]The Competition Act incorporated EU legislation on cartels and the abuse of dominant positions into UK law.

[47]Published by the OFT, with whom Ofwat had concurrent powers.

[48]A restrictive Act was passed in 2003.

[49]As suggested in the CAT case on Shotton, the section could be interpreted more widely, but Ofwat seemed to settle on a narrow interpretation, namely the Efficient Component Pricing Rule (ECPR) already rejected when argued in a case in New Zealand.

[50]The Competition Appeals Tribunal criticised Ofwat for not providing proper cost analyses.

His final report, recommended the introduction of competition at the retail level, further lowering of the threshold for insets and the development of greater trading of bulk water supplies,[51] perhaps along the lines suggested by Severn Trent Water.

Progress on inset appointments continued to be slow, although they have now become a useful regulatory tool, and after 20 years, there is now a firm promise from Government further to reduce the threshold and perhaps abolish it.[52] Government, however, is reluctant to do anything that might prejudice the ability to raise money, off-its-own-balance-sheet, for environmental projects.[53]

10. SCOTLAND

In 2006, I was appointed as the first chairman of the Water Industry Commission for Scotland, a body appointed to regulate a Public Corporation in a devolved jurisdiction, formed in 2002 out of a merger of the three Water Authorities which, in turn, were formed out of the municipal water and sewerage departments in 1996. Our prime task was to set limits to at Scottish Water's tariffs – a radical departure from the position where Ministers limited the prices that Public Corporations could charge.

The Commission took over from the Water Industry Commissioner[54] for Scotland, who was appointed in 1999 publicly to recommend price limits to Ministers. The Commission was also charged to implement the provision in the 2005 Scottish legislation

[51]Cave Review of Competition & Innovation in Water markets. Final report 2009.
[52]Government has shown extraordinary reluctance to use secondary legislation to reduce the threshold; despite continuous pressure from the regulator; changes have been both tardy & hesitant.
[53]The City has been strongly opposed to any vertical dis-aggregation of the water companies on the grounds that it could increase risk.
[54]Alan Sutherland was appointed Commissioner in 1999 & became the first Chief Executive of the newly formed Water Commission in 2005.

for the introduction of retail competition for all non-household customers.

When I came onto the scene, there were awkward tensions between the Chief Executive of Scottish Water and the Commissioner, now Chief Executive of the Commission. They had similar objectives, but incompatible styles. And there had been a clumsy assessment[55] of the water and environmental obligations of Scottish Water, which was then translated by Scottish Water into a hugely expensive capital programme that Scottish Water alleged would push up prices by 88%. The (former) Commissioner correctly believed that this involved gold-plating; the Commission proposed, and the company eventually accepted, a much lower figure for capital expenditure, which was consistent with modest reductions in tariffs.

This assessment was accepted with some reluctance; Scottish Water would do its best, but offered no guarantees. The upshot was the resignation of its Chairman, followed shortly afterwards by that of its Chief Executive. Scottish Water nevertheless continued both to cut its costs and dramatically to improve its customer service. Relations with the Commission improved and, under its new Chairman, Ronnie Mercer, Scottish Water developed its role as a successful business.

Rapid progress was then made on the introduction of competition, for all business and non-household customers. This has reduced costs, in both Scottish Water's wholesale and its ring-fenced retail business and reduced the costs incurred by customers.[56] There have also been improvements in customer service.[57]

---

[55]The Quality & Service (Q&S) assessment that parallelled the definition of quality obligations made in E&W at each price review.
[56]Glasgow City Council alone is already saving £1 million a year on its water bills.
[57]*Retail Competition in Scotland: an Audit Trail of the Costs incurred and the savings achieved* Water Industry Commission for Scotland (2011). See also *Regulation of the Water Industry and Competition in Water Markets – the Case of Scotland (UK)* Dipl.-Wirt.-Math. Nicole Annett Müller (PhD candidate, TU Dortmund) 2011 IWW Rhenish-Westphalian Institute for Water Research.

Recent events are casting a shadow. Scotland now faces public finance constraints and the Scottish Government has cut its lending to Scottish Water, reducing its investment programme while expecting it to contribute to reductions of carbon emissions by generating, directly or indirectly, electricity from renewable sources.[58]

11. CONCLUDING THOUGHTS

Regulation should start with high-level principles. They are conveniently set out in a UK government statement in April 2011.[59]

This involves goals: in the case of water, the overriding goal of the total regulatory system was the improvement of water and environmental quality to the benefit of customers. As this would involve higher and higher prices, it seemed appropriate for the economic regulator (Ofwat) to concentrate on customer protection and the promotion of efficiency.

Within this framework, regulation is about people as much as about process and about how the two interact. A balance needs to be struck, but it is subject to constant change: notions of equilibrium and optimality provide poor guides to action.

Regulation is politics as well as economics. Regulators have a

---

[58]See the Scottish Government's Hydro Nation paper. An alternative approach would have been to finance a public interest company from the capital markets. For this see my article in *The Scotsman* 23rd August 2011.

[59]The purpose of the Principles for Economic Regulation is to:

- reaffirm the importance of, and the Government's commitment to, stable and predictable regulatory frameworks to facilitate efficient investment and sustainable growth;
- set the framework for delivering greater clarity about the respective roles of Government, regulators and producers, and greater coherence in an increasingly complex and interlinked policy context; and
- set out the characteristics of a successful framework for economic regulation to guide policy makers in assessing future developments. Department for Business, Innovation & Skills (BIS) April 2011.

different constitutional position from politicians, enriching the separation of powers.[60] They must, however, be constantly aware of political issues, looking-out for political surprises while keeping their eyes on economic and business issues. Governments should set outcomes, not delve into implementation.

Consistency is a virtue, but circumstances change and regulators must adapt. They must stay flexible and respond in a timely way. They should, however, try, wherever possible, to act predictably. This implies constant explanation of what they are trying to achieve and why they have taken action. This must be sufficiently simple and sufficiently succinct to be properly accessible both to top decision makers and to the general public.[61] In Ofwat, we used the press, in addition to regular contact with individual companies, to raise issues, to indicate options and to promulgate decisions and policies.

Regulation itself will influence the operating environment; indeed to work well it must exercise a discovery function. Regulators, regulated companies and governments must learn to adapt to the interacting dynamic of change.

The regulated company, not the regulator, delivers services to customers. The regulator is only successful when the company is successful, i.e. when it is an efficient business unit providing satisfactory service to customers, measured by achieved performance. Regulators are, however, necessary to protect customers from both monopoly suppliers and from ambitious governments, notably, in the case of water services, in the environmental area.

Regulators must have a strategy that drives the regulatory relationships. Discussions (and negotiations) must involve key

---

[60]See Frank Vibert *The Rise of the Unelected; Democracy and the New Separation of Powers* Cambridge 2007.

[61]This requires presentational skills that are very different from the stream-of-consciousness consultation papers that have become increasingly unwelcome because too detailed in content and too vague on intent.

decision-makers and not become lost in regulatory detail; it is important always to remember that the most powerful deterrent to bad behaviour is a (public) threat to revoke the company's licence.

7.2   25 Years of Regulation of Water Services; looking backwards and forwards[1,2]

Utilities Policy 48, 2017

ABSTRACT

Sir Ian Byatt was the first regulator of the water and wastewater industry in England and Wales (Director General of Water Service) from privatisation in 1989–2000. He examines the experience of a quarter of a century of the regulation of water companies, concentrating on what worked well and where further developments are needed to deal with changing circumstances. He concludes that while RPI-X regulation, combined with comparative competition, worked well with respect to operating expenditure, the regulation

---

[1]This paper is an extension of the notes I delivered at the annual conference of the Regulatory policy Institute held at Merton College Oxford on 12/13 September 2016 I amended the notes in the light of the discussion at Oxford and further helpful comments on an earlier draft. An important contribution could be made by adoption, or adaptation, of a new procedure devised for the Australian electricity market, made in a lecture by John Pearce, Chair, Australian Energy Market Commission, and an insight by Stephen Smith in his presentation on the Evolution of Network Price Determination Processes. Further points emerged at a subsequent presentation by Thames Water at a European Policy Forum Roundtable on the financing of the Thames Tideway Tunnel. I am particularly grateful to Alan Sutherland, John Smith, Colin Skellett, John Banyard, Remy Prud'homme, Rupert Darwall, Martin Cave, Stephen Littlechild, Sonia Brown and Jonson Cox and to three anonymous referees for help in the drafting of this paper and to Julia Havard in editing the text.
[2]See my article on the Regulation of Water Services in the UK in *Utilities Policy* 24 (2013) for my account of my term of office from 1989 to 2000.

of capital expenditure needs enhancement to avoid overcharging of customers. He advocates the development of performance regulation, backed by project competition, where customers pay for quality enhancement only when they receive it.

Observing the progress of the revolution in Paris in the 1790s, Mme de Stael wrote:

Theory without experience, is only a phrase; experience without theory, is just prejudice.[3]

1. Early-stage liberalisation and market opening
The privatisation of Water Services (both water supply and wastewater disposal) in England & Wales[4] in the year 1989 was very unpopular, despite providing incentives for a large improvement in water quality. Ofwat, the newly created economic water regulator, helped to make it work by publicity and explanation. Explanation (transparency) was critically important, in simple ways that could be understood by a wide range of interested parties, not in the form of long and complex papers. The key audience was the paying customer.

This involved using the media. Not easy, but you can learn. A media presence is essential for an independent regulator. Regulators must manage the public agenda and deliver public signals to all stakeholders.

Did privatisation work well? Replies should be more nuanced: nothing stands still – nor should. Some things went well, and policy still needs to move on.

The politics is as important as the economics. It was not wise, at the privatisation settlement in 1989, to allow water companies

---

[3] *Of Present Circumstances.*
[4] Water services were not privatised either in Scotland or in Northern Ireland. They remain publicly owned but in both cases are regulated independently of Ministers.

to use their ungeared balance sheets to undertake often unwise diversification.[5] The more recent take-over of many companies by private equity infrastructure funds has also led to problems of perception, and so public acceptability. Institutions, along with personal and institutional networks, are crucial. So are personal and institutional incentives, often pulling in different directions.

At a periodic price review, the major issues need to come together and be considered in the round. Too much detailed modelling can inhibit wider customer involvement.

1.1. The regulatory office

The quality of the regulatory office is key; I was fortunate to have skilled and creative senior staff. Focus on the straightforward regulatory objectives was vital; mission creep was to be avoided. The regulator only does a good job when the companies do a good job.

We devised systems for collecting information, which stood us in good stead when making decisions. We appointed independent Reporters to challenge company information.[6]

We addressed four major issues in the early days; publishing consultation papers, with clear proposals for action:

- Paying for Water; Video, Analytic Papers and Director's conclusions (1991):
- Cost of Capital (1991) & Assessing Capital Values (1992):
- Cost of Quality (1991, 1993):
- Paying for Growth (1993).

Taking due account of the main responses, set the scene for our future work.

---

[5]Much money was lost in ill-conceived overseas ventures e.g. by Thames Water and North West Water. Welsh Water made politically unwise diversification into hotels.

1.2. Working with companies

I declined to work with the Trade Associations normally used by Government, preferring direct personal touch with the companies, visiting them regularly and always being open to their visits. I established working groups to test regulatory strategies. Things need to be talked through; regulators and companies need to listen to each other.

I visited the European Investment Bank to encourage it to finance privatised as well as state-owned utilities. We regularly briefed the financial analysts in the City of London, including Rating Agencies, on regulatory intentions.

Utility companies seem to respond better to challenges than to opportunities; the prospect of loss seems a more powerful incentive than the possibility ofgain. Managements deal with difficulties, but hesitate to innovate.[7] Regulators need to consider how best they can present challenges to drive better performances.

1.3. Working with regulators, ministers and parliament

The key networks relate to customer representation, water and environmental quality as well as to Ministerial policy. Good relations with, not subservience to, Government Departments (not only the Department of the Environment), were the key to accountability; remembering that there are different emphases between different Departments. The emergence of formal interactions between regulators and Parliament, which has its own, often conflicting, priorities, was a significant step in the public governance of utilities.[8]

---

[6]These Reporters were independent consulting engineers appointed in consultation with Ofwat, with a duty of care to the regulator. I would have preferred to pay them from Ofwat funds, but we had to make the best use of our budget.

[7]Sir John Hicks famously said that the pro fi ts of monopoly were a quiet life.

[8]Starting with *The work of the Directors General of Telecommunications, Gas Supply, Water Services and Electricity Supply Report by the Comptroller and Auditor General HMSO 1996.* An all-party Group was a useful pre-curser.

Ofwat cooperated with the Environment Agency[9] to check that big investment projects were on course. In Scotland, the Water Industry Commission for Scotland (WICS) developed an output-monitoring group to track capital expenditure. But recent events (see below) show that monitoring of environmental performance should be strengthened.

1.4. Working with customers

Initially customer representation was closely linked to regulation. The Chairmen of the Customer Service Committees (CSCs), appointed from across the political spectrum, came together in an Ofwat National Customer Council, which played a major part in the Ofwat consultations on metering, and attended the meetings where companies made representations on the 1994 draft price determinations. In contrast, the independent Consumer Council for Water has progressively lost authority, and influence, since its creation in the early years of the new century.

1.5. Paying for Water

At privatisation in 1989, household customers, with rare exceptions, were charged in relation to the domestic property tax, the rateable value (RV)[10] of their houses, irrespective of consumption. For many people, this was a matter of principle[11]; but the privatisation legislation forbad the use of RV after the end of the century.

[9]The regulatory functions of the nationalised Water Authorities (created from the water supply and sewerage functions of the Local Authorities in 1974) were removed at privatisation in 1989 and put in the hands of a newly created National Rivers Authority. (NRA). Five years later the NRA was incorporated into the newly created Environment Agency (EA). Neither the NRA nor the EA was formally independent; unlike Ofwat they reported to Ministers.

[10]Last assessed in the early 1970s based on the rental value of property in a situation where government policy had destroyed the rental housing market.

[11]A long-standing debate is whether water supply and wastewater disposal are economic or social services. Privatisation stressed the economic and business aspects.

Our consultation revealed different preferences, particularly between different regions and different tenure groups.[12] We advocated customer choice,[13] but found the metered tariffs in use were loaded against metering. Acting under our nondiscrimination powers, we required companies to reduce their volumetric charges so that the metered bill for average households was not significantly higher than the average RV bill. This led to significant reductions in metered bills and to an increased take-up of metering.[14]

The gradual switch to metering (still not complete) had a major impact on the demand for water, considerably reducing the scale of investment needed for enhancement of capacity, and so moderating general increases in customers' bills.[15]

1.6. Governance?

I believe that the single regulator, involving personal responsibility, is to be preferred to the Board. Regulators need advisers; I appointed a group of business advisers when Ministers decided to separate CSCs from Ofwat. But politics is personal, and wide visibility is essential to independence from Ministers.

People are crucially important. An interesting change in governance followed the break-up of the Welsh multi-utility Hyder. A public interest company was created that is much more customerfocussed than the impersonal, finance dominated infrastructure companies that have now taken over most of the industry. Particular individuals have played a key role.

[12]Fixed charges were favoured in the North, and among local authority tenants, while the South and owner-occupiers preferred volumetric charges.

[13]Under nationalisation, customer already had a legal right to have a meter, but tariffs were in the hands of companies.

[14]This also depended on the policies of individual companies. While, Anglian Water moved quickly to encourage metering; Thames Water waited for customers to take the lead and Severn Trent Water made a policy change at the time of the 1995 drought.

[15]A study by Wessex Water showed reductions in demand of around 17%, irrespective of tariffs. See Wessex Water website.

1.7. Industry structure

The privatisation structure of the ten water & sewerage companies and the remnants of 19th Century private water companies, mainly owned by French water companies, was (sensibly) derived from the transformation of the municipal supply of water and sewerage into nationalised authorities in the early 1970s.[16] Subsequent changes, such as the development of multi-utilities, did not prosper and were abandoned.[17]

A major change at privatisation was to take regulation of their environmental activities away from the authorities and put it in the hands of an environmental regulator, initially the National Rivers Authority, and subsequently, although not entirely happily, the Environment Agency.

A special merger policy was also introduced to preserve comparative competition. This ensured that any merger would be accompanied by a prior transfer of "claimed" efficiency to customers. Valuable to customers, it was regularly attacked by the City of London for limiting its mergers and acquisition activity.[18] Without those special legislative provisions, the ten regional monopolies, with the scope for comparative competition, could have been amalgamated into a single national monopoly.

There is little evidence of economies of scale in networks beyond a low level; indeed there are arguments for dividing the biggest company, Thames Water, into separately listed London

---

[16]The nationalisation of the municipal water supply and sewerage activities in 1974 into Water Authorities based on river basins, subject to the nationalised industry control regime, was the key organisation change of the second half of the 20th Century. The investment plans subsequently formulated by the Authorities and the National Water Council were aborted by the public expenditure cuts following the UK application to the International Monetary Fund in 1976.

[17]Both Welsh Water and North West Water bought electricity companies becoming, respectively, Hyder and United Utilities. Both were subsequently dissolved.

[18]Econometric analysis has failed to find economies of scale beyond a small size and there is some evidence of scale diseconomies.

and Oxfordshire companies, regulated under separate Licences.[19,20]

1.8. Incentives & efficiency

The UK introduced price cap (RPI-X) regulation for privatised utilities, in order to provide incentives for private sector enterprise and skills. Profit regulation was explicitly rejected. In water, this became RPI ± K, where RPI (the retail prices index) was a proxy for inflation and where K equals –X (efficiency) and + Q (water & environmental quality).

Prices were reviewed every five years and set for five years ahead. This provided powerful incentives to reduce operating expenditure (broadly a third of total costs of supply) and allowed for a substantial increase in the quality of drinking water and wastewater discharged to rivers and coastal waters.

Quality, both of drinking water and wastewater, rapidly improved. Customer service improved. Output, when adjusted for quality, rose by nearly 50% in the first decade of privatisation. Thanks to incentives, operating costs fell significantly although there was an increase in annuitized capital costs as a result of a doubling of investment.[21]

Experience showed, moreover, that the sticks of tough price review proved more powerful incentives to efficiency than the carrots of higher profits.[22] In setting price limits, regulators should

---

[19]See Financial Times 5th May 2017 p.9 for analysis of the performance of Thames Water. The issues confronting London and Oxfordshire differ in many respects.

[20]See *Thames Water ownership structure criticised after record fine*. Financial Times 24 March 2017.

[21]Saal, Parker and Weyman-Jones, *Determining the contribution of technical change, efficiency change and scale change in the English & Welsh water and sewerage industry*, *Springer* Science + Business Media LLC June 2007.

[22]See Saal, Parker and Weyman-Jones, *ibid*, Erbetta and Cave 2007 *Regulation and efficiency incentives: evidence from the England and Wales water and sewerage industry*. Review of Network Economics, Vol.6 (No.4) and Charlotte Pointon *Essays in the Measurement of Efficiency for the English and Welsh Water and Sewerage Industry*, *Ph.D.* Thesis, Cardiff University 2014.

aim towards the side of severity. Companies are, rightly, protected from arbitrary regulator behaviour by the scope for appeal to the Competition and Markets Authority.

The benefits of lower prices were duly passed on to customers at successive price reviews; in both 1994 and 1999, broadly half in the form of lower prices, and half in the form of better water and environmental quality.

RPI– (X + Q) was also a formula for transparency, so that customers would know how much changes in their bills were attributable to greater efficiency and how much to the cost of enhanced water and environmental quality.

1.9. Regulation of capital expenditure

Regulation of capital costs (capital enhancement & capital maintenance) proved more difficult. Following work in the Treasury on nationalised industry finance,[23] Ofwat developed capital base regulation, involving the estimation of a capital value – the Regulatory Capital Value/Regulatory Asset Base (RCV/RAB). This was based on the sale price of the companies at privatisation, updated for new net (i.e. after depreciation) capital expenditure and by inflation, as measured by the RPI.[24]

To this was applied a uniform, national cost of capital, the weighted average cost of capital (WACC). However, cost-based comparisons of standard capital projects were made to reflect differences in efficiency across the companies.

This dealt with the differences resulting from the sale of assets, valued in the books at £50 to £100 billion, net or gross, and privatisation proceeds of around £5 billion, and provided a

[23]See, especially. *Accounting for Economic Costs & Changing Prices: A Report to HM Treasury by an Advisory Group*. HMSO, 1986.

[24]We considered that the implicit WACC used by the Secretary of State in setting the privatisation K factors for ten years was much too high, leading to unacceptable increases in prices for customers. Our consultation paper on the cost of capital was received with horror by the City; we consulted, with only limited dissent, on the capital value to which the WACC was applied.

system for incorporating future capital expenditure. It provided an incentive for companies to choose their most efficient capital structure. But it has also been used as a cost-plus tool, storing up problems for the future (see below).

1.10. Ring fencing of the licensed business

Ring fencing of licenced water companies has been an object of policy from privatisation onwards. This prevented recourse to the revenues of the regulated monopoly by a company pursuing expansionary but unprofitable diversification.

The ring-fence was strengthened at the time of any take-over and was particularly valuable in the case of Wessex Water when taken over by Enron. After the Enron fiasco, its bonds became junk, while Wessex bonds retained investment grade status.

I argued that water companies that formed part of a group could better serve the public if they had a separate listing.[25] What happened, however, in the early years of the new century, following the soft price review of 2004, was the take-over of most of the industry by private equity/infrastructure funds, with immensely complex ownership structures; these were dominated by those financing the industry, without being subject to the disciplines placed on them by listing on the London Stock Exchange.

I tried to develop the position of non-executive members on the Boards of Licenced Companies, as part of the policy of treating them as freestanding Plcs. But I was disappointed at their quality; it was still necessary for the regulator to deal with the ultimate owners.

After a long delay, Ofwat is now dealing with these issues by ensuring better stakeholder, especially customer, representation on Utility Boards. Principles of leadership, transparency and governance have been developed and are being enforced.[26]

So far, so good.

---

[25]*The case for an amicable separation.* Financial Times 9th January 1996.
[26]*Board leadership, transparency and governance – principles* Ofwat January 2014.

2. RESPONSES TO VARIATIONS IN REGULATORY CONTEXTS AND THE EMERGENCE OF NEW ISSUES

2.1. Problems of capital-base regulation

Capital base regulation (RAB/RCV) has become overly concerned with rewarding inputs. It provides financial incentives for proposing new projects, whose cost effectiveness is dubious.

The water and wastewater quality objectives at the time of privatisation in 1989 were achieved by the early years of the new century. But new ones were always emerging; capital schemes that primarily benefit investors were developed under the badge of "infrastructure". Under capital base regulation, they all generate dividends for investors.

Estimates of the cost of enhancement projects are inevitably uncertain. This gave rise to the extensive use of contingency allowances, where companies had an information advantage over the regulator – and an inventive to use it.

Infrastructure projects could be privately financed by setting obligations and relying on capital base regulation to set customer prices which would produce an adequate return to investors, whether or not the project was in the interest of customers. The first example came when Chris (now Lord) Patten, then Secretary of State for the Environment, advanced the implementation of the EC Urban Waste Water Treatment Directive. The Thames Tideway Tunnel (TTT) is now the outstanding water example, mandated by Ministers, involving spending £4 billion for zero or minimal customer and environmental benefits.[27]

There are useful lessons to be learned from this scheme:

- The Tunnel was never properly appraised against a **combination** of options, some of which were already in train:

---

[27]Chris Binnie *Thames Tideway; Measures to protect the river from the adverse effects of waste water discharges* January 2014.
Chris.Binnie@btopenworld.com.

- There was an accountability vacuum. Ministers did not formally instruct Ofwat. Nor did the then Chairman deem this necessary, despite his unhappiness with the scheme:
- Thames Water's modelling was flawed; actual fish kills fell well short of predicted fish kills:
- While useful work was undertaken by Ofwat to ensure competition for the cost of the scheme and for the cost of financing it, What did **not** take place was a competition for alternative schemes for achieving better wastewater quality:
- The involvement of the National Audit Office (reporting to Parliament, not to Ministers) in identifying a catalogue of risks could be a model for the future.

2.2. The cost of capital

Experience in financing privatised utilities has shown that the supply price of finance (the cost-of-capital) has been very much lower than was thought possible in the 1980s. Over the last 25 years, interest rates (nominal & real) have fallen dramatically. But their financing duty has made regulators cautious; they have taken advantage of lower interest rates, but not to the extent that would have been possible.

The use of a single cost-of-capital figure at a five-year price review, plus the scope for increased gearing, meant that the (future) marginal cost of finance was below the average. Increases in gearing also allowed for further increases in dividends.

2.3. Overcharging and poor service?

- Customers have been overcharged, both because the investment allowed for has become too high (and project choice not subject to competition) and because the cost of capital allowed for has also been too high:
- Capital maintenance policies can put future customers at risk of companies cutting corners. The political flurry concerning leakage, induced water companies to improve their network management; but infiltration of groundwater into sewers

can also be a serious problem, involving costs for future customers:

- Thames Water's systematic abuse of the storm overflow systems at treatment works ("flow-clipping") has recently revealed a poisonous effect of monopoly.[28]

2.4. Dividends

Dividends paid by regulated water companies to their parents have far exceeded what shareholders paid at privatisation. They increased dramatically after the acquisition of the water utilities by private equity/infrastructure companies.

Companies seem unwilling to retain funds for future investment. While one company, Welsh Water, has shared financial gains with customers in the form of price reductions, and some other companies, e.g. Wessex Water, have made additional investment, it would be foolish to rely on this in the case of private equity infrastructure funds.

Pressures from the capital market can be very strong.[29] I responded with a tight price review in 1999, involving large price reductions but subsequent events show that something more systemic is needed. Now is time to explore adding a price/dividend sliding scale to the regulation of prices, whereby dividends above those assumed at price reviews would be accompanied by lower prices to customers, providing a fairer division of gains. It would also give companies an incentive to plough back profits to finance future investment.[30]

[28]See Judgement in Abingdon Crown Court March 2017.
[29]See John Kay *Other People's Money: Masters of the Universe or Servants of the Public*, London 2015 for a scholarly, and highly critical, account of the wider failures and poor contributions of the developments in capital markets in the last 25 years.
[30]See Philip Burns, Ralph Turvey and Thomas G Weyman Jones The *Behaviour of the Firm under alternative Regulatory Constraints* Scottish Journal of Political Economy 1998.

2.5. Retail competition

Separation of retail supply for non-household customers of publicly supplied water services took place in Scotland in 2008, followed in England nine years later. In Scotland, it yielded substantial savings for customers, often from better service; customers became much more aware of the importance of measurement, for economising on usage and reducing leakage.

Meanwhile, the spread of domestic metering has increased choice for household customers and reduced their bills, but many companies have been slow and governments have been unhelpful. While welcomed by environmentalists, customer bodies seem hesitant. Specific regulatory action is needed where companies have plans for major new projects, such as Thames' Abingdon reservoir.

2.6. Wholesale competition

Progress on wholesale competition has been painfully slow, reflecting both regulatory inertia and Ministerial reluctance.

- The inset appointments devised at privatisation had modest results, by allowing geographically specific retail competition:
- Common carriage has not taken off: time has been wasted on fruitless debates:
- The government adopted a retail-minus approach, passing an unhelpful Act in the early years of the century, which Ofwat interpreted as the minimally effective Efficient Component Pricing Rule:
- Ofwat failed to give proper attention to the case involving the supply of water to Shotton steel works.

Was this inevitable? Not all of it.

2.7. Geographical transfers

Water trading has scarcely developed despite geographical differences in supply & demand; companies prefer to build reservoirs rather than buy from neighbours. Regulatory action is needed to facilitate trading (of water or of licences), and to stimulate the spread of household metering before adding potentially unnecessary facilities into the capital base, such as desalination plants.

2.8. Customer engagement

Company-wide customer challenge groups were important bodies in the 2014 price review in England and Wales; the technique was also employed in Scotland.[31] It has the merit of taking account of local circumstances and forces companies to be more transparent with their customers.[32]

In one case, where prices were already high, customers rejected the company plan because it was too expensive. But in many cases, Ofwat ultimately set prices below those "agreed" between customers and their companies.

Most of the obligations' imposed on water companies come from governments; the ministerial process also needs formal customer engagement.

To be fully effective, customer challenge groups need sufficient information, successfully to challenge companies' financing costs and their efficiency. Meanwhile, the regulator must retain a "financier-of-last-resort" capability.

3. THE EVOLUTION OF NETWORK PRICE DETERMINATION PROCESSES

Retail competition for non-household (Business & Public Bodies such as local authorities & the NHS) should produce benefits of the kind resulting in Scotland. It seems sensible to extend it to household customers, especially those on a meter. But the big

---

[31]The Consumer Forum for Water in Scotland. *Legacy Report: Lessons learned from Customer involvement in the 2015–2021 Strategic Review of Charges* February 2015.

[32]Private communication from Sonia Brown who led the analysis for Ofwat in the 2014 price review.

money, and the big savings, are in wholesale, particularly in meeting new objectives economically, where there is a bias towards capital expenditure. It is only too popular among operating staff (who see their costs reduced), among ambitious engineers (who like prestige projects), and financiers (who then earn higher dividends). Under present arrangements, customers have to pay the bill in advance.

3.1. Performance regulation

Regulation should shift towards the principles of performance based regulation, where customers would pay only when they receive the benefits of enhanced quality, and where the choice of solutions to new objectives would be opened to competition. This could generate substantial savings. Ofwat is now developing a regulatory approach that will require companies to use direct procurement for high-value infrastructure projects. [33]

Regulators should continue to identify significant activities within the overall monopoly that can be contracted out and exposed to competition. Retail is one successful example. Sludge treatment may be another.

Competition should take place in the market place, not in the government office.[34] Potential suppliers would be encouraged to specify schemes that would deliver the desired outputs/outcomes. Bids would show their estimates of the total expenditure (totex)[35] involved, both operating and capital expenditure, suitably discounted at a cost-of-capital figure.

---

[33]*Water 2020: our regulatory approach for water and wastewater services in England and Wales – overview.* Ofwat May 2016.

[34]The use of cost-benefit analysis by government has proved to be open to abuse, being designed to defend rather than to challenge ministerial views. Competition in the market would be more open & more objective.

[35]Totex is only a useful tool if the time aspects of expenditure are explicitly allowed for in the calculation. Adding capital and current expenditure without discounting would distort incentives and repeat one of the past errors in the financial control of Nationalised Industries.

This approach could be phased in, starting with big schemes, such as new reservoir development, or new areas of company activity such as flood control. With experience, it could be extended to more potential schemes, so that the use of competition became the norm.

Large schemes should be open to consultation, involving customers and other interested parties; this should include local views. The regulator should ensure that proper information, on a consistent basis, is available, and help with the technical and economic aspects of the bids.

3.2. Overall financing implications

This should be reflected in a development of cost of capital analysis. The continued low-risk provision of existing services could be bond financed while the provision of new services would be evaluated using a cost of capital that was established in the market through competitive arrangements. Private companies should not, as a matter of course, make high-risk profits out of low-risk activities.

These steps should be supported by a re-establishment of the cost of quality debate; environmental pressure groups are too often dismissive of trade-offs with other human objectives. Ofwat papers in the early 1990s set the stage.[36] Environmental priorities should now be defined in terms of outcomes and regulators should consider how competition could be used to deliver cost-effective and innovative solutions.

Performance measures are available in the form of the drinking water standards devised by the DWI, the wastewater standards devised by the NRA/EA and the customer service standards devised by Ofwat. Where new obligations are imposed on the industry, such as managing flood defence, new indicators need to be added, and their delivery costed in competitive markets.

---

[36]Ofwat. *The Cost of Quality; A strategic assessment of the prospects for future water bills.* August 1992. Ofwat. Paying for Quality; the Political Perspective July 1993.

Performance against these measures would become a key element in regulation. Companies must face financial penalties for failure to deliver. This should go well beyond ticking the progress of capital projects.[37] Vague talk of "resilience" will not do; Ofwat is now identifying specific objective indicators & the mechanics of a competitive process.

3.3. A framework for negotiation

The missing part of the privatisation settlement was to create a framework for regulators to talk to, and negotiate with, each other.

The Environment Agency should formulate and declare its priorities over a specific time scale. This need not be in cost-benefit format; but environmental objectives should be ranked within affordability envelopes.

Prices should be an objective in their own right. This would change incentives and could halt the creep, whereby new environmental objectives are added without proper costing. Brexit also offers opportunities to re-consider the outcomes of EU Directives.

Affordability envelopes should be created by a simpler form of RPI ± K, (where a par position was set early in a price review), enabling the regulator to show the consequences for prices of rolling forward neutral K factors.

Customers should be involved in discussions from the beginning. Ofwat and WICS devised ready reckoners, derived from bigger regulatory models, to show the consequences of regulatory options and regulatory decisions. They were designed to allow consultation with customers (and to facilitate discussions within and between regulatory offices) on the effect on prices of different input and output assumptions, including different environmental policies.

A forum for discussion is needed. This should cover the interests

---

[37]This should build on the work of the WICS Output Monitoring Group in Scotland, developing into a Performance Monitoring Group, involving the quality & economic regulators and reporting publicly on progress.

of a range of parties: customers, (including local customers): environmentalists: companies: regulators: governments: etc. It should be open and independently chaired, with the ability to require companies and regulators to provide information and the results of analysis. The Regulator is well placed to undertake this role.

An open system for consultation has been devised in the electricity market in Australia that should have valuable lessons.[38]

3.4. Bottom line

Privatisation, combined with incentive regulation was a major step forwards in improving customer welfare. But we live in a world of constant change, requiring constant re-appraisal of regulatory arrangements. Customers have been over-charged; dividends have been excessive; there is a bias towards capital expenditure. Failure to develop fresh approaches would undermine the legitimacy of the private provision of monopoly services.

Living standards have not been rising satisfactorily. Utility regulation has a role in raising them by redoubling the search for efficiency – higher productivity and better value for money in an important area of consumer expenditure. New approaches for doing so need to be widely debated in the light of experience, particularly that of customers.

Competition needs to be extended to capital investment, particularly big new schemes. Currently, capital regulation remains largely cost-plus – and verges on rate of return regulation. Regulators should be constantly searching for other contestable activities that can be separated out and made subject to market competition.[39]

---

[38]Steve Smith of Lloyds Bank made an important contribution to the debate by pointing out that present arrangements have created a monopoly of ideas for dealing with problems. Such problems would include how best to deal with urban drainage in more sustainable ways.
[39]See above. There is much opposition to the TTT, but no satisfactory framework for discussion of the pros and cons.

Regulation needs to shift towards performance regulation, linked to enhanced competition, replacing the primacy of cost-base regulation. Customers should pay for enhanced quality only when they receive it. Consultation should help to select the best project in the local circumstances. Problems of excess dividends could be dealt with by a dividend/price sliding scale.

This would involve switching risks from customers to companies and distinguishing between the risks of the continued provision of standard services and the provision of enhanced services, (such as ensuring protection from flooding). Companies appear to be sufficiently well rewarded to deal with these issues.

This approach should go, of course, go much wider than water; it is also important, perhaps in different ways, in energy, railways and airports.

September 2017 Ian Byatt Director-General of Water Services (Ofwat), 1989–2000 and Chairman Water Industry Commission for Scotland, 2005–11.

CHAPTER 8

"Events" and People

8.1 "Events"

Good regulation depends on the goals set for the regulator and on how they are implemented. The process of explanation, listening, consultation, and response to the unexpected is crucial. Individual people matter both in how goals are implemented, and on how to deal with "events"[1]. Rules and process are necessary but not sufficient.[2]

I like to stress the importance of "events" and the importance people make in coping with them. Good process only takes you so far.

The big events in my periods of office were:-

- the recognition that the privatisation settlement was too generous,
- the dangers of unwise diversions by water companies into unregulated business,
- the rapid escalation of water prices in the Southwest sparked by Chris Patten's environmental enthusiasm,
- the near exhaustion of water supplies in Yorkshire in 1995,
- Labour's utility tax following their 1997 General Election victory,
- Ofwat's own event, the 12% price reductions of the 1999 Periodic Price Review.

In retrospect, we were quick to see that the cost of utility capital was much lower than generally believed in the City. We also

---

[1] Harold Macmillan, when asked what drove the policies of his government is alleged to have said "Events, dear boy, events"

[2] Rules and process are dealt with in the various papers in this volume.

succeeded in ring-fencing the regulated businesses and were able to deal with the collapse of Enron and the failure of Welsh Water. We did not handle the situation in the Southwest in the early days, very well. We could have made more use of competition for capital projects, although we did make use of the political consequences of environmental enthusiasm for the price of water services in the run-up to the1994 Periodic Price Review.

Our response to the near debacle in Yorkshire was, I like to think, correct and showed the advantage of regulatory independence. The price cuts of 1999, were, in part, a correction of the generosity of the 1994 Periodic Price Review and in part a response to the continued fall in the cost of capital resulting from continuing increases in the acceptance by financial markets of higher gearing of debt to equity.

8.2   Ofwat's Media Profile

Back in 1989, public regulation of private monopolies was new. There was much scope for the media, directly and indirectly to raise issues and to criticise the new regulators for their alleged failures. This was both healthy and offered scope us regulators to explain what we were doing, especially to protect the customers of utility companies from excessively high prices. Customers were, in general, and certainly in water services, disadvantaged by the inevitably generous privatisation terms. In water, the privatisation settlement involved price increases of 5% a year above the rate of inflation for five years and subsequently 4% a year for the next five. This was scarcely a recipe for customer satisfaction and we in Ofwat had no opportunity for correction of this until the 1994 Periodic Price Review.

The media response included many TV and radio programmes, and newspaper articles. It also included many cartoons, which used to decorate the walls of the Ofwat office. I have included three of them in this book. Figure 1 shows a 1992 cartoon from the Times, showing me in front of a maze of water pipes. The message

Fig. 1. He only produces paper, *The Times*, 20th July, 1992

is that he produces only paper; the companies provide service to the customer. Quite right; but well-judged and well-exposed information is critical to objective regulation of a monopoly supplier. In Figure 2, another early cartoon from the Times shows the long lasting dissatisfaction of the largest Water and Sewerage Company with its regulator. In Figure 3, the 666th edition of the industry's weekly magazine Water Bulletin, we see the industry's response to the "diabolical" 1999 Periodic Price Review, which reduced prices by 12%.[3]

---

[3]"And that no man might buy or sell, save that he had the mark, or the name of the beast, or the number of his name. Here is wisdom. Let him that hath understanding count the number of the beast: for it is the number of a man: and his number is Six hundred, threescore and six." The Revelation of S. John the Devine Chapter 13. verses 17 &18.

325

Fig. 2. Thames Water's Mike Hoffman, left, finds Ian Byatt of
Ofwat hard to please, *The Times*, 1993

Fig. 3. The Indusgtry's view of the 1994 Price Review.
Water Bulletin, August 1995

8.3 The Ofwat People[4]

I am most grateful for the support of colleagues in Ofwat and WICS. Everyone played a part, although some stand out because of the significance of their contributions. Below is my list of key people, with my view of their contributions.

The work of the administrative staff underpinned our achievements, particularly, **Neil Jackson**, **Roger Dunshea**, **Roy Wardle**, and **Anneke Vermeer**, who ran my private office brilliantly: our key consultants, **Ann Bishop** and **Clive Sparrow**, helped to make Ofwat a productive, challenging, innovative, and effective organisation – a great place to work in.

Tony Ballance who succeeded Chris Bolt as chief economist, came from the economics of textiles. He, **Scott Reid** and I wrote a paper which is included as 3.4 in this book.

I had worked with **Chris Bolt** in the Government Economic Service, where he had served in the Treasury, the Home Office and the Department of the Environment (DoE). At the DoE, he was responsible for the modelling work undertaken at privatisation. He brought with him a wealth of information and experience, leading Ofwat's work on the cost of capital, the financial modelling of the individual water companies and undertaking the operational management of the first Periodic Price Review in 1994.

I first knew **Phillip Chappell** when he was working for Morgan Grenfell. He joined Ofwat as Chairman of the Customer Service Committee (CSC) for the Thames region. His key contribution was on financial matters, in particular the efficient financing of the environmental obligations of the Companies. He also found financial advisers for Ofwat who were independent from the big City firms advising the companies.

Bill Emery came to Ofwat from Yorkshire Water where he was a qualified engineer with an MBA. He designed the annual collection of the information on the outputs of the water companies, putting it on a comparable basis and linking it with the financial

[4]Rules and process are dealt with in the various papers in this volume.

information in the regulatory accounts. He worked closely with the Environment Agency and the Drinking Water Inspector, becoming Ofwat's chief engineer.

Richard Fowler, our brilliant QC, worked closely with as well as for the Office.

Jim Gardner was Chairman of the Northumbrian CSC. He came with wide experience in the local authority world, having been Chief Executive of Tyne and Wear Metropolitan County. He became Chairman of the Ofwat National Customer Council (ONCC), comprising the ten CSC Chairmen, at its formation. He led the work by the ONCC to draw attention to the consequences for customers of the poorly costed EC water and wastewater quality Directives.

Fiona Pethick came to Ofwat from the Government Statistical Service. She illustrated the best traditions of that service, getting the numbers appropriate and right, always completing practical tasks, dealing very ably with Ofwat's side of appeals to the MMC and helping to co-ordinate internal policy across the various Ofwat Divisions.

Dilys Plant came to Ofwat from the Government Information Service. She understood the importance of wide communication with the public in understanding the role of regulation. She had the media skills to deliver Ofwat's policy successfully, understanding both the need hold companies to public account, and how to do it. Dilys was ably followed by **Julia Havard,** who handled public relations excellently in the 1999 Periodic Price Review.

David Rees came to Ofwat when Chris Bolt left for the Office of Rail Regulation. Coming from a City background, he masterminded the financial analyses underlying the 1999 Periodic Price Review, when customers' prices were reduced by 12%. His work was subsequently upheld by the Monopolies and Mergers Commission.

Michael Saunders began by advising Ofwat on the implementation of the consumer protection provisions of the privatisation legislation. He then became Ofwat's Director of

Consumer Affairs, advising the CSCs and making the approach of Ofwat's regulatory experts, increasingly consumer friendly. He well understood the necessary links between economic and consumer policy and excellently supervised the investigation of the failures of Yorkshire Water during the 1995 drought.

I had worked with **David Walker** after the nationalisation of local authority water services in 1974, when he became Deputy Director of the National Water Council. We worked together on the application of the then Treasury rules to the Water Authorities. On privatisation, David became a much valued consultant to Ofwat over more than a decade, bringing knowledge of both engineering and economics, experience and fresh air to the office.

Clive Wilkinson, former leader of Birmingham's Labour Council and Chairman of the Central (Midlands) CSC, was a key influence, always stressing the plight of the poorer consumers and pointing to practical ways of helping them in a privatised world.

Martin Cave[5] joined the Ofwat team after I had left. His report on competition indicated a practical way ahead. A former Treasury colleage, **Jon Stern,** usefully reminded us that the single server was a monopolist.

8.4 The Government People

Outside Ofwat, I am grateful to **Patrick Brown,** the Deputy Secretary leading the privatisation process, who taught me that in the new world of privatisation, I would be more a minister than an official, to **Nicholas Ridley**[6] and **Michael Howard**[7] who saw

---

[5]Martin Cave, Independent Review of Competition and Innovation in Water Markets, April 2009.
[6]Secretary of State for the Environment at the time of privatisation. He was particularly important for insisting that independent regulation of quality was a necessary part of the privatisation of suppliers and in stressing the benefits of comparative competition in the privatised industry.
[7]Water Minister at the time of privatisation.

the great advantage of an independent regulator, and to successive junior Ministers in the Department of the Environment: in the Major government. They all saw their role as setting strategy, not interfering in implementation.

At official level, I am particularly grateful to **Neil Summerton**, the Undersecretary heading the Water Division in the Department of the Environment. He was a positive influence on the development of water regulation; unlike many officials, he understood how independent regulation could improve conditions for customers by limiting prices, while still improving environmental quality. He and I met frequently to exchange views, about the progress of our work, its political impact and approaches to emerging issues.

Neil and I did much work together in the run-up to the 1994 Periodic Price Review to deal with the unhappy political and customer consequences of the unexplained escalation of the estimated cost of EC obligations, from £2 billion at privatisation to £10 billion 5 years later. We jointly reviewed the totality of environmental obligations and trimmed them to an affordable cost.

8.5   The People in the Water Companies

Nigel Annett was a City analyst who, together with **Brian Charles**, masterminded the conversion of the failed Hyder multi-utility into the public interest company Welsh Water/Dwr Cymru, ably chaired by **Terry (later Lord) Burns**, including the raising of bonds. Under him Welsh Water became a form of co-operative, paying dividends to customer rather than shareholders.

John Belloc was a business man who became Chairman of Severn Trent Water Authority, and, at privatisation, Chairman of Severn Trent Water. He was a libertarian in economics and was relieved to discover that I was not, as he had assumed, a social engineer.

Kevin Bond ran Yorkshire Water after the debacle of the near failure of the water supply in the Bradford area. A former policeman, he had a wide view of the public interest and understood the need for prices to be reduced in 1999.

Vic Cocker, who had worked for British Gas was a key person working for the companies during the privatisation negotiations on the content and drafting of the Licences to be held by the Appointed Companies. He became Chief Executive of Severn Trent Water, always able and ready to take a statesman-like position.

Bill Fraser came to South West Water as Chief Executive from the north sea oil industry. An ebullient capital investment champion, he was not, perhaps, as focussed on customers as might have been appropriate. He unwisely took on Ofwat at the 1994 Periodic Price Review.

John Hargreaves was Chief Executive of Northumbrian Water before its take-over by Lyonnais des Eaux. He later became first Chief Executive of Scottish Water where he masterminded the merger of the three Scottish Water Authorities, and greatly improved their performance and efficiency, despite quarrelling with Alan Sutherland, the regulator.

Bernard Henderson, appointed Chairman of Anglian Water Authority becoming Chairman of Anglian Water Company at privatisation, was a businessman and great networker, who did much to bring regulation and business onto parallel tracks.

Mike Hoffman, another businessman, came to the water industry as the powerful and lively Chief Executive of Thames Water. Much of his energies went into the non-regulated business, but he was clearly in charge of the utility. He liked a good argument but saw the need for agreement.

Nick Hood, a business man appointed to be Chairman of Wessex Water Authority met me on the station platform at Bath as I toured the newly privatised companies. While having a clear point of view, he was always diplomatic.

Mike Kinski revived the neglected capital programme of Southern Water after it was taken over by Scottish Power. He worked very hard to catch up on lost ground and to carry out the full programme to improve the treatment and disposal of sewage on the holiday areas of the South Coast. He was ready, with

331

Guy Hands to take on the management of Welsh Water after the collapse of Hyder.

Sir Gordon Jones was the Chairman of the Water Authorities/ Water and Sewerage Companies' trade association before and after privatisation. He helped to develop the new system in co-operative ways, but, as Chairman of Yorkshire Water, he was devastated by the 1995 drought.

Ronnie Mercer was both Chief Executive of Southern Water, following Mike Kinski, under Scottish Power, and Chairman of Scottish Water after the enforced resignation of Alan Alexander in 2006. An experienced businessman, he had earlier managed Ravenscraig Steel Works and knew how to "make a swerve" when politicians came over the horizon. He recognized that companies did better when they took sufficient account of their regulators.

Christine Moran-Postel worked for Lyonnais des Eaux when they, Generale des Eaux and SAUR[8] each took over a number of Statutory Water Companies following their entry into the new regulatory regime, where prices rather than dividends were controlled. She, and the indefatigable **Jean-Claude Banon**, her counterpart at Generale, took an active part in the strategic management of the French owned companies in North London, the South Coast, Essex and the North East. I also visited Paris to discuss regulatory issues with senior management and to learn about the well-established regulatory system for water in France

Trevor Newton was Chief Executive of Yorkshire Water at the time of the drought. He maintained supplies of drinking water by tankering up the Dales; something which the Treasury would never have financed in the nationalised days. Unhappily he fell foul of the media over where he took his baths.

Desmond Pitcher came to North West Water from the betting industry in Liverpool. He was focussed on customers, but bitterly attacked by the media for his high salary. He was one of the instigators of the progressive dividend policy of the second half of

[8]A French Construction Company

the 1990s, a policy which got out of hand under the private finance ownership of the water companies following the easy Periodic Price Review of 2004.

I first met **Colin Skellett** when, on appointment, I visited Wessex Water. He is still there after a successful time in management, having endured the period of ownership by Enron; then working successfully with the new Malaysian owners to manage an efficient and customer-friendly business. He and his Finance Director, **Keith Harris** made a formidable combination.

Alan Smith was Chief Executive of Anglian Water. He came originally from a local authority background and led the welcome transformation of the company to a meter based charging system. Unfortunately, ill health forced him to retire early.

John Smith, previously a member of the Government Economic Service, was always an excellent commentator on the privatised water industry; he was always worth listening to.

Sir John Wills, of tobacco fame, was Chairman of Bristol Water who saw the role of business in a Statutory Water Company as making a contribution to social objectives. He was characteristic of those who raised funds for the local water company and held the management to account – a very different world from that of the water authorities and their privatised successors.

Andrew Winkler, who I had worked with in the Treasury, was an excellent advocate for the former Statutory water companies, very usefully challenging Ofwat.

8.6   Other Regulators

National Rivers Authority (NRA)/Environment Agency (EA)
Nick (becoming Lord) Crickhowell, who had been Secretary of State for Wales in Margaret Thatcher's administration, became Chairman of the newly created National Rivers Authority. He and I had a tense relationship. When I called on him in our shared offices on the Albert Embankment, I suggested that environmental improvements should be subject to cost-benefit analysis. He

told me that he did not see it that way; that he would push for environmental improvement whenever money could be found. So it proved.

John de Ramsey, a hereditary Member of the House of Lords became the Chairman of the EA, when it took over the NRA. He was more interested in the good management of the countryside than in championing environmental causes.

Drinking Water Inspectorate

Mike Rouse was appointed as a free-standing and independent Drinking Water Inspector soon after privatisation. He took the work very seriously, checking installation as well as doing laboratory tests, driving up quality to very high standards.

Monopolies and Mergers Commission (MMC)

Sydney (now Sir Sydney) Lipworth chaired the first of the MMC analyses into cases arising under the special merger regime established at privatisation. This concerned the proposed take-over by Generale des Eaux, of three Statutory Water Companies in North London, to form the Three Valleys Company.[9] The Commission accepted the arguments that Chris Bolt and I put to them, namely that promise of greater efficiency was not sufficient; prices to customers had to be reduced *in advance* of the merger.

Graeme (subsequently Sir Graeme) Odgers, a businessman chaired the hearing of South West Water's appeal against the Ofwat price limits set in the 1994 Periodic Price Review. The Commission felt that the primary regulator had been too kind and reduced them, costing South West £1 million and the cost of the inquiry. No Water and Sewerage company subsequently appealed against an Ofwat price determination.

---

[9]The privatisation legislation provided for compulsory reference of mergers between larger companies to the MMC, lest they reduce the capability of the Director General to make comparisons.

Dan Goyder, one of the Deputy Chairman of the MMC, chaired a succession of water merger cases, notably the proposed take-over of the wounded South West Water by both Severn-Trent Water and Wessex Water, both geographical neighbours. The Commission's recommendations supported the thrust of Ofwat policy, namely price reductions **before** merger.

8.7   The People in Scotland

Neil Menzies came from a business background to be the Chairman of Alan Sutherland's Advisory Committee before the formation of the Water Commission. After my appointment he was most helpful in taking me on visits to customers in various parts of Scotland and introducing me to key people.

Andrew Scott, ably assisted by **William Fleming,** was a key official in the Scottish Executive, who masterminded the appointment of Alan Sutherland as Commissioner: the creation of the Water Commission: and the legislation set to introduce retail competition in 2008. They both recognized to importance of creative thinking within the bureaucracy.

I met **Alan Sutherland** while I was still at Ofwat, when he was appointed Water Industry Commissioner for Scotland. He was developing comparisons between the costs and performance of the publicly owned Scottish Water and the privatised companies in England and Wales, using the results to challenge Scottish Water's outrageous costings, especially of its capital programme. After leaving Ofwat, I was delighted to work with him, first as a member of his Advisory Council and subsequently as Chairman of the newly constituted regulatory Commission.

Alan masterminded the separation of retail and wholesale services and the introduction, in a publicly owned service, of effective competition for retail services a decade in advance of England and Wales.

I am also grateful to **Katherine Russell,** Director of Corporate

Affairs at WICS for her outward vision and efficient management, to **John Simpson,** who served in both Ofwat and WICS, and to my non-executive colleagues on the WICS, **John Banyard,** former Director of Severn-Trent Water, **Mike Brooker,** former Chief Executive of Welsh Water, **Charles Coulthard,** previously with Energywatch and **David Simpson,** a former Professor of Economics at Strathclyde and Economic Adviser to Standard Life.

I am also grateful to **John Simpson** who served both in Ofwat and WICS, ably supporting, in different ways the regulatory approaches of both offices.

8.3 The City

I am grateful to the work of City analysts who were valuable critics of the industry and its regulation. In particular, **Robert Miller Bakewell** was always a wise, albeit challenging critic. Lakis Athanasiou was also helpful.

EPILOGUE: THE AUTHOR

Figure 4 shows me as Chairman of WICS, standing in front of Edinburgh castle.

I was born in Preston, Lancashire in 1932 and educated at Kirkham Grammar School, Oxford (St Edmund Hall and Nuffield College) and Harvard Universities. I began my working career at the Durham Colleges in the University of Durham, where I taught the History of Economic Thought.

In 1962, at the invitation of Alec (later Sir Alec) Cairncross, I joined the Economic Section of HM Treasury, where I spent two exciting years working on microeconomic issues, including regional

Fig. 4.

policy, competition policy and policy towards Nationalised Industries.

In 1964, I joined the London School of Economics to teach public finance and industrial policy, while serving on the Plowden Committee on *Children and their Primary Schools*. In 1967 I was appointed to the new Planning Branch as Senior Economic Adviser to the Department of Education and Science by Anthony Crosland, then the Secretary of State.

In 1969 I became Director of Economics and Statistics at the Ministry of Housing and Local Government, becoming a Director of Economics when it was merged with the Ministry of Transport and the Ministry of Public Buildings and Works.

In 1972 I transferred back the Treasury to set up the Public Expenditure Economic Unit. After six years I was promoted to the post of Deputy Chief Economic Adviser dealing with microeconomic issues and supervising the management of the Government Economic Service.

In 1989, I was appointed by Nicholas Ridley, then Secretary of State for the Environment, to be the Director-General of Water Services, the Economic Regulator of the to-be-privatised Water and Sewerage Companies, and of the existing private Statutory Water Supply Companies. I was appointed a Knight Bachelor in 2000, in recognition of this work

I left Ofwat in 2000 and in 2001 joined the newly founded Frontier Economics as a Senior Associate; I gave numerous lectures in various countries in Asia, including Malaysia and China.

In 2006 I was appointed Chairman of the newly-formed Water Industry Commission for Scotland, where I worked with successive Labour and Nationalist Governments until 2011.

I am currently member of the Public Interest Committee of RSM Audit UK, concerned with the application of the public interest to audit. I am also a member of the Advisory Council of the European Policy Forum, with whom has worked for many years, and a member of the Political Economy Club.

I has been involved in charitable activities, notably with the Holy

Cross Centre Trust in King's Cross, working for disadvantaged people. In Birmingham I became Chairman of the Friends of St Philip's Cathedral.

In 1959 I married Susan Drabble (subsequently the novelist A S Byatt) and in 1997 Deirdre (now Professor Deirdre) Kelly CBE, founder of the Liver Unit at Birmingham Children's Hospital. I have had two children, Antonia, who is now Chief Executive of English PEN, and Charles, tragically killed when only 11, have two stepsons, Eoin and Lochlinn Parker, three natural grandchildren, Saul, Clara and Saskia Collyns and three step-grandchildren, Finlay, Nina and Niamh Parker.

When not working, or involved with family activities, I enjoy drawing and painting (usually, I hasten to say, not water colours).

Ian Byatt
2019